Dancing
on the
Glass Ceiling

Dancing on the Glass Ceiling

Tap into Your True Strengths,
Activate Your Vision, and Get What
You Really Want out of Your Career

Candy Deemer and Nancy Fredericks

Contemporary Books

Chicago   New York   San Francisco   Lisbon   London   Madrid   Mexico City
Milan   New Delhi   San Juan   Seoul   Singapore   Sydney   Toronto

The *McGraw·Hill* Companies

Library of Congress Cataloging-in-Publication Data

Deemer, Candy.
    Dancing on the glass ceiling: tap into your true strengths, activate your vision, and get what you really want out of your career / Candy Deemer & Nancy Fredericks.
        p.   cm.
    Includes bibliographical references and index.
    ISBN 0-07-140694-8
    1. Vocational guidance for women.   2. Career development.   3. Women executives.
I. Fredericks, Nancy.   II. Title.

    HF5382.6 .D44   2002
    650.1′082—dc21   2002067667

Permission to reprint copyrighted material can be found in the Credits section on page 271, which is to be considered an extension of this copyright page.

1 2 3 4 5 6 7 8 9 0   DOC/DOC   1 0 9 8 7 6 5 4 3 2

ISBN 0-07-140694-8

Interior design by Hespenheide Design

McGraw-Hill books are available at special quantity discounts to use as premiums and sales promotions, or for use in corporate training programs. For more information, please write to the Director of Special Sales, Professional Publishing, McGraw-Hill, Two Penn Plaza, New York, NY 10121-2298. Or contact your local bookstore.

This book is printed on acid-free paper.

*To Mom and Dad, who always encouraged
me to follow my heart and pursue my dreams.
With love and thanks,*

CANDY

*To my sister, who is my safe harbor; and to Uncle Bill
and Aunt Judy, who demonstrated the joyous harmony
possible through being fully male and fully female.
With love and thanks,*

NANCY

CONTENTS

ACKNOWLEDGMENTS

Getting a book from initial concept to final publication involves so much more than merely writing it. Behind every chapter, story, and insight are dozens of people who gave so generously of their time, experience, and expertise. Can we thank them all? Probably not, but we shall try.

To Monique Raphel High, our guide and mentor: your help with both our material and our search for an agent made our impossible dream possible.

To Joanna Brody: we gave you a cheap margarita, and you gave us a priceless title.

To Jill Smolinski, Sandra O'Briant, and Christine Canabou, our "support group" of writers: for your caring yet honest criticism on every chapter.

To Chelsea Roe, Audrey Eisner-Hoeller, Linda Watts, Marianne Ellis, Caryn Wiley, Beverly Popielarz, Liz Montgomery, Debra Rainier, Silver Rose, Kieta Fox, Jill Nowak, Jan Barcus, and all of the other unnamed women who shared their stories and their expertise.

To all of the men who supported this book with their thoughts and encouragement: Bob Goldstein, Dave Park, Jim Fredericks, David Ellis, and Ed Carlson.

To Mitchell Waters, our agent at Curtis Brown, Ltd.: Working with you has been a joyful experience. And on top of all that, you never gave up!

To Michele Pezzuti and Katherine Hinkebein, our editors at Contemporary Books: you were thoughtful, demanding, reasonable, and delightful taskmasters.

And from Candy: To my husband, Ken, for your unwavering belief in me and for making me feel, every day, that I am your grandest adventure. And to Kevin, Andy, and Brian, the best cheerleaders a mom could ever have.

And from Nancy: To Mom and Dad, Ed, Jim, Fran, and everyone else in the family, for your unwavering love and support.

INTRODUCTION

Once upon a time there was a beautiful little wooden peg and an alluring little square hole. This little peg watched for years as all of the other little pegs slipped effortlessly through the little square hole. When they got to the other side, they would shout back, "We're having a great time on this side of the little square hole!" And the lonely little peg would just sit there, peeking through at all of the other pegs busily working away, wishing she could be on the other side too.

Then one day the little peg decided that she would do whatever it took to get herself through that hole. She positioned herself perfectly at the edge of it, and then she began to shove . . . and shove . . . and shove. She kept twisting herself around, trying to find a way to fit through. All of the other little pegs had gone through it so smoothly! What was her problem?

Well, you may have already guessed. This one little peg wasn't square like the hole. She was round! So you can imagine how much she had to struggle and how painful it must have been for her to shove her way through that little square hole. It took many days, but eventually she made it! Some of her nice, smooth curves had been shaved into sharp edges and she looked a little scarred. She certainly wasn't a perfect little round peg anymore! But she was on the other side where the happy square pegs were.

"Hurray!" shouted the other wooden pegs. "You made it! And look at you. Now you're *almost* like one of us." Secretly, though, some of the other pegs couldn't help thinking that this one particular peg should have stayed on her own side of the hole. After all, with her odd shape, she would never really fit in with the rest of the perfectly square pegs.

For a while the little almost-round, almost-square wooden peg was happy. But she never felt as if she really fit in with the other pegs. She finally admitted to her best little square-peg friend that she liked herself a lot better when she was round. Boy, was she surprised when *he* told her that he liked her better when she was round too! She was easier to talk to when she was a round peg, he told her. Something just seemed to be missing now that she was neither square nor round. She didn't seem quite herself anymore—just a little less real and authentic.

That night, as the little peg was going to sleep, she dreamed of being round again, of having her whole self intact once more. Then she dreamed that the hole might be just a little bit bigger. That way both the square pegs and the round pegs could easily slip through it just the way they were! Working on the other side of the little hole would be a lot easier—and more fun—for everybody.

For as long as women have been in business, we have struggled within a world dominated by the subconscious belief (and occasionally, the stated conviction) that women are somehow "less" than men. So instead of recognizing our strengths, we have obsessed over our weaknesses. Instead of daring to stand out, we have "shaved off" little pieces of ourselves so we could fit into the square hole—the accepted, masculine-driven pattern of business.

We wrote *Dancing on the Glass Ceiling* for all of those women in business who feel like that perfect little, round, wooden peg, struggling to squeeze through the hole into upper management. We wrote this book for the women who struggle every day to win more acceptance and success in their companies, yet wonder how they can get it without fundamentally altering who they are. And we wrote it for those women who have already sacrificed some part of themselves in their quest for professional advancement and wonder now how they can regain what they lost.

The original idea for *Dancing on the Glass Ceiling* was Nancy's. After several years of one-on-one executive coaching with both men and women, she began to notice patterns. While the male and female executives had a great deal in common, a number of unique issues occurred within each group, which she could only attribute to gender differences. For example, several success concepts that were almost instinctive for men—such as managing up and out-of-company networking—were counterintuitive for the women, who were consistently adamant in their belief that "doing a great job should be good enough" to earn a promotion. Correspondingly, women seemed to gravitate instinctively toward certain leadership behaviors that were not even on the radar screens of most men, such as intuitive decision making, the special talent for nurturing subordinates, and the automatic ability to interpret both the verbal and nonverbal layers of communication. Yet neither the women nor their organizations recognized the powerful role these assets play in fueling the companies' success.

Long before we became writing partners, we came together as client (Candy) and consultant (Nancy). Even then, we recognized that our personal paths had taken us on very different career journeys. Nancy had spent twenty years in corporate America, managing staff and operational functions; Candy had spent twenty years in marketing and client-management functions. Nancy had worked in a variety of conservative, left-brain, logic-driven law and accounting firms. Candy's career had been in highly creative, emotional, right-brain advertising agencies. Nancy left corporate America to become a successful entrepreneur as a corporate consultant and executive coach. Candy spent seventeen years steadily working her way up the ranks of the same company as a "trailblazer"—the first woman to reach each executive position.

We both have had extensive experience managing men and women and have observed firsthand the differences between them. We have observed the special struggles of other women as they strive to succeed in a world still governed by male virtues and values, and we have both lived through those struggles ourselves. We know how it feels to be the only woman in the executive boardroom.

Despite our separate pathways, these common experiences have resulted in our arrival at the same viewpoint regarding the power of the feminine perspective in corporate America and the need for that perspective in the twenty-first century: *Yes, women are different from men. But we are not deficiently different. We are grandly different!*

This book is a celebration of these grand differences. It is also a reality check (because let's face it, nobody's perfect!). As you complete the various exercises we've provided, you will learn to revel in and rely on the inherent power of your feminine qualities. You will also identify those internal attitudes and behaviors that can undermine your success and learn how to transform them into supporters rather than saboteurs.

Dancing on the Glass Ceiling has been designed to combine the philosophical with the practical. It pairs sophisticated insights with down-to-earth exercises to help you discover what you really want in your career and what you need to do to get it. Our mission is twofold. First, we want to help you recognize, celebrate, and nurture those inherent feminine-based strengths, which truly are your keys to career success. And second, we want to help you construct an additional foundation of attitudes and behaviors that will empower you to fully capitalize on your strengths. This is the feminine pathway through which you can achieve even the most impossible of dreams, with less struggle and more joy in the process.

In the conception and writing of each chapter, our collaboration yielded exponential—and often surprising—realizations. We began calling them "Aha!"s. Each time one happened to Candy, she would gasp, shake her head, and exclaim, "I just can't believe I didn't *do* this (or *know* this, or *say* this)!" She likened her reaction to the character in the 1980s commercial who would smack himself on the head with the palm of his hand and say, "WOW, I could have had a V8!"

As you read this book, you will probably experience a few "Aha!"s of your own. You may realize, "WOW, I could have had a great relationship and really learned something from my not-so-great boss." Or "WOW, I could be a lot more successful if I just stop trying so hard to be a 'good girl' in my job." Or "WOW, networking can actually be fun if I just allow myself to do it in a way that is more natural for me." The good news about all of these thoughts is that *you still can*! Even if you have already squeezed yourself through that little square hole, you still have much of your career ahead of you. It's not too late to make those incremental shifts that will enable you to *dance on the glass ceiling* rather than muscle your way through it.

You may think that an infinitesimal shift will make little difference in your life and career. Think again! Minuscule shifts can have an enormous impact on the outside world. It's called the "butterfly effect." Research has shown that a single butterfly fluttering its wings in China has the potential to magnify the resulting airflow throughout the world, even affecting weather in the United States.

Now, if a butterfly can do all of that, imagine the power that you have to create results in your own career and in your own company simply by allowing yourself to follow a more natural pathway to success—a feminine pathway.

As you read this book and complete the exercises in it, you will experience the feelings of freedom and comfort that arise from the flutter of more feminine wings. You will undoubtedly decide to change some aspects of your own career trip. As the authors, we are honored to be making this journey with you.

CHAPTER 1

WHAT'S SO POWERFUL ABOUT FEMININE LEADERSHIP?

Dance Lesson #1: To become a true leader in your life and in your organization, you must honor the natural rhythms that exist within you. For women, these rhythms have a distinctively feminine tone; they are the foundations of our success, fulfillment, and joy.

Let's play a game before we talk about theories, shall we? We'll start with a little word association.

Leader = [list the first three or four descriptors that pop into your head]
Great Business Leader = [list the first three names that come to your mind]

Now, take a moment to look through these two lists for patterns or similarities. Could it be that the names on your list belong to only one gender (and chances are, it's not female)? And could it be that your descriptors of a leader are primarily *masculine* traits (for example, aggressive, decisive, competitive)?

If the leaders we admire are men and the traits that we identify with leadership are masculine, where does that leave women? Unfortunately, far too many working women have chosen a pathway of emulation rather than differentiation. They have modeled their own style of leadership after the men who occupy the top positions that they want so badly to attain.

This desire to be like the majority is a normal response. We have also been steadily guided, pushed, and prodded in this direction for the past thirty years by most books on the subject. A whole variety of "experts" have advised working women that to win this particular game called business, we must learn to "play like a man."

But if you happen to be female, fitting into the male model of leadership is the most unnatural course for you to take. It is the square hole, and fitting through it requires you to devalue, deny, and even destroy the unique, feminine-based strengths and contributions that you can bring to the masculine world of business. And that is precisely why this "macho" success formula has actually turned out to be somewhat of a sabotage formula for the women who have devoted themselves to it. It makes us appear to be in alignment with the business world around us, but ultimately it leaves us out of integrity with ourselves—that is, out of alignment with our internal being. Instead of standing powerfully on the feminine foundation that resides in our right brains, we place our entire business future on the more masculine thought patterns and skill sets of our rational left brain.

"Researchers refer to the left brain as the dominant hemisphere and the right as the nondominant one, because the skills of the left brain are dominant in our society," write Jacquelyn Wonder and Priscilla Donovan, the authors of *Whole-Brain Thinking*.[1] They developed a list of left- and right-brain qualities that includes these:

Left		*Right*
Positive		Intuitive
Analytical	Spontaneous	Holistic
Linear	Emotional	Playful
Explicit	Nonverbal	Diffuse
Sequential	Visual	Symbolic
Verbal	Artistic	Physical
Concrete		
Rational		
Active		
Goal-oriented		

In our drive to accentuate these left-brain traits, we inevitably lose touch with those fundamental feminine parts of ourselves. We silence the voice of our intuition; we stifle the expression of our emotions; we harden the tenor of our communications; we close down the flow of our creativity. Yet these are the success qualities that any business leader—male or female—must demonstrate at the very top levels of management.

In focusing so single-mindedly on the left-brain skills (and ignoring the need to develop the softer, feminine-based assets of leadership), women have failed to build the complete package of talents required for leadership. They have denied themselves the power that comes from using their inherent, right-brain strengths—and unwittingly held themselves in check, confined to the ranks of middle management.

The proof of the folly of this "play like a man" formula lies in the continuing dearth of women's presence at the top rungs of our companies. In 2001, women represented roughly half of middle management positions in corporate America but just 12 percent of all corporate officer positions in the Fortune 500. True, the figure has grown (from 2.6 percent in 1990)—but at a rate that only a snail would be proud of. And among the Fortune 500's CEOs in 2001, only six were women. Six![2]

Those few women who have made it into the rarified air of top executive positions (and managed to stay there) are further proof of the importance and power of feminine-based skills. Just read *Fortune* magazine's profiles of the fifty most powerful women in business over the last couple of years. They are aggressive and hard-charging, but what truly distinguishes them as leaders is their blend of these masculine traits with their feminine-based talents. They are nurturers of their companies and their fellow employees; they are extensive communicators; they build relationships; they inject passion and emotion into long-cold corporate environments to transform and rejuvenate the fortunes and the futures of their companies:

- Barclays Global Investors (BGI) chairperson Patricia Dunn is the quintessential nurturer. Her distinctly feminine method of supporting her senior managers runs directly counter to BGI's technically driven culture. But it works! Here's a story from the company's head of global risk management, Andrea Zulberti, about a business deal that required her to make a tense, middle-of-the-night conference call with Barclays's top management in London. The nature of her boss's support was unique—and distinctly feminine: "Pattie said to me, 'Come to my house. Bring your jammies.' She knew I could handle it, but she wanted to be there supporting me." And after the deal closed, Zulberti said, "I got a nice note and flowers from Pattie within hours."[3]

- Paramount Motion Pictures chairperson Sherry Lansing has a reputation for graciousness that makes her unique among studio executives. She is renowned for returning phone calls promptly, and she proudly labels herself a nurturer. According to actor Michael Douglas, who has produced several hits with Paramount, "Sherry's graciousness is beguiling. She's always more than willing to share credit. In fact, she's great at giving credit where it isn't even deserved, just to assuage egos."[4]

- Advertising agency McCann-Erickson's chairperson and chief creative officer Nina DiSesa intentionally controls her masculine tendencies and relies instead on her extraordinary relationship-building talent. "I'm very much in touch with my male side. I'm really competitive, and I find confrontation stimulating. But I keep those qualities in check. I use my feminine traits—empathy, collaboration. . . . I'm dealing with big egos, big personalities. . . . If I didn't have a strong nurturing component, I couldn't do it."[5]

These women are real-life examples of the first lesson of true leadership: be who you are. And who you are is a woman! Allow yourself to accentuate those right-brain skills that the world perceives as feminine. For, in reality, these are the core skills of leadership, whether the leader is a man or a woman.

Let's test this premise with some of your own real-life examples.

Step 1: On a piece of paper, quickly write down the names of three male or female leaders from your *personal* experience who were really extraordinary.

Step 2: Now quickly write down three characteristics for each leader that he or she demonstrated to you (that is, the reasons you admire this person).

Step 3: Next to each of the nine qualities put an *L* if it is a left-brain/logical/rational/analytical trait, or an *R* if it is a right-brain/creative/emotional/intuitive/communications trait.

Finished? We'll bet that you have both *L*s and *R*s on your list. We'll also bet that at least five (or more) of your nine letters are *R*s. How can we be so sure? Well, we've probably asked more than three hundred people in our speech audiences and training programs to answer this question. The predictability of "R dominance" in their answers never ceases to amaze us . . . and them.

So what does this tell you? First, leadership is not an *either/or* choice between masculine- and feminine-based strengths. It is an *and* equation, because it requires both sides of our brains, both aspects of our energies and talents. Second, the feminine side of leadership is not just an equal partner with the masculine; it is the majority partner. So while the perception of leadership is overwhelmingly masculine (as demonstrated by the exercise at the beginning of this chapter), the actions and experiences of leadership are primarily feminine.

Herein lies the first "Aha!": the pivotal assets of great leaders are not the hard-and-fast qualities of rationality, objectivity, and analytical prowess. Rather, they are those subtler skill sets including intuition, emotionality, and creativity that arise from the emotional right side of our brains—the feminine side. Great leaders are communicators and relationship builders; they are creative and intuitive; they are collaborative; they are occasionally emotional; and they are always supportive. Great leaders are also visionaries and risk takers; they are decisive and highly competitive. In short, they are a blend of skill sets where the formula tends to be masculine minority/feminine majority, even if they are men (and especially if they are women!).

As women—innately feminine beings—we have a sort of instinctive orientation toward these softer skills. But in working our way upward through our companies, we assimilate into the culture of the masculine majority because theirs is the time-honored style of doing business. In our eagerness to develop those masculine skills that make us look and feel just like the men around us, we take a step too far. Instead of adding masculine skills to our feminine foundation, we subjugate our instinctive feminine characteristics—an unconscious choice that eventually costs us dearly. We deny our intuition and focus on our logic; we bury our emotions and force ourselves to excel in our rationality. In this rush to conform, we strip ourselves of the very core of our future power: our feminine energies and talents. And without this side of ourselves fully functioning, we are unable and unqualified to take that final step into top-executive leadership.

Here's just one real-life story to illustrate the toll that a masculine-driven pathway takes on a woman's career advancement as well as her feminine psyche.

In September of 1990, a bright young accountant named Martha Evans began her career in a Big Six firm, her MBA and briefcase in hand and her hopes riding high that someday she would make it all the way to partner. During the first few proving-yourself years, Martha (and all of the other young accountants), worked seventy to eighty hours each week on huge client audits. Her problem-solving abilities, her talent for building strong client relationships, and the outstanding quality of her work soon made her a standout among her peers.

After two years, Martha was assigned to manage a group of accounts. Six years and three promotions later, Martha made it to manager. It wasn't until she was sitting in the first staff meeting with her new peers that Martha realized how suddenly "unique" she had become. She looked around the room at the other nine managers and discovered not one female face in the crowd.

"Hey, Martha, great to have you here!" was her greeting from Jerry, her former boss. As she settled into the chair next to him, he leaned over and whispered, "Don't worry about a thing. You're every bit as tough as any of these guys."

Martha wasn't worried at all. She knew that she was just as aggressive and competitive as any of the male managers. After all, these qualities were part of the skill set that had gotten her promoted this far. She just had to keep up the hard work, she thought, and she would continue moving up the ranks.

But she didn't keep moving up. She got stuck in the middle.

"The year that Rick spent in our London office just gave him the edge over you," Martha's boss told her, when the firm decided to promote a less-senior manager to partner. Naturally, Martha responded by taking on more responsibility and working even harder.

But when another younger manager, Joe, was promoted, Martha challenged the decision.

"I've always kept my billing hours higher than anyone else," she told the senior partner who was her boss. "I manage more clients than anybody else, and every client has given me the highest ratings. I know it, you know it, and the other partners know it. So what possible reason could all of you have for promoting Joe instead of me?"

"Nobody's arguing with your capabilities, Martha," was his patient-but-slightly-irritated response. "And your clients have told me how essential you are to them. Joe just had several managing partners in his court. Over the past year, his networking paid off and he brought in a couple of new clients that were real gems. That really made an impression on all of us."

Well, after losing to Rick and Joe, Martha decided to do something about it. She left.

Leaving the company was not Martha's first choice. She would have preferred to stay and make that last promotion to partner. But she simply didn't know how. Martha made the same mistake that millions of other women have made. In her quest to rise, she chose the pathway of assimilation: she relied—consciously or not—on her masculine energy, molding herself into an aggressive, competitive, tough manager so she could "out-macho" her male colleagues.

By the time Martha reached midmanagement, she had focused so single-mindedly on these left-brain skills that they weren't merely her primary assets; they had become her only assets. Martha continued to ignore her feminine-based skills, while the male managers around her were devoting more time and energy to building relationships with key senior managers.

When her male peers began to pass her by, Martha focused even more zealously on the logical, left-brain world of her work. She took on more work from more clients and signed up for several extended education courses. Her life became just two components: work and study.

Martha never realized the critical importance that the right-brain world of relationships and communication have on top management's promotion decisions. So instead of creating relationships with the senior partners above her in the hierarchy, she devoted more energy to strengthening the relationships and skills of her subordinates. When it was her turn to be named partner, she was judged as lacking because she had not bothered to develop and use those innate, feminine talents that would have qualified her for a leadership position.

What could Martha have done differently to achieve the outcome she desired? Plenty. For starters, instead of struggling so hard to fit into the masculine system that surrounded her, what if Martha had honored and nurtured her feminine qualities? What if, instead of relying exclusively on her tangible, quantitative work to achieve success, she had also developed her innate right-brain qualities of relationship building, holistic communication, creativity, and intuition? What if, instead of devoting herself to *doing* the work, she had also concentrated on *being* the leader?

Here are four critical choices that Martha would have made had she been functioning with the mind-set and behaviors of a feminine-based leader:

1. *Be proactive.* Instead of passively standing by, waiting for each promotion decision, Martha would have communicated her expectation clearly to her boss (and the appropriate partners) and enlisted him as an ally. Here, once again, Martha's single-minded focus on the work undid her. She was so intent on *doing* that she forgot the critical importance of *communicating* (and how much easier it is!). She simply expected her boss and the other partners to notice her. She would have had far more control over her future if, instead of waiting for their acknowledgment and approval, she had asked for what she wanted and explained why she deserved it . . . *before* they began their decision-making process. For Martha, a little direct communication would have accomplished far more than a lot of unnoticed work.

2. ***Build relationships upward.*** Instead of blindly focusing on the quality and quantity of her work, Martha would have looked for ways to connect with the key partners who would eventually make the decision to promote her. One of the common characteristics of women who get stuck in the middle is their stubborn belief that it is *what* they know (and what they *do*), rather than *whom* they know, that earns them their promotions. This belief works for a while. But women like Martha don't realize that once they are in middle management, the factors determining their promotability to a top executive position undergo a fundamental shift: It is not what you know, but whom you know and how strongly those people believe in you that figures most prominently in your continued advancement. If Martha had been firmly grounded in her feminine-based skill sets, she would have instinctively built relationships with the partners who were pivotal in promotion decisions. Then, the next time she was in the running for that final step into top management, she would have had the support of the quality of her work as well as the quality of her relationships.

3. ***Build a network.*** At a much earlier point in her career, Martha would have used her natural ability to build supportive, nurturing relationships and would have created a wide variety of networking activities with potential new clients. Because Martha (like so many women in business) viewed networking as a selfish and self-serving pursuit, she avoided it. She chose, instead, to dwell in the safety of her existing client relationships. Oh, if only she had recognized the possibility—and the value—of being a supportive networker! If she had merely approached potential clients from a feminine-based viewpoint of "how can I help you?" they would have embraced her. Human beings love to be nurtured, no matter how rich or confident or smart they may be. Eventually, at least a few of Martha's contacts would have become new clients for the firm. This would have proved her ability to grow the bottom line—a core mandate of leadership in any business.

4. ***Find the solution within yourself.*** Instead of focusing on "them" (and the wrongness of their decision) when top management didn't approve her promotion, Martha would have focused on herself and

what she could do differently to get the outcome she desired. Was top management showing their gender bias by choosing more-junior men over her? Perhaps. Was there a glass ceiling operating at the very highest levels of her accounting firm? Perhaps. But the moment Martha began concentrating her attention on these external factors, she doomed herself to fail in achieving her goal. Organizational barriers are negotiated more successfully by going around them rather than by charging headlong into them. Martha couldn't possibly have changed the historical and cultural ethos of her organization; yet she did have total power to change her own future within it. But once she began blaming "them"—every male partner who voted not to promote her—for her inability to make partner, Martha lost the perspective and the political support that would have enabled her to solve the problem and succeed.

This last point brings us to that ever-present business fact of life: the glass ceiling. Even after thirty years of government-sponsored studies, lawsuits, and formal legislation like the Civil Rights Act of 1991, a body as formidable as the United States Congress has failed to do much more than make a dent in the glass ceiling. Like most other external barriers, this one too stands strong when attacked.

In fact, attacking an external barrier to your progress is precisely the way to perpetuate it. For example, when Martha spoke to her boss and accused the partners of bias in their promotion decisions, their natural instinct was to defend their decision rather than admit wrongdoing. This doesn't mean they're bad guys; it simply means they're following an instinct of human nature. Instead of attacking the barrier, remain focused on finding the solution within yourself. What attitudes, skills, or behaviors do you need to change—within *you*—to get the result you desire? Take this path and you will find success far more often and with far fewer battle scars.

The final twist to our tale of Martha—and the millions of women like her—is the unalterable fact that, regardless of how masculine these women become in attitudes, actions, and skill sets, the delivery system for all of this is still feminine. Even if a woman exhibits strong, masculine attitudes and behaviors, she is still seen by those around her as a woman. As a result, each of us walks the tightrope that authors Pat Heim and Susan Golant describe in their book *Hardball for Women*:

> *If we become the aggressive, no-nonsense, win-at-all-cost players that our male counterparts pride themselves in being, then we are labeled "bossy," "obnoxious," "ambitious," or "strident bitches" who are "just mouthing off," and our input or achievements are summarily dismissed. If, on the other hand, we adhere to our childhood training and continue to be passive, nurturing, and cooperative in the business setting, then we're labeled "weak," "overly sensitive," "unambitious" females, and again, what we perceive of as important contributions and successes are dismissed. What a double bind!*[6]

This "double bind" scenario is still a fact of life for women in business. Acquiring the skills to plot an accurate career course and successfully steer yourself through the journey presents a particular challenge. Instead of struggling along the masculine pathway like Sisyphus, shoving that boulder up the mountain, you can choose to be like Alice, strolling down a more feminine road. You can go *through* the looking glass and into the wonderland of top management. The key to change is always internal. Instead of focusing on what's wrong *out there*, start accepting and nurturing what's right *in here*—those feminine talents that already exist inside you. This is your true, natural pathway to success, fulfillment, and joy!

Following this pathway does not mean abandoning the masculine-based skill sets. Rather, it requires you to respect and use both your left- and right-brain talents. And in a male-dominated business world, your feminine strengths can develop to their full potential only if you give them special consideration and extra attention.

For women especially, these feminine skills create the power behind a truly great leader. They are what makes a leader charismatic, inspirational, and powerful enough to move an entire organization onward and upward into the future. And they are more in demand now than at any point in the history of American business. The combined forces of corporate expansion and globalization have created a twenty-first-century business environment that is multiethnic as well as multicultural. Work teams are no longer composed of like-minded American Caucasian males; they range across genders and generations, ethnicities and ethos, countries and continents. In this diversified and global human landscape, the softer, right-brain skills required for communication, relationships, and community building are even more critical requirements for effective leadership.

The information, examples, insights, and tools in this book are designed to help you define your own career pathway from the middle to the top of corporate America—if that is what you choose. And because the male majority still runs corporate America, part of the process has got to be about helping you succeed in a man's world without compromising the most important and valuable feminine qualities that make you a woman. Certainly, thought and behavior patterns that originate in the logical world of the left brain are mandatory skills to have in today's workplace, but not to the exclusion of your softer, right-brained skills. These are your true, valuable assets for leadership. Our aim is to give you a larger appreciation of your powers—and your challenges—as a woman working in a business world that is still primarily defined through the eyes of the men who run it.

So do you really want to take charge of your career? Of course you do! The first step is to celebrate and honor who you truly are. The second is to build the internal attitudes and behaviors that will support you in becoming who you aspire to be.

Only when we begin acknowledging and using those unique strengths and skills that come from our feminine side will we reach our true potential as professional women. Only then will we achieve that blend of masculine and feminine that marries the rational with the creative, the powerful with the sensitive, and the struggle with the joy as we pursue our individual career dreams. This is the innovation that is our unique gift to our organizations. Once we focus on the added value that we, as women, bring to corporate America, we step onto the pathway that will propel more of us to the tops of our companies. And this is how we can begin *dancing on the glass ceiling*.

CHAPTER 2

KNOW YOURSELF AND YOUR DESTINATION

Dance Lesson #2: If you want to be both successful and happy at the end of your life, you've got to start at the beginning, with a deep understanding of who you are today and who you want to become.

The two *whos* in this Dance Lesson are the alpha and the omega of your professional and personal life journey. Once you have a clear understanding of them, you have taken the first critical step to defining the pathway that you will follow in life, as you confront the different dilemmas and the myriad choices that occur along the way.

Developing this understanding of your present and future selves is not such a simple task. To truly know who you are and who you want to become requires your commitment to a process of thought and reflection. The journey begins in the world of your values, passions, and dreams. These are the keynotes that define your character and guide your accomplishments. Without them, you are a body adrift, a dancer in need of the rhythms and melodies of the music.

As women, we are especially prone to embarking on our career pathways without much forethought about where we want to go or who we want to become in the process. Most of us don't have an overall career plan, so we simply respond to opportunities as they occur. Those few among us who are truly proactive may plan their careers a year or two at a time. But finding a woman with a clearly defined endgame is about as rare as uncovering a diamond in the sands of the Kalahari Desert.

Whether driven by nature or nurture—or a little bit of both— women are reluctant vision builders. The seeds of our resistance rest partially in the lessons we learned in our childhood play and partially in our genetic encoding.

Although more girls than ever play team sports, the competitive playing fields of baseball, soccer, football, basketball, and so forth remain the primary domain of boys. For them, playtime is devoted to learning about strategy, taking risks, setting goals, and building the leadership skills that bring victory. Even off the sports playing field, the play of boys is a competitive, one-upmanship pursuit. Boys crave victory. Not so with girls. Our play domains tend to be egalitarian and grounded in cooperation (rather than competition), as Pat Heim and Susan Golant write in *Hardball for Women*:

> *Girls grow up in a flat organization rather than hierarchies. It doesn't take long for a little girl to discover that if she wants to be a leader and she starts pushing her playmates around, relationships will suffer; friends will call her bossy and avoid her. As a result, she tries to keep the power dead even.*[1]

The patterns we learned from years of childhood play are difficult to abandon as adults. Setting our sights on a vision represents a fundamental change in how we see ourselves in relation to our peers. Choosing to pursue a vision is *not* keeping the power dead even. It is a conscious choice to become somehow bigger and better than we—and our peers—are today.

Creating a clearly defined vision is a fundamental step that sets the course of your career (and life) journey. Just imagine yourself in Los Angeles, about to begin a trip east, with no specific destination in mind. You get into the car and simply start driving east on the main freeway out of L.A. Each time the road forks, you choose to stay on the main highway. These large interstates, you reason, will get you there faster, wherever "there" may be.

Four days later you arrive at the East Coast end of your last interstate highway: Miami. The newness is exciting at first. But after a few days the novelty wears off, the permanence of the heat and humidity and big-city crowds sets in, and you realize that you are miserable! Miami isn't where you wanted to be at all. You start thinking, and for the first time you consciously envision what you want: to watch the leaves turn red in the fall, to downhill ski in the winter, to be surrounded not by crowds but by nature. As you peruse the map for those towns that fit your vision, your finger finally lands on Lake Placid, New York. This is the destination you really wanted! So you pack up your car and drive north to New York State. Eventually you reach Lake Placid, and your life is full of joy and contentment again. It just took you longer to get there.

A career journey has many similarities to this hypothetical trip from L.A. to Lake Placid. Most women will travel down many roads, making choices at each fork but without a clear idea of exactly where they're headed. And because a career covers far more time and distance than our example, the opportunities to go off course are amplified exponentially. As advertising agency founder Bill Bernbach once said, "All roads lead somewhere, if you don't know where you're going."

Even if you've already traveled down several roads, it's never too late to stop and think about where you truly want to end up. If you want a career that gives you joy, both during the journey and at your final destination, spending time in reflection is a critical requirement. You need to understand who you are, who you want to become, what you want to achieve in your career, and how you want to do it. For you are reinventing your future, and these are the guideposts for every decision you'll make along the way. They'll help you recognize and avoid the detours that could take you off course. When you have these guideposts solidly in place, you will achieve your dreams with less effort. Your journey will become one of joy and discovery rather than stress and uncertainty.

By the time you finish reading this chapter and completing the exercises, you will have the following guideposts in place:

- *Defining Values:* These are the six or eight operating principles that you hold most dear, the touchstones of all of your future decisions. They are a critical component of that nebulous quality called character. They define the essence of who you are and how you choose to travel on your life and career pathways.
- *Heart's Purpose:* This is the expression of your passion, that category of *doing* that is most fun and fulfilling for you. It is the why that explains the Activating Vision you choose to pursue. It's the burning drive—the fuel—that connects your energy to where you want to be.
- *Activating Vision:* This is the broad accomplishment that you want to achieve with your career. It is not merely a goal; it is your endgame. And it will take at least fifteen to twenty years to accomplish. Your Activating Vision is the single statement that represents your grandest dreams of who you want to become as a final result of your efforts. It is a dream of *being*, rather than simply *doing*.

The absence of any of these three guideposts has a definite impact on the executive's career results. It could be a disappointed vice president who grabbed the brass ring only to be disillusioned; or the mediocre performance of a "worker bee" stuck in the grayness of a midlevel job that brings no satisfaction. The symptoms may look different, but the root issue is the same. Each woman failed to spend the time to truly explore these three critical components for creating the life she wanted.

In Nancy's coaching work over the years, she has found that most female executives have done only a small portion of this course-setting work, if they've done it at all. Most professional women are creatures of action. They put far more value on doing than on being in their careers. Taking time out to think, which is so important when crafting a career pathway, looks and feels like inaction to them. So they bypass it.

Spending the time to think, reflect, and develop a clear, written definition of each of these guideposts is an ongoing process and a critical first step if you want to live your life by design rather than by accident.

When one or more of these foundations is missing, the pragmatic urgencies of today will dominate your field of focus, and the output of your efforts will be deficient. You will begin to drift as you settle into a pattern of reacting to the present rather than proactively creating the future you desire. The dance that is your career will begin to feel more like an endless dirge than a joyous opus. Herein lies the root of our unhappiness and dissatisfaction with our careers, our lives, and our deepest selves.

If we simply spend the time necessary to develop the three foundations of our Defining Values, Heart's Purpose, and Activating Vision, we can put our lives on a pathway of self-fulfillment, effortlessness, and joy. Robert Louis Stevenson described the benefits most eloquently: "To be what we are, and to become what we are capable of becoming, is the only end in life."

The Power of Patchwork Quilting

While women may be reluctant vision setters, we have historically off-set that weakness by adopting a different pattern of achievement that is uniquely feminine. George Mason University professor Mary Catherine Bateson calls it "patchwork quilting," a process of putting life together one piece at a time, often in a random pattern created from the odds and ends that life offers us.[2] While this kind of patchwork quilting sometimes appears to be accidental (or even chaotic), it is a powerful secret weapon that has enabled women to excel at making the best of whatever problems and opportunities come their way.

The patchwork-quilting process is a unique gift and a highly effective strategy that should be retained. It can be seen at work in the lives of many women who were pioneers in achieving success in various fields. Precisely because these women were "firsts," they had no role models to guide them on their own pathway to success. They couldn't envision some grand, crowning achievement for their careers. They simply overcame barriers and took advantage of whatever opportunities presented themselves along the way. Each new step represented the achievement of a small goal—a first-ever foray into unexplored career territory.

Their route upward was taken one step at a time, based on making the best of what life offered them. It was an improvisational dance, created in response to the music of life.

Cathleen Black, president of Hearst Magazines, described this pattern when Oprah Winfrey interviewed her in 1999:

> *For a lot of women [careers] are more sequential. . . . You got into one job and you looked at who was around you, at who had the offices if you didn't, and said, "Well, I can do that!" And then you got into that job. And you said, "How about the next one?" . . . Not maybe three levels up, but the next one. . . . For a lot of women it kind of unfurled.*[3]

The stories of the following two women illustrate the randomness, the flexibility, and the potency of this patchworking pattern of career building.

As the daughter of *Washington Post* publisher/owner Eugene Meyer, Katharine Meyer grew up in a world that expected her to marry well and take her place as a socialite wife and mother. She quit her job at the *Post* soon after marrying Phil Graham, and over the years that followed, they had four children. Phil became the newspaper's publisher, eventually buying Eugene's voting stock. By her own admission, Katharine was "quaking in her boots" when her husband died suddenly in 1963. After almost twenty years as the socialite wife and mother, she assumed control of an international media empire, which included the *Post*, *Newsweek*, *Times-Herald*, and several broadcasting companies. When she took over her husband's position as president, she had no expertise and no respect from her employees. But over time she developed both, eventually becoming chairperson of the Washington Post Company and one of the most powerful—and admired—leaders in the publishing world.

Another woman who utilized the patchworking method is Sandra Day O'Connor. In 1952, she graduated third in her Stanford Law School class. But no firm in Los Angeles or San Francisco would hire a woman as a lawyer. Life didn't offer her a private-sector job, so she took one in government as deputy county attorney in San Mateo, California. Over the next few years, while her husband was building his career, she adapted hers. She was a civilian attorney in the army's quartermaster corps in Germany, and when the family moved back to Arizona she had several nonpaying civic positions. From there, she became an assistant attorney general, then on to the Arizona senate. Later, she was elected as a Maricopa County Superior Court judge. Her career pathway looked more like a zigzag than a straight line shot, but in hindsight, her zigzags wove neatly together into one clearly upward career pathway. In 1981, she became the first female justice on the United States Supreme Court.

These two women's stories are proof of the potency of patchwork quilting in building a successful career, even when the world offers handicaps rather than helping hands. When you add the three-pronged powers of Defining Values, Heart's Purpose, and Activating Vision to your ability to make the best of what life offers, you will accelerate your career progress because you will be honing in on your ultimate destination from the very onset of your trip. In merging these two patterns of quilting and visioning, you free the opportunist and the idealist within you to work hand-in-hand. You give yourself a distinct advantage over your male counterparts, who are not as schooled in capitalizing on the opportunities hidden in the patchwork quilt of corporate life.

Developing Your Defining Values

Life is a never-ending cycle of thought, decision making, actions, reactions, and evaluations. Nobody has the all-purpose guidebook that gets you from birth to death with a flawless record as a human being. We are each bound to have lives filled with triumphs and mistakes. It is our values that influence every "yes" and "no" in our lives. They are the daily compass points that guide our every choice and action as we journey toward our Activating Vision.

The first step in your vision-building process is to identify those Defining Values that represent the essence of your character: who you are and what you stand for. They are the operating principles that govern your professional and personal lives. They determine how you will travel the pathway between where you are now and where you will be once you achieve your goal. They are the values you hold most dear, that truly distinguish you—for better or for worse—as you pass through this world. Defining Values have no timeline. Oftentimes, they were formulated early in your life but not always. Once formed, they forever own a piece of your heart. They are enduring.

Jackie Schiff was almost thirty when she first discovered one of her most important Defining Values. Even as a small child, Jackie had followed in her father's footsteps. He held a Ph.D. in electrical engineering and taught at a prestigious midwestern university. Encouraged by her father, Jackie aimed for M.I.T., where she earned bachelor's and master's degrees in his chosen field. Her father valued financial stability, so Jackie spent the first ten years of her career working for Fortune 500 companies. She was highly paid, highly successful . . . and profoundly unhappy. But she didn't really know why.

Then the Internet exploded. One night over drinks, Jackie and Eric, a close friend and colleague, began fantasizing over the e-companies they would create. After several of these "drinks and dreams" sessions, their ideas became more realistic, and they began getting more serious. Then they hit on the "big idea." Over the next three months, Jackie and Eric spent every spare hour developing a full-fledged business plan while they continued working full-time in their current jobs. A small venture capital firm agreed to make a large start-up investment, but only if Jackie and Eric were devoted full-time to the new company. Now the two would-be entrepreneurs faced their defining moment.

"Jackie, the only way we'll ever make this company happen is if we both give it 100 percent," Eric told her. "I'm ready and willing to quit my job tomorrow . . . but only if you quit too."

"But what happens if we fail?" Jackie replied. She was worried about her ability to rejoin the ranks of corporate America if her bid to become an entrepreneur failed.

"I'd rather think about what happens if we succeed," Eric said. "But even if we fail, we'll add some great experience to our résumés. So the way I see it, no matter what, we'll end up in better jobs than we have right now! And this will be so much more fun!"

In that moment, in hearing that one word, Jackie got her "Aha!" She would, for the first time in her career, be doing work that was fun. Jackie finally realized that one of her Defining Values was entrepreneurship. Oh, if she had only known this from the beginning of her career! Just imagine how different the last ten years of her life would have been.

Defining Values can cover a wide range of possibilities. And because each one is a broad term, the description of precisely what that particular value means to you and how it will operate in your life will be unique to you. Building your list is the first step; below are a few options to get you started:

Honesty and integrity: I will be truthful and fair.

Independence: I will take care of my own wants and needs.

Personal responsibility: I will take responsibility for my actions and fulfill my commitments to myself and to others.

Equality: I will not engage in discriminatory practices, and I will work toward the elimination of such practices in others.

Adventure: I will lead a professional and personal life that is rich with the adventure of new experiences.

Continuous personal growth and learning: I will always work on improving myself in some way.

Family: I will be a faithful, loving wife and mother, putting these relationships first among all others in my life.

Spirituality: I will spend time developing my personal relationship with God and with others in my faith community.

Creativity: In whatever career/profession I pursue, innovation and imagination will be central to my activities and at the heart of my personal performance.

Philanthropy: I will devote time and money toward improving the lives of others.

Personal wealth: I will have all the money I need to fulfill my wants and needs, and those of my family.

The willingness to identify with this last value, in particular, seems to be yet another differentiator between men and women in the world of business. The value of money is almost instinctive for men, who proudly include it in their lists of Defining Values. After all, they have been raised to believe that achieving financial success is a responsibility, part of their career purpose, and an indicator of their level of success as a person. Women, on the other hand, often visibly flinch in our seminar program when we begin probing them for personal wealth as one of their Defining Values. They seem to feel that money is an unworthy value—too shallow, too selfish—and therefore not acceptable to include. Yet by the end of our seminar discussion, most women have admitted that it does belong on their list as well.

Once you have built a list of the values that are important to you, use these two techniques to verify your choices and reduce your list to the six or eight most essential:

1. *Contemplate:* Think through several "challenge" scenarios, in which you would make a decision that is in opposition to this value. Would you feel a true sense of loss, guilt, or wrongdoing? If yes, then this is probably a Defining Value for you. Pretend, for example, that you receive a tremendous job offer in a new company—your first chance to actually manage an entire division. It includes a significant bump in both salary and bonus potential, but 50 percent of your time would be spent on the road. Imagine yourself working in the new job, and then compare this to your feelings if you stayed in your current position. Perhaps you have young children at home. Your choice may depend on the priority of your value for personal wealth compared to your value for family. Either option comes at a cost. If you take the job, you will have less family time. If you don't take the job, you will have less income (and perhaps less future career success). You can only choose one value, and in making that choice, you have accepted the cost for holding on to that value. This is one of the surest proofs of a Defining Value.

   Holding on to a Defining Value often looks to the outside world as though you are making a highly irrational decision, because you are using your feelings—not your logic—to sort the priorities in your life. But once you begin to rely on these operating principles in your decision making, you will experience less struggle and more flow in your career and your life.

2. *Listen:* Keep a thirty-day journal of your thoughts and business decision-making experiences. At the end of the thirty days, review your journal to glean any new insights on what your defining values really are versus what you thought they would be.

This process is, at its very core, about knowing yourself. It is about making career and business decisions based on your own, enduring, internal foundation of values, rather than the fickle, fleeting circumstances of your external environment. It is about remaining true to yourself throughout your career journey. And this is where true joy can be found.

Discovering Your Heart's Purpose

The simplest way to understand the difference between your Activating Vision and your Heart's Purpose is to imagine yourself on a long sailing voyage. Your Activating Vision is the ultimate destination, so far away and seemingly impossible to reach that you can only imagine it as you sit in the harbor, preparing to start your trip. But you know that once you reach that destination, you will be someone bigger than you are today, and you will have accomplished something extraordinary. Your Heart's Purpose is the inner drive that compels you to embark on a particular journey in the first place. It's the reason you want to make the trip. And when this trip is completed, this same Heart's Purpose will be the reason you plan another one. Because while an Activating Vision can eventually be achieved and replaced with a new one, Heart's Purpose is a specific, ongoing desire that you can never complete or finish. It just is, and it always will be.

We call it your Heart's Purpose because it is rarely rationally driven. Instead, it has an emotional center that arises from your own need to fulfill your reason for being. It is why you've been placed on this earth, and your giftedness is the acting expression of this reason.

Learning to identify your own Heart's Purpose may be a little easier once you see what it looks like for someone else. When you think of Lucille Ball, for example, you might conclude that her Heart's Purpose was acting or performing. Yet if you look deeper, you realize that virtually her entire career was spent in a certain kind of acting and performing: comedy. So her Heart's Purpose may have been to bring joy into the lives of others by making them laugh. Thomas Edison is another example. He was an inventor, but his inventions were of a certain type. Perhaps his Heart's Purpose was to invent things that improve the quality of ordinary people's lives.

Uncovering your Heart's Purpose is an uncomplicated but deeply contemplative process. It happens not in a single session but over time. Start by taking a trip through the memories of your life. From childhood, you have been gifted with special interests, natural skills, mental acuity, physical prowess, and so on. Because these gifts are built into your being to a certain extent, they are easily taken for granted. But examining what you're good at, what fascinates you, and what feels most fun and rewarding will give you the clues to your Heart's Purpose—that central, driving reason for being that expresses both your unique giftedness and your special passion.

Candy spent about six months contemplating these three areas in her own efforts to identify her Heart's Purpose. Here is a condensed version of what she discovered about herself:

- *What fascinates her:* People and prose have been a lifelong obsession. Even as a child, Candy was a passionate reader. She loved not just the stories but also the way language was used. And she has always been fascinated by the unique inner workings of people—how they think and why they feel a certain way, what causes them pain and what brings them joy.
- *What she's good at (her giftedness):* Candy's strongest qualities include unflagging optimism, strong speaking and writing skills, and mentoring and motivating others toward success.

- *What feels most rewarding to her:* Nurturing others, writing, and speaking to large audiences bring Candy joy. Candy began writing stories in third grade and human-interest articles for her school quarterly in the fourth grade. She wrote for her high school newspaper and was the editor in chief her junior and senior years. In college she majored in journalism. Her most joyous activities as an advertising executive centered on the development of new strategies and ad campaigns, and the "on-stage" thrill of new business presentations.

When Candy traveled back into her childhood and began looking at these three areas, she found the recurrent themes that led her to her Heart's Purpose: to create stories and ideas that inspire people to believe in themselves and to reach for their dreams. This, then, is the *why* behind her public speaking, her seminar/coaching work, and her writing, both fiction and nonfiction.

To identify your own passions, ask yourself the following questions. Give yourself time and a peaceful environment in which to contemplate the answers, and a good pen and plenty of paper on which to write down all of your thoughts. This process may take you several days or even several months. Capture every one of your thoughts and ideas and avoid any desire to edit your initial thinking:

- What activities fascinated me as a child? What was the most fun?
- What am I good at?
- What issues or causes am I passionate about?
- As an adult, what activities are most fun for me?
- As an adult, what activities are the most rewarding for me?
- How do I want to be remembered?

Within this list, the most important questions are those that focus on what is fun, rewarding, and what you are passionate about.

Fern Blackwell's story gives us a real-life example of the discovery of Heart's Purpose, as well as the special talents that aligned with her Heart's Purpose. Fern was born in 1940 in a rural part of South Dakota that was buried in poverty. Everyone was poor, so the deprivation she felt as a child was more physical than psychological. Fern's energies were spent discovering ways to serve the purposes of her stomach rather than her heart.

Fern managed to graduate from high school, and then she hitchhiked to L.A. where she worked full-time as a waitress for the next eight years to put herself through a local state college. Fern was a whiz at math and accounting. These were her built-in skills, so naturally she majored in business. At the time, she wasn't thinking about her Heart's Purpose. She was only thinking about getting a good-paying, secure job when she graduated so that she'd never feel poverty again. Hers was strictly a "head's purpose." At twenty-six, she took an accounting job in the space division of TRW, where she stayed for the next twenty-three years. She never rose higher than project analyst, and she was never really happy or particularly fulfilled with the work. But the hours were a predictable eight-to-five and the pay was enough to support her and her two kids after she was divorced.

In the late 1980s space exploration became an unpopular defense budget item. Fern, like thousands of others, was laid off and given a severance package as consolation. She was forty-nine. After spending a year searching unsuccessfully for another accounting job, Fern was forced to rethink her career. For the first time in her life, she began to reflect on what she loved to do rather than simply what would pay the bills.

Fern had always had a vegetable garden and fruit trees in her yard. She seemed to have been born with a green thumb, and as a child her happiest moments were tending the vegetables in her family's tiny front yard. As an adult, she spent most of her free time in the garden. Tending the corn, tomatoes, and carrots had become a family affair for Fern and her little girls. These were, Fern realized, her happiest hours. Helping things grow was her Heart's Purpose! So she called her brother in Colorado and put her house up for sale. She bought a small farm next to his and a dozen good books on farming and raising cattle. She even bought an old tractor. Then Fern and her daughters started raising chickens and cows and planting vegetables. Today, she is not rich and she's not poor. But finally, she is truly happy.

Choosing to ignore your Heart's Purpose may seem like an easier, safer, or more lucrative pathway in life. But as Fern's story shows us, it always demands the most severe sacrifice: a career that fails to give you a full measure of joy, success, or self-esteem. These benefits can enter fully into your life only when you are in touch with your Heart's Purpose and intently going after it. It's simple, really: pursue your passion, and joy and success will surely follow.

Activating Vision: What Is It and How Do You Get It?

Your chances of reaching your desired destination in life rise exponentially when you have created an Activating Vision for yourself rather than randomly tossing a coin each time you are faced with the difficult barriers and crossroads that life so often throws your way. In the absence of an Activating Vision, your personal life and your career can become like the poetic wanderings of a little calf:

The Calf-Path

One day, through the primeval wood,
A calf walked home, as good calves should;
But made a trail all bent askew,
A crooked trail as all calves do.

Since then two hundred years have fled,
And, I infer, the calf is dead.
But still he left behind his trail,
And thereby hangs my moral tale.

The trail was taken up next day
By a lone dog that passed that way;
And then a wise bell-wether sheep
Pursued the trail o'er vale and steep,
And drew the flock behind him, too,
As good bell-wethers always do.

And from that day, o'er hill and glade,
Through those old woods a path was made;
And many men wound in and out,
And dodged, and turned, and bent about
And uttered words of righteous wrath
Because 'twas such a crooked path.
But still they followed—do not laugh—
The first migration of that calf,
And through this winding wood-way stalked,
Because he wobbled when he walked.

This forest path became a lane,
That bent, and turned, and turned again;
This crooked lane became a road,
Where many a poor horse with his load
Toiled on beneath the burning sun,
And traveled some three miles in one.
And thus a century and a half
They trod the footsteps of that calf.

The years passed on in swiftness fleet,
The road became a village street;
And this, before men were aware,
A city's crowded thoroughfare;
And soon the central street was this
Of a renowned metropolis;
And men two centuries and a half
Trod the footsteps of that calf.

—Sam Walter Foss, 1858–1911

The reality is that without a defined "going to" place, you become like the primeval calf, and circumstances rather than your own conscious choices control your journey. An Activating Vision is the third foundation in your career and life planning. Going through the process of determining what you really want provides clarity to all of your future decision making. And the sheer act of vision building generates a concentration of energy that stimulates you to move from complacency to action. It *activates* you. When life's unexpected twists and turns inevitably occur, it is your Activating Vision that keeps you directed toward your ultimate destination—your Lake Placid.

The Activating Vision is a statement that describes who you will be and what you will be known for after you have devoted fifteen or twenty years to achieving this identity for yourself. One of the key criteria for an Activating Vision is that it must be bigger and bolder than you are today. As a result, it is absolutely unbelievable *today*. The moment you establish this vision for yourself, you start living in two worlds, your *today* and your *tomorrow*. Tension occurs between your existing comfort zone and where you are going. This tension comes from the beliefs you hold about your own unworthiness to live in the impossible dream that is your Activating Vision.

This steadfast belief in our own unworthiness is a characteristically female trait. It has been bred into us throughout history, across cultures, and in the core tenets of many of the world's religions. We have been taught to think of ourselves as subservient, weaker, requiring protection, even somehow innately evil by nature. Even today, in the modern-day culture of North America, we carry these feelings as if they were genetically encoded.

The first step to overcoming this so-called unworthiness coding is to understand—and believe—that in fifteen or twenty years, all things become possible. Your Activating Vision statement is where you take ownership of what is possible for you to achieve.

Your vision of that end point is what activates you to begin your trip. You see, the very act of defining your vision sets off an entire chain reaction of both cognitive and cosmic energy that will propel you toward the achievement of your dream, even if you have doubts about your ability to complete the journey. Both your own brain and the universe will support you in powerful but often unseen ways. Radiating from the oldest part of our brain stem is a small network of cells called our reticular activating system (RAS). The RAS has a unique function of filtering incoming information. It is a sort of subconscious navigation system that automatically supports our goals and dreams so we can produce the results we desire with greater ease. The unique aspect of the RAS is that it is always working; when you don't consciously use it to support yourself, it will take its lead from your subconscious. International consultant Carol Kinsey Goman, a recognized expert on change, describes the process: "When you are committed to a clearly envisioned goal, your brain will act like an autopilot, steering your perceptions and behavior toward success."[4]

Another facet of the raw power of the unconscious mind is its sheer speed. Mathematician Peter Ouspensky has estimated that the subconscious mind functions up to thirty thousand times faster than the conscious mind. So harnessing its power is the key to effortless achievement. And giving your unconscious mind the gift of an Activating Vision is what harnesses that power.

Creativity consultant Robert Fritz explains the special power of vision in *The Path of Least Resistance*: "Vision has power, for through vision you can easily reach beyond the ordinary to the extraordinary. . . . Vision also has a magic quality. I define magic as seeing the results without seeing the entire process leading to those results."[5]

The second force that supports us is the entire field of energy that surrounds us in the universe. Whether you name that field of energy God or Higher Power or Nature, it is there. It expands your imagination and enlarges your dreams of the future. As values and vocations expert Jacqueline McMakin explains:

> *[Once] we have truly committed to follow our dream, there exists beyond ourselves and our conscious will a powerful force that helps us along the way and nurtures our growth and transformation. Our journey is guided by invisible hands with infinitely greater accuracy than is possible through our unaided conscious will.*[6]

Developing your Activating Vision is akin to being Hamlet and going through a thought process of "to be, or not to be." There is no tried-and-true process that will get you to a final, magical statement. It is a journey of discovery, of searching through scads of alternatives and then creating more. When one of them gives you that deep-breath, goosebumps reaction and you feel a slight flutter in your heart (joy, perhaps?), then you've got it.

While there is no prescribed method for developing your Activating Vision, there is a basic formula that you can use for the statement itself: "To be [insert how you would want to be described], whose work [describe what impact or contribution you want your work to be known for]." Add two or three sentences that enhance this first one, including vivid visual and emotional components.

This statement describes what you must accomplish with your work, which will enable you to become the person you desire to be. If you cannot explain your vision in clear, precise, well-chosen terms to a friend, then you haven't actually created a motivating vision. You need to go back to the drawing board. You must both believe in and be motivated by your vision if you want the universe to support you in achieving it.

Once you have developed these components of your Activating Vision, write them down and then speak them out loud as a way of constantly committing yourself to the journey.

Your Activating Vision should be a vivid picture that you hold in your mind's eye as you go through the thick and thin of life. Achieving this vision of your "going to" place will necessitate sacrifices—often time and interim pleasures—along the way. So it needs to be strong enough and satisfying enough to hold you on your path and motivate you to continually stretch yourself to achieve your dreams.

Candy's Activating Vision, for example, is this:

To be an internationally respected, bestselling "renaissance author" and public speaker whose various works of fiction and nonfiction have a positive, life-changing impact on people around the world.

This particular vision describes what Candy wants to achieve over the course of the next fifteen to twenty years. It is a new Activating Vision for her because she has embarked on a new career. It bears absolutely no resemblance to any vision statement she would have concocted for the first twenty years of her professional career, when she was steadily working her way up the ranks of the advertising industry.

Although Candy and Nancy are writing partners, their vision statements are not exactly the same. Nancy's is the following:

> *To be an internationally respected agent of change for business in the twenty-first century, whose writing, lectures, and personal coaching encourage people to become more open and joyful in their work and to achieve bigger results with less effort.*

When this book was about two-thirds written, Candy and Nancy realized that the material would translate into a powerful and transformational seminar program for women. Since they both loved to lecture and make presentations, they created the program in May of 2000. Suddenly, Candy and Nancy were no longer simply writing partners; they were also business partners.

As with any service business, marketing consumed a great deal of time. In fact, for the next six months, the majority of their efforts were focused on marketing and sales rather than writing, teaching, and speaking. Tension began to occur in their relationship. Nancy was frustrated about how little time and effort Candy was devoting to the business; Candy was frustrated about how much time and effort Nancy was demanding of her. Realizing that they needed to identify the root of the problem, and then solve it, Nancy took on her familiar coaching role. She asked Candy to spend some of her upcoming four-week vacation in Montana thinking about what she really wanted to do in the business and how much time she wanted to spend.

Dutifully, Candy did. After mulling things over from every left-brain angle she could find, Candy still could not put her finger on the problem. So she pulled out her Activating Vision statement to see if it could help her. And sure enough, she got her "Aha!" Her statement contained not a single word about business!

As soon as she returned from her vacation, she called Nancy.

"So, what decisions did you make?" Nancy asked Candy. "How much time are you comfortable spending on the business?"

"I'm not sure you're going to like the answer," Candy began.

"Hey, you know that any answer will be OK with me, as long as you live up to whatever time commitment you make," Nancy told her.

"OK. Well, how does *zero* sound?" Candy laughed as she said it, but Nancy knew that she was 100 percent serious.

"Umm, well, that's a little less than I expected," Nancy answered. "So tell me, how did you get all the way down to zero?"

Candy told Nancy to pull out their two Activating Vision statements and look at what was different about them. Nancy saw it right away: Candy's vision was about writing and speaking, not business; Nancy's vision, on the other hand, had business at its very center!

"What I realized when I read it was that I'd already spent twenty years in marketing, and I was tired of it! I don't want to be in that kind of business anymore. I just want to write and talk!" Candy felt both happy and relieved. (And to tell the truth, Nancy was too!) So Nancy took over the business, and Candy got back to writing her first fiction book. She takes a royalty on the seminars and occasionally helps Nancy lead them.

And they lived happily ever after . . .

In developing your own Activating Vision, you must be willing to set your target high in the stratosphere and go for it with all of your power. Then, just as women have been doing successfully for generations before you, weave the glorious fabric of your life with every colorful thread that it offers up to you. And remind yourself that anything is possible for someone who believes in her vision and acts in alignment with that desired end result.

Putting It All Together

Developing your Activating Vision, your Heart's Purpose, and your Defining Values is a demanding, nonlinear process that does not come easily for most people. It takes time, and you will probably have plenty of scribbled on, wadded up pieces of paper covering the floor before you're through. A technique called Mind Mapping may help you discover these insights.

Mind Mapping helps you tap into your brain's natural "radiant" thinking pattern, which is a more integrated left-brain/right-brain thought process so critical to identifying your vision, purpose, and values. Creating a Mind Map is an unfolding process that opens your mind to exploring connected concepts and then capturing these thoughts on paper. You can use the Mind Map to reveal your dreams for both your professional and your personal lives. All you need is a large sheet of paper, colored pens or pencils, and a willingness to allow yourself to be creative.

Begin by writing in the middle of the page the issue you wish to explore. In this case you would write something like "Successful, Joyful Life" and circle it. The main goals of this exercise are to collect and record all of your thoughts as they bubble up to the surface, discover how they are connected, and then see what emerges from those thoughts and connections. There are no rules, except that you be as creative and colorful as possible while your Mind Map unfolds. For example, drawing pictures rather than simply writing words will add value to your map. Use symbols, arrows, and lines to show connection.

Allow yourself to work on your Mind Map over several days or even several weeks to give your subconscious mind a chance to influence your ideal career vision and your dreams for your personal life. This is an exploration, not a timed exercise with right or wrong answers.

Once completed, your Mind Map will provide the basis for you to either extract the values, purpose, and vision that have been directly expressed in the map, or to back into them based on your map's content. Put your Mind Map in a place where you will see it every day. This frequent reminder will help your conscious and unconscious mind stay focused on achieving your vision.

If you want to explore the concept of Mind Mapping in further depth, read *The Mind Map Book* by Dr. Tony Buzan. He is both the originator and reigning authority on this subject.

Following is an example map based on Nancy's work in discovering her own Defining Values, Heart's Purpose, and Activating Vision. We have described Nancy's mapping steps below to give you an idea of the thinking process that goes into the building of a Mind Map and how these three outputs emerge from that thinking.

At the center of Nancy's map, she has placed the words "My Life: Fully Passionate, Fully Alive." The key sections of her map are Defining Values, Heart's Desires, and Spirit Life. As she developed her map, her Heart's Purpose arose from the Heart's Desires section, and her Activating Vision grew from a combination of the Spirit Life and Heart's Desires inputs.

When Nancy began to build her Mind Map, she revisited her past and discovered those gifts and talents that made her unique and delighted her heart. She remembered the pot holders she had diligently woven every night when she was in third grade, which she then sold to neighbors the following afternoon. She initiated the first pot holder mass-production line in her neighborhood when she convinced three friends to join her, and she began to make a profit. Through this memory, Nancy found her first clue about her Heart's Purpose: a love of business and a talent for managing people and achieving results.

She remembered that when she was a teenager friends would call her for support and wisdom with their daily heartaches. Here was the second clue: a desire to support people through difficulties and help them respond more powerfully to life's challenges.

Nancy's third clue emerged from her experience in acting classes: the joy she felt when she was connecting emotionally with an audience. This gave her a glimpse of who she could be, despite her current terror of standing up in front of people.

Her fourth clue introduced writing into the picture, when she came across a 1983 journal entry: "I want to make a difference in people's lives through speaking and writing. I'd like to write a book that will transform people in business."

Thus, Nancy found her Heart's Purpose: to introduce new concepts to people in business that expand their perceptions about themselves and their work, and help them reach entirely new levels of enthusiasm and empowerment.

This Heart's Purpose drove her Activating Vision: to be an internationally respected agent of change for business in the twenty-first century, whose writing, lectures, and personal coaching help people become more open and joyful in their work and achieve bigger results with far less effort.

When you make the decision to follow a career pathway that is guided by your Defining Values, Heart's Purpose, and Activating Vision, you become the master creator of your own life. You define the alpha and omega of your career and the foundations that will guide your journey. Once these foundations are in place, as Walt Disney said, "If you can dream it, you can do it." What you dream is what you will become.

For each of us, the dream is different. And it doesn't have to be about getting rich or being famous or running a big company. It has to do with achieving something that will bring you bundles of joy and perpetual satisfaction.

Nancy's Mind Map

SPIRIT LIFE
God
Contribution to others
Finances
Time
Talents
Prayer life
Community

My Life
Fully Passionate
Fully Alive

DEFINING VALUES
Honesty
Growing and learning
God in everything
I'm responsible
Honor others
Stand for beliefs
Walk your talk
Your vote counts
Time for contemplation

HEART'S DESIRES

Passions

Selling
Managing people
Influencing
Creating
Making money
Building profitability
Change/new

Learning and growing
New ideas
New experiences
Asking questions
Sharing concepts
Open mind and attitude

Family
Friends
Building
Adapting
Growing

Skiing downhill
Biking
Reading
Swimming
Arts and crafts
Knitting
Macrame
Crochet
Pottery
Cross-country skiing
Hiking
Movies
Theater
Great food

Loving
Giving
Interdependence
Through thick and thin

CHAPTER 3

PLOTTING YOUR CAREER COURSE

Dance Lesson #3: Your career is a long journey. To keep yourself on course and on schedule, you need a step-by-step plan. You need to monitor your progress, and you need to be willing to make adjustments along the way.

Now that your Defining Values, Heart's Purpose, and Activating Vision are complete, your career is headed toward a clearly defined destination, and the guideposts are in place to keep you on course. But the journey is a long one. It will have many interim stops where you will restock your supplies, evaluate your progress, and examine your plan for the remainder of the trip. As you encounter each new barrier and opportunity, the decisions you make will determine the speed, accuracy, and ease of your progress. You may set a particular course, but once you have followed it for a year, some unforeseen change in conditions may require you to rethink your direction and perhaps plot a new one. Precisely because the world around you is not static, your progress toward your final destination will not be a straight shot. Rather, you will follow a sailor's path, constantly tacking back and forth as you shift with the winds. Ironically, these zigzags are what keep you on course, always moving toward your Activating Vision.

Each interim stop in the journey represents a midterm Destination Goal. As you progress toward your Activating Vision, these Destination Goals mark the key segments of your course. They are the essential *what's next* in managing the gap between where you are today and where your vision is taking you over the next fifteen to twenty years. The space between one Destination Goal and the next represents a specific achievement gap. To successfully cross this space, simply measure your progress on a weekly, monthly, and quarterly basis. As long as you keep focused on where you're going, plan what's next, and take the necessary actions along the way, you are assured of arriving at your envisioned future.

Although you have a single Activating Vision, the pathways to reach that vision are many. Some will certainly be better than others—faster, easier, more direct, or more fun. Once you have a clear understanding of what kind of Destination Goals are most effective and how to use them to monitor your progress, you will be fully in charge of both the direction and the speed of your career journey.

By the time you finish reading this chapter and completing the exercises, you will have accomplished the following:

- Learned to develop context-driven goals, which are more empowering and more flexible than label-driven goals in steering you toward your Activating Vision
- Learned how to use Golden Thread Goal Setting, rather than linear goal setting, to more easily break down your career journey into segments that are manageable, trackable, and achievable
- Developed a personalized set of Destination Goals, which will be the key stepping-stones of your journey

Becoming skilled in setting your goals and holding yourself accountable for achieving them is how you take personal responsibility for your future. Successful women don't look to others to determine where they are going or how they will get there. They look to themselves.

Numerous research studies validate the theory that having precise, written goals with supporting action steps is the most powerful single exercise you can do for long-term success. One study followed the Yale University class of 1953. Upon graduation, only 3 percent of the class had clear, concise, written goals for their future and plans for achieving those goals. When the surviving graduates were interviewed twenty years later, not only was this 3 percent happier (based on their own criteria), but they were also worth more in financial terms than the entire remaining 97 percent of the class.[1]

Taking a lesson from the class of '53 and writing down your list of Destination Goals will support you in achieving your Activating Vision expeditiously—and effortlessly. These goals link your present to your future by defining the key stepping-stones on your road to success. They enable you to be selective and discriminating in your work choices. Without them the only way to get ahead is to continually handle as much work as you can as fast as you can in a constant drive for results, results, results. It is a hard-work, high-stress formula for success.

Written goals offer an easier way. They can grease the wheels to achieving your dreams and desires with less effort and less stress. So you can have the life you love instead of feeling like you're living in a pressure cooker.

Writing down your goals and speaking them aloud, as you did when developing your Activating Vision, is the first step to reaching them and creating a future where your dreams really will come true. This is a rare and life-changing gift that we all have, yet so few of us use.

The Value of Context Versus Labels in Goal Setting

Most books on goal setting concentrate on the analytical approach that originates in the left brain. Since most executives are result-oriented, this logically driven thinking process leads to a list of Destination Goals that are sequential, fact-based, rationally oriented, and quantifiable. Such a list might include:

- Work for a Fortune 100 company
- Vice president by age thirty-five
- $250,000 salary, senior vice president by age forty
- General manager of a division by age forty-five

These goals meet all of the left-brain criteria and appear to be perfectly valid destinations on the way to your future dreams. But something critical is missing. You see, they are merely labels—shorthand, "frosting on the cake" descriptions that sit atop an entire layer of meaning. The meaning that lies beneath the label is something deeper, more profound, and more satisfying: *context*. This is what you really seek. In reality, it isn't the concise, specific label that you are striving for but the effect that achieving it will have on your work and your life. Consider the label "Work for a Fortune 100 company." You can discover the underlying context by understanding your motives in choosing this particular label as one of your key Destination Goals. What *exactly* do you want? The following questions can help you discover the real context that you desire in your professional life:

- *Why do you want to work at such a large company?* What benefits do you get? Is it stability, the benefits package, the possibility of working and living internationally, the variety of work? Is it the prestige of working with the biggest and/or best in the industry? Is it a résumé-building step that you plan to trade in for a bigger job in another, smaller company? Is it the comfort—or the challenge—of working in a structured, hierarchical corporate environment?
- *What kind of work and work environment do you want?* Do you want work that has a narrow focus or work that offers broad exposure and experience? Do you want a high or low level of interaction with fellow employees? Will your environment be cutthroat, competitive, or collegial? Will the pace be fast or slow? Will the hours be long or standard, fluctuating or predictable?
- *What kind of personal satisfaction do you want?* Do you want constant challenge, risk, and rapid advancement? Or do you want the safety, ease, and predictability of spending a long time in the same position? Do you want to expand your experience or bask in the glory of your existing knowledge and expertise?

The "Fortune 100 company" goal represents something deeper to you, and that "something" is the context that you are really striving for. If you express your Destination Goals only in their label form, you are likely to miss the real point—your real desires—in setting those goals in the first place. Labels have little depth. They are so easy to understand that they lull you into a false sense of self-confidence about their validity and about the happiness that you will find once you achieve them. Rachel Naomi Remen, M.D., a pioneer in the mind-body health field, describes the illusive power of labels:

> *Labeling sets up an expectation of life that is often so compelling we can no longer see things as they really are. This expectation often gives us a false sense of familiarity toward something that is really new and unprecedented. We are in relationship with our expectations and not with life itself.*[2]

Allowing yourself to focus on the label rather than the context of your goals is like choosing to eat cotton candy instead of a filling, nourishing five-course meal. That huge mass of fluffy pinkness looks so gooey and satisfying. But the minute you've stuffed a big hunk of it into your mouth, it dissolves into a minuscule lump of sugar. The reality of the bite was far less fulfilling than the magnificence of the sight.

Genevieve Kwan can tell you exactly how fluffy and pink and disappointing a label-driven goal can be. As a young turk in one of the Big Six accounting firms, she had a crystal clear goal: to become the youngest person to ever make partner. This was her brass ring, and at age thirty, it became hers. As Genevieve tells it now, "At what should have been the happiest day of my professional life, I was surprised at how depressed I felt." She had expected elation and instead found disappointment. A "what have I done?" feeling consumed her. When she shared these feelings with her older male mentor, he dismissed her misgivings and reassured her, "Everyone goes through it. Don't worry, over time you'll feel fine."

But Genevieve didn't feel fine. As the realities of her newly acquired partnership settled in, she realized the reason for her depression. She had set her sights on the label, without realizing the context that accompanied it. As a partner, she could look forward to an endless future of predictable responsibilities and routine. She'd achieved the label, but the context behind it didn't sing to her soul. What Genevieve truly loved was challenge and unpredictability, growth and change, things she would never have as a partner in her Big Six firm. What she really wanted—her Activating Vision—was to be a financial innovator and decision maker who would build a new company rather than simply perpetuate an old one. So she traded in her partnership and took a new job as controller of a Fortune 500 company. Over the next few years, as she rose to become the company's CFO, she was instrumental in several key divestitures, as well as the development and explosive growth of a new technology division. When this new division was spun off into a separate company, Genevieve chose to go with it, as CFO. She faces a new set of challenges every day in this evolving industry. And she loves it!

To ensure that your Destination Goals are based on context, you must be concerned with more than simply naming specific end results. These are merely the labels of your goals. Instead, make sure you understand why you want to reach them and how you want to feel when you do. Uncovering your context desires requires you to ask tougher, more invasive questions. It requires you to understand what your labels represent so that you can identify your true desires—not what you think you should want, or what others think you should want, but what will give you fulfillment, challenge, and joy.

Caroline fell prey to the illusions of label-driven goals from a very early age. Like many other young women today, she grew up in a household with two career-driven parents. Both were highly successful attorneys at prestigious New York law firms. She was an only child, raised to have a high regard for education, success, affluence, and social standing. Caroline never questioned these values during her teenage years in an exclusive girls prep school nor when she went to college. She established her Destination Goals using the same labels that her parents valued: Ivy League university, law degree, job with prestigious big-city law firm. Caroline never took into account context states of being such as joy, contentment, and satisfaction. (Well, she did dip her toe in the waters of context just a little, when she accepted a job with a large firm in Los Angeles instead of her native New York. She said she was tired of snow and wanted to feel what it was like to have warm weather and sunshine all year.)

Caroline had worked for several years at this L.A. firm when her father suddenly passed away. Without his constant reinforcement, Caroline began to realize how discontented—and bored—she had always felt with her job, and how little life existed outside her work. Corporate law was dry and uninteresting to her. She hated the cold, impersonal environment of her firm. And after completing the required eighty- to ninety-hour workweek, there was no time left to spend on fun activities (which were *what*, by the way?). The treadmill of Caroline's life was moving at a brisk pace, but she wasn't enjoying any of it.

It was at this low point that Caroline heard about executive coaching. She was introduced to Nancy, who began by asking Caroline to envision the kind of life she would like to live. What were her likes and dislikes about practicing law? What other kind of work would she like to do? What kind of work environment would she thrive in and enjoy?

Caroline's answers were the first steps in creating context-driven Destination Goals. She enjoyed the challenge of the problem-solving aspects of law and the intimacy of representing individuals rather than companies. She wanted to use her skills as an attorney to improve people's lives rather than corporations' balance sheets. She wanted a more reasonable workweek and a more relaxed environment in which people were honored more than billable hours were.

Today, Caroline works at a center for women where she uses her Ivy League education to help women and families through difficult legal-related crises. She gave up the big paycheck, but in return she put large amounts of joy and satisfaction back into the balance sheet of her life.

Settling for labels without attaching your context desires to them means that you don't ever scratch below the surface. It means you never ask yourself the really tough, invasive questions. It means replicating a life by simply marching in lockstep toward the next label of your career, without considering what sings to your heart and soul. Taking time to explore your inner needs, rather than simply the external labels, is an essential component in designing a fulfilling, joyous journey.

To develop context-driven Destination Goals, allow your right brain to lead the way. The thought processes that emanate from this hemisphere are intuitive, nonlinear, feeling-based, and visceral. This style of thinking is where images are most alive and fantasies spring forth.

Context-driven Destination Goals are more natural and in sync with the unpredictable way that life itself evolves. David Whyte, author of *The Heart Aroused: Poetry and the Preservation of the Soul in Corporate America*, explains it this way:

> [A]lmost everything we come across in life is nonlinear, that is, the shortest point between A and B is not a straight line. . . . The line is an evolving path that actually changes according to the first steps we ourselves take to begin the journey. Most paths . . . take the form of an iterative equation, an equation where the values and events it produces are continually fed back into the equation again and again. . . . Every action, then, no matter how small, influences every future action, no matter how large.[3]

The specificity of label-driven goals engenders a more rigid, narrow pathway of pursuit, which is easily blocked when external factors change. For example, if you are striving to reach a label goal of becoming president of your company when suddenly the company is sold and someone from the acquiring company gets the job, this particular label Destination Goal is now an impossibility. Your career may drift for a while as you search for a new goal. But if you had developed a clear understanding of the context-driven goals that lay beneath this label (for example, using your visioning and strategy skills to develop a bigger future for a company; being a top-level decision maker), then you can more easily seek out alternative labels that will allow you to achieve your context needs. Perhaps you become the director of strategic planning or the general manager of a division or president of a different company.

The more general "feeling" nature of context-driven goals enables you to identify a pathway that has multiple options and is, therefore, flexible. So you can continue the pursuit of your goals in that "iterative equation" described by Whyte.

The pathway that Nancy took, from a career in corporate America to an entrepreneur/founder of her own company, illustrates the portability of context-driven goals in this iterative equation of life. Early in her career, long before she had thought through the theoretical differences between context and labels, Nancy created three goals by which to mark her career progress:

1. To be respected by all levels of the organization
2. To improve the quality of her own life through a flexible work schedule
3. To work for a large international corporation

Shortly thereafter, Nancy was offered a prestigious position at a large, multinational accounting firm, which met her third goal. As she thought about the job, though, she realized that it failed to fulfill her other two objectives. "Thank you, but no thank you" was her response to the offer. That "no" took her into a world of trust: she didn't know what lay ahead, but she was willing to believe that it would appear.

Nancy shared her goals with several close friends, seeking their advice and counsel. The common thread among them was their belief that Nancy would be most successful, powerful, and fulfilled if she started her own consulting business. So she faced her fears, embraced her desires, and struck out on her own.

A year later she was in the women's bathroom of one of her larger client companies when she heard an unidentified employee's voice through the door: "Thank you so much for the work you're doing with my boss. He's so much calmer and more even-tempered. I just want you to know that it's made a major difference in my life too."

Later that day the president of the same organization stopped her in the hallway and told her, "You've helped bring a *can-do* attitude back into this office. People are excited about coming to work again. Whatever you're doing, keep it up!"

While driving home, Nancy realized that by turning down that job and starting her own company, she had abandoned the pursuit of a label-driven Destination Goal in favor of fulfilling her two context-driven objectives. She had achieved them both, but certainly not through the expected corporate pathway. Instead of pursuing the straight course, she had tacked her career sailboat by creating her own business. It was through this process of speaking her goals aloud and then trusting her surroundings and herself enough to shift her course that she got it all.

So often, life surprises us. The universe's plan for us is far bigger and better than our own imaginations could ever conjure.

In today's American work environment, a new employee can expect to have eight to ten jobs and as many as four different careers in her lifetime. Here, context-driven Destination Goals are especially relevant because they are stand-alone goals—independent of any specific industry or company. When you change companies or careers, these goals move with you. You can choose from a variety of different pathways to achieve them.

Janet Ming was senior vice president of sales and marketing with a prestigious international organization when she decided that her next career position was not the kind of work that would interest or excite her. So she decided it was time for a dramatic career redirection. Her Destination Goal was to create a position for herself in new-product development. There, she felt, was the place that would give her the excitement and creative fulfillment she craved. She would be able to utilize all of her knowledge: widespread industry experience, creativity in solving problems, ability to influence change, strategic thinking, and, of course, salesmanship.

But in the midst of her own career planning, Janet's company went through a massive reorganization that permanently closed the door to her dream job and even threatened her continued employment. At this critical juncture, if Janet's only goal had been the label-driven one (a job in the New Product Development department), she would have been unable to achieve it. Her only option would have been to leave the company. But instead Janet calmly kept the context of her Destination Goals in mind throughout the reorganization, and eventually she was given an important opportunity in another department. It wasn't New Products, but she soon realized that her new job utilized every bit of her skills, experience, and expertise. And just as important, it has enabled her to make a major contribution to her company. Janet is now executive vice president of organization and development. Her new job meets all of her context-driven goals, and it has moved her closer to achieving her Activating Vision: being an innovator who is an instrumental decision maker in crafting the long-term future of an international company.

Successful people, like Janet, react with flexibility and agility when life hits them with unexpected events. They maintain their innate sense of trust that all will be well. Their ability to triumph over any adversity emanates from their commitment to the end result they seek. As Janet's story demonstrates, context-driven goals enable you to choose from many pathways and still reach your desired career destination.

Some questions that might help you uncover your context-driven goals follow:

- What kind of boss do I want?
- How do I want the company to respond to me?
- What attributes do I bring to the picture that nobody else can?
- What do I want to feel about the work I do?
- My typical day will include what activities that bring me joy?
- Do I prefer working with people or alone, independently or interdependently?
- What are the important aspects that I admire in a company?
- When I sit in my office, what does my ideal environment look, feel, and sound like?
- What does earning $____ mean in my life, in terms of the external world and also my internal feelings of freedom, self-worth, and so on? ("Try on" different levels of income to find the best fit for you.)
- What level of influence and power do I want to have in my company?
- What level of balance do I want to experience between my personal and professional life?
- What makes me happy?
- What am I really good at?
- What do I like doing?

Once you define a goal, decide whether it is label-driven or context-driven. If it is label-driven, ask yourself why you want to achieve it and what benefits you expect to gain from it. Keep asking these questions until you have discovered an answer that resonates with your emotions—not just your mind. Imagine yourself actually experiencing your goal. Does it feel fun, exciting, and adventurous? Do you feel happy, stimulated, and fulfilled? These are the signals that you have arrived at the root of your desire.

Brianna O'Leary was a product manager in the retail division of a large U.S. financial institution, and one of her key Destination Goals was to become the director of corporate marketing. When she began asking herself why, here were her answers:

- I want to be the ultimate person responsible for leading all of my company's marketing programs.
- I am happiest when I am the leader of the team; I enjoy the broader responsibilities of handling people and relationships as well as marketing and financial decisions.
- Having final control over the implementation and financial success of the programs that my team develops is most exciting and personally satisfying for me.

What Brianna realized through this process was that as the corporate director of marketing, she would influence the marketing programs for all divisions, but she would have no actual decision-making power over their design and implementation. The job as director of retail marketing better satisfied her context-driven goals. There she would be the final authority, with direct control of the marketing programs for all of the division's products—the responsibilities that she had identified as most exciting and fun for her. This division was also the largest financial contributor to her company's bottom line, so it would give her the opportunity to make the most significant financial impact as well.

Golden Thread Goal Setting

Getting from where you are today to the ultimate career destination that you created in your Activating Vision is a long and winding journey—at least a fifteen- or twenty-year trip if your vision is truly visionary! Once your planning process is completed, you will probably have ten to twenty Destination Goals that mark the key ports of your voyage. They are the incremental steps between where you are today and your envisioned future. Because the journey is so long and the final destination is far in the future, you may find it difficult to actually choose those ten to twenty key goals from the myriad options that your mind and imagination will conceive.

So then, how do you choose wisely?

First, give up the idea that your Destination Goals must be established chronologically. While you will undoubtedly arrange them this way at the end of the process, this is rarely how they occur to you. Goal setting is a creative process. Forcing your mind into the rational, left-brain world of linear thinking will shut down the flow of your creative mind.

To keep the flow of creativity open, look again at your Activating Vision statement and identify its two or three core components. The goals you develop will lead you to the achievement of each of them. To begin, ask yourself the following questions and write down your answers as they occur to you. In other words, don't force your mind to answer all in a single sitting; allow your mental energies time to digest and go a bit deeper in delivering an answer. This may take a couple of weeks or even a month:

- *What do I already know or do that is in alignment with achieving this vision?* This question reveals what you already own in terms of knowledge and proven expertise and simply need to continue owning to achieve your Activating Vision.
- *Is there someone else who has already achieved this position or lifestyle whom I can look to as a guide?* Finding the people who already live the life you have dreamed for yourself and then analyzing those people's pathways will help you plan your own journey. What pathways did they choose? What were their strengths and weaknesses? In hindsight, what were the key Destination Goals that marked their progress?
- *What do I need to learn, perform, experience, or achieve to become fully qualified and deserving to live in my Activating*

Vision? A large part of the answer to this question will emerge from the previous two. Here, you are precisely defining the actions that you must take to travel from where you are today to where you want to be in your envisioned future.

Your key Destination Goals will emerge from your answers to these questions. Each Destination Goal is a pathway—a golden thread—that connects your present to one of the key components of your Activating Vision. When you identify a goal, write it down without worrying about where it fits into the timetable. When the process feels complete to you, simply rearrange your goals in chronological order; weave your golden threads together. Then take one more look at the pattern that you have created. Do you see any holes where you need to add more thread—additional Destination Goals—to complete the connection that will take you from who you are today to who you want to become? Reflect on what those goals should be and then simply add them. Now your pattern is complete.

The first step to accomplishing your Destination Goals is to put them in a place where you can see them every day: in a small frame on your desk or next to your phone, on the screen saver of your computer, on the little plastic divider of your weekly planner, or in that teeny leather case that holds your Palm Pilot. This frequent reminder will help your conscious and subconscious mind hold its focus on achieving these milestones in your career journey.

While writing this book, we realized that we needed to build a dual vision for ourselves as long-term partners. Instrumental in our discussion was defining the set of Destination Goals that we would pursue together. First, we broke our dual Activating Vision statements into their core components, shown below.

Candy's Activating Vision

To be an internationally respected, bestselling "renaissance author" and public speaker whose various works of fiction and nonfiction have a positive, life-changing impact on people around the world.

Nancy's Activating Vision

To be an internationally respected agent of change for business in the twenty-first century, whose writing, lectures, and personal coaching encourage people to become more open and joyful in their work and to achieve bigger results with far less effort.

Our visions share two common components, which we realized are the core of our partnership:

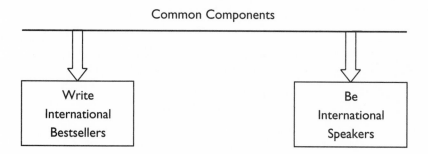

Common Components

Write International Bestsellers

Be International Speakers

Our next step was to develop the pattern of Destination Goals that would take us from where we are today to the achievement of both aspects of our combined vision. We began with the end in mind: what would it take for us to be legitimate, bestselling authors fifteen years from now? The answer became our final Destination Goal: Write ten bestselling nonfiction and fiction books (some as coauthors, some as solo authors). From this final goal, we jumped from the end to the beginning—an action we could take *now*. This became our first Destination Goal: Write a breakthrough business bestseller that positively changes women's lives. Then we simply filled in the hole between these two goals, until we had captured the entire list. Only then did we begin weaving these golden threads together into a chronological pattern.

In building the Destination Goals for our second core component (to be internationally respected speakers and lecturers), we simply repeated this process. As a last step, we merged the two sets of goals into a single chronological pattern, shown below from the end backward to the beginning:

Write ten bestselling nonfiction and fiction books
(coauthor and solo)

↓

Be internationally acclaimed authors receiving
six-figure advances by book three

↓

Receive international marketing requests to appear on
television, radio, and Internet events by book three

↓

Widen sphere of influence with syndicated column
after publication of first book

↓

Make triumphant and influential interview appearances
across the United States ("Oprah," "The View")

↓

Sign with a prestigious publisher that supports and vigorously
markets its authors with time and money

↓

Sign on with a well-respected agent who is thrilled
to be representing us and our book

↓

Write a breakthrough, bestselling business book that is wise,
warm, insightful, funny, and positively changes women's lives

Each Destination Goal incorporated some elements of context. We didn't just set a goal of "signing with a publisher," for example. We actually described some of the emotional elements that we desired: supports and vigorously markets the authors with time and money. There are hundreds of potential publishers of business books. With our context in place, we were equipped to find the publisher that could meet our needs at this particular Destination Goal.

When we first set these goals, we had neither agent nor publisher. And look what happened! We found an absolutely first-rate agent in Mitchell Waters of Curtis Brown, Ltd. His expertise and "never give up" mentality were pivotal in securing a publisher. And what about that publisher goal? Well, McGraw-Hill is one of the larger houses, with an outstanding sales force, deep pockets, and a true desire to work with us as a team to create a highly successful book. We got everything we asked for! So you see, when we talk about vision and goals, about context and golden threads, we really do practice what we preach. And it really does work!

Guidelines for Powerful Goal Setting

Choosing wisely is a challenge for all of us, both male and female, when it comes to the open-ended world of goal setting. The trick is to choose exactly what to include in each goal, what language to best express it, and how you will pursue it. These are the subtle cues that can either motivate or misdirect your conscious and subconscious energies. With the right goals in place, you will be able to leap from where you are to where you're going with less effort, more speed, and more joy and fulfillment along the way. These five guidelines will help you. Each one is explained in detail in the following pages:

1. Move toward something, not away from something.
2. Remember to ask for everything.
3. Be persistent about measuring your progress.

4. Relax and release it.
5. Visualize yourself living in the outcome.

Move Toward Something, Not Away from Something

Many professional women, particularly those with several years of corporate experience who are now ready to change careers or companies, have a tendency to define their goals in terms of what they *don't* want more often than in terms of what they *do* want. These "going away from" desires include everything that hasn't worked in their professional and personal lives. They either seek to escape from something that is already present (a nasty boss, a boring career, a particularly distasteful assignment), or to prevent some negative element from occurring. This is misdirected goal setting, and in the end it will lead to a lack of fulfillment.

In a 1997 article in the *Journal of Small Business Management*, authors E. Holly Buttner and Dorothy P. Moore included the findings of several research studies on the reasons women have left corporate America to start their own businesses. In a 1985 study of women's entrepreneurial motivation:

> *Hisrich and Bush asked their women business-owner respondents for the reasons they started their businesses. Most frequently cited were "push" factors of frustration and boredom in their previous jobs, with "pull" factors such as autonomy a distant third.*[4]

Several studies between 1975 and 1994 compared the role of "push" versus "pull" factors in male and female decision making. Buttner and Moore state:

> *In general, researchers have found that men start their businesses primarily as a result of such "pull" factors as the opportunity to work independently, to have greater control over one's work, and to earn more money. There is less influence from such "push" factors as limited advancement opportunities, job frustration, and avoiding an unreasonable boss or unsafe working conditions.*[5]

Although "push" factors may be more prevalent than "pull" factors for women, it is possible to overcome their negative thrust. To make this transition, simply use the "pull" factors as inputs into your goal setting rather than structuring your actual statements in the same, negative framework.

Here are some examples of "going away from" goals, with a sister solution that easily refocuses the thought on "going toward" something. As you read this list, ask yourself which perspective you tend to favor in your own goal setting.

Going Away From	*Going Toward*
By fifty I won't have to rely on anyone else financially.	By fifty I will have complete financial independence.
I don't want a boss that takes credit for my great ideas.	My new boss will support my long-term career growth.
I don't want to work for an organization that is losing market share.	I will be employed by a leading organization in a growth industry.
I don't want to be part of an organization that is only concerned with profitability.	I will be part of an organization that honors people as its most important asset.

Using "don't" or "won't" language in your goals will invariably sabotage your efforts. This is directly related to how the human brain functions. Certain parts of the brain have evolved very little over the course of human existence. Today, these functions are still highly unsophisticated. Research has documented that the brain does not distinguish nuances of language. As a result, a "don't" goal often sets in motion the very thing we are trying to avoid. This is why parenting experts advise that when a child is standing on the curb, the most dangerous thing to tell that child is "Don't go into the street." The brain tends to omit the "don't" and the child steps into the street. More effective, advise the experts, is to simply say, "Stay on the curb." Planting an image in the child's mind of what to do (rather than what not to do) is a verbal expression of the parents' goal for their child's behavior, which increases the likelihood that it will be achieved.

Even as a logical, higher-thinking adult, creating a verbal "don't" statement to express a goal will set you in motion toward the very thing that you are trying to escape. This point was vividly illustrated in 1978 when Karl Wallenda, patriarch of the world-renowned trapeze family the Flying Wallendas, fell to his death. When his wife was interviewed afterward, she told the reporter that for the first time in her husband's long career, all of his thoughts and preparations for his San Juan aerial performance were about *not falling* rather than about walking on the high wire.

As you begin writing down potential Destination Goals, focus exclusively on positive, "going toward" statements. Translate any "don't" goals into "do" goals, as we have done in the preceding list. When you switch your focus to the "do"s in life, your goals can propel you in the direction you really want to go, toward the powerful, positive results that you truly desire.

Remember to Ask for Everything

How often have you gone to the grocery store and forgotten to restock one of your staples, such as flour, sugar, or salt? Why? Precisely because they are staples: you always have them in the cupboard; you rarely run out. So it's easy to forget to buy more when you're in the store shopping for a multitude of other (usually far more interesting) items. Yet these staples are the true necessities in your kitchen. Without them, your meal options are more limited, and the food simply won't taste as good because it will be missing a key ingredient.

This same forgetfulness, or taking for granted what has always been present, is an important factor when establishing your goals. It is critical that you pay particular attention to what you already have "in the cupboard" and wish to carry forward into your future. All too frequently, as women become immersed in the goal-creation process, they forget to include what already exists in their lives—those jewels and joys of their present that will also enrich their future. We call this the Microwave Theory because it came as a result of Nancy's direct personal experience when she bought her first townhouse.

Nancy had envisioned every contextual detail of what she wanted: she saw herself swimming, walking up and down stairs, parking her car in the garage, and lolling around in a lush patio area. Her real estate agent walked her through the townhouse that she would later buy, and Nancy saw her dreams come to life. It felt right, it looked right, it even smelled right! She happily moved in.

Then, on her first night, she went to the kitchen to microwave her dinner. Oops! No microwave!

Nancy had assumed that because a microwave oven had been a permanent, long-term fixture in her life, one would automatically be in her new townhouse. The oven hadn't even made it onto her context list because it was such a given in her mind.

We have often talked with others who have made this same mistake of leaving behind important aspects of their own lives simply because they failed to include these items in their future goals. One woman, who took her large and luxurious office for granted, started a new job only to find herself in a cubicle in a temporary trailer. Another wanted to work in an energy-packed entrepreneurial environment, but forgot to include the goal of working for a boss who would be just as good as the one she was leaving behind.

As you create the contexts of your Destination Goals, remember not to take your existing treasures for granted. Be purposeful about taking them with you.

Be Persistent About Measuring Your Progress

Once you have established your Destination Goals, it is not unusual to almost immediately face difficulties that challenge your commitment. It's a test! Life is asking, "Do you really want to do what it takes to achieve your vision?" Now you face a defining moment: you can either become persistent and commitment-based, or you can allow the ebb and flow of your emotions to determine your future.

Emotions are usually externally focused. They react to other people's thoughts, ideas, and actions. They change from moment to moment, and thus are unreliable gauges that can derail your progress. This is a particular issue for women because we are innately more emotional beings than our male counterparts. To keep ourselves on course in our career journeys, then, we must be even more persistent and commitment-based. When these twin traits become our internal foundation, they keep us in action, moving ever forward toward our goals, regardless of what or how we are feeling today.

At its heart, persistence is about doing whatever it takes to overcome any obstacle. It is an especially important quality for women, since we face more (and often bigger) barriers to success than do men. If you want to become more persistent, start measuring your progress. This does more than tell you where you are. It focuses your efforts and fuels your dedication to keep working so you can get to where you want to go. The first step is to put a time frame in place for each of your Destination Goals. Simply ask yourself, "By when should I expect to reach this goal?" Then commit yourself to a regular check-in process. Every one or two weeks, revisit your most immediate Destination Goal and note the progress you have made. Then write down the specific action steps and tasks that you will complete by your next check-in date.

For example, to reach our own first Destination Goal—writing a breakthrough business book that positively changes women's lives—we built the following list of action steps and tasks:

1. Take classes and read books to learn about writing a nonfiction book.
2. Brainstorm key concepts our book will explore, and figure out how to merge our two viewpoints into one cohesive book.
3. Create an outline of each chapter.
4. Gather and analyze existing writing and research on each key concept.
5. Check Amazon.com, libraries, and bookstores to determine what other competitive books exist, and verify the extent to which our topic and our point of view on the subject are unique.
6. Revise the initial chapter outlines in response to the new information we learned from steps 4 and 5.
7. Establish tasks and timetables for completion of each chapter.
8. Recruit other businesswomen to share their stories so that each concept can be brought to life with real examples.

9. Expose our written chapters to a preselected focus group of career women for feedback and refinement.
10. Review final polished draft with writing coach for further refinement and make last round of changes.

We set a specific due date for each step, and we measured our progress weekly. Once all of the steps were completed, we had achieved our first Destination Goal.

If this practice of regular, frequent measurement is new to you, remember that it takes time and diligence to build a new habit. We recommend that you set up a system that holds you accountable for specific results on a weekly basis, to ensure that you are making regular progress. Take one evening a week to assess your work schedule, and then plug in your weekly "to do" list of action steps and tasks. These are your guarantees—promises to yourself about specific work that you must complete before week's end, come rain, shine, crisis, or natural disaster. Taking personal responsibility for consistently achieving your weekly results will create a habit of diligence that will help you reach your Destination Goals, and in turn your Activating Vision, more rapidly.

Be diligent, but also be aware of one pitfall: Don't use your measurements as yet another way to beat yourself up; when you measure yourself for failure, you will surely achieve it.

Nancy unwittingly fell into this negative pattern when she took a business development course that required participants to call in weekly and report important statistics pertaining to building their businesses. One of the numbers Nancy used in her self-reporting was weekly income. As the weeks went on and she tracked her paltry income, Nancy began feeling more uncomfortable and unqualified. If she didn't make her target result of $2,500 in additional income and three new clients, it didn't matter to her that she had brought in $2,000 more than the previous week or that she signed on two new clients. Instead of celebrating her success in reaching three-fourths of her goal, she dwelled on her failure to meet 100 percent. She was using the numbers to invalidate herself: to measure what she had *not* achieved rather than what she *had*.

From this experience, Nancy came to understand that measuring sticks are most helpful when they are used as a game, to let you know how far you've come and what you need to do next. It is done with fun and joy in your heart because you are in the process of creating the rest of your life. This unique creation ability is one of the greatest gifts of being human. And by committing yourself to a goal and then simply refusing to quit, your eventual success is guaranteed. The only unknown is the time and effort it will take you to get there.

Relax and Release It

This guideline is central to determining how effortlessly you are able to achieve your goals. Sometimes in the creation process we overload our thinking with emotional energy that is grounded in thoughts like "must have" or "got to get." These thoughts emanate from our need to control, and they stem from a fear that we cannot get that control. This thinking creates dense energy that closes off the flow of help and support from the world around us. To turn on the flow in your life, you must dissipate this dense energy by doing less working and more relaxing, less worrying and more trusting, less controlling and more releasing. In other words, the time comes in every journey when you need to jump into the middle of the river and let the water carry you along!

This book was born out of our own relaxing and releasing process. Before we even had the idea to write it, we had developed an extensive research and training project to help women become more effective in large corporations. We were excited about the opportunity to make a true difference, and we did everything we could to make the project happen: researching, writing a detailed proposal, intensive marketing. Then we relaxed and released our emotional attachment to the outcome. We stopped worrying about it and started believing in it—that somewhere, somehow, it would occur.

Nothing happened. The project never even received a nibble from a paying prospect. To the outside world this may have looked like a waste of time. But for us, it was the beginning of this book. What we released, in our dreams for a single corporate project, was returned to us a hundredfold with the gift of the idea for *Dancing on the Glass Ceiling*. We created a space, and the universe added to our dreams.

Creative energy is light, relaxed, and quiet. It trusts that once you have bound yourself to your destiny, it is already yours. So after you have found your Activating Vision and committed yourself to pursue it, to paraphrase a famous poet's words on love, "Set it free. If it returns to you, it is yours."

Visualize Yourself Living in the Outcome

Your subconscious and central nervous system cannot distinguish between a vividly imagined event and the actual event itself. Your body experiences both as reality. This is why visualizing your outcome is such a powerful tool to assist you in manifesting the results you desire. Visualization is creating, or living, your planned future right now in your mind's eye. Using this unique human capacity has been proved to speed up and improve the quality of the outcome.

Years ago, research was conducted to test the effectiveness of visualization on the performance of basketball players. Three groups were studied. The first threw one hundred practice free throws every day; the second did absolutely nothing; the third visualized themselves throwing successful free throws without actually doing it. The group with the most-improved results was the one that visualized the ball swishing through the net on each free throw, yet never actually tossed the ball!

This is an example of the human mind functioning to support you in achieving your desired goals. Just think of your brain as a marvelous system of biochemical/electromagnetic pathways. These are roads, waiting to be traveled. The first time a thought travels down one of them, it is an explorer, finding its way. But with each subsequent journey down the same path, the thought moves with more speed and ease toward its destination. Visualization, then, is a sort of "programming tool" that prepares your brain to fully support your physical efforts—to magnify their power and effectiveness—as you strive for your goals. Why not use this powerful tool to achieve the life you desire? Have fun. Play with your future in your mind. Imagine different scenarios until you are comfortable with the results. Would you prefer working in a large urban city with its frantic, energizing pace, or is the slower, suburban town more to your liking?

Envisioning your future is effortless since all of the practice and improvement of your end results take place in your mind first. When you actually see yourself accomplishing, performing, or living in your Activating Vision, you are creating the most effortless pathway to achieving it.

CHAPTER 4

REINVENTING YOUR ATTITUDES
BUILDING A SUPPORTIVE SELF

Dance Lesson #4: Achieving your career dreams is far easier when your internal attitudes are supporting your external actions. With this support system in place, your efforts in the external world will gain their full measure of success.

By now you should be looking at yourself and your career with fresh eyes, an open mind, and a perspective that is present- and future-oriented rather than rooted in the traditions of the past. The various exercises in the last three chapters have been designed to help you develop a deeper understanding of your dreams, your passions, and your pathway to achieving them. We have taken your heart and mind through a process of tuning into the grand possibilities that you can create in your career and in your life. But even if the outside world fully assists you in your journey, you can still be sabotaged by your inside world—unconscious thoughts and attitudes that undermine your ego, your self-confidence, and even your best efforts. By redesigning these negative attitudes and creating an internal world that nurtures and supports you, achieving your dreams becomes truly effortless.

Your Defining Values, Heart's Purpose, Activating Vision, and Destination Goals are the big-picture constructs that will draw you toward your envisioned future. What remains to be built into this system is your internal framework: the attitude and belief patterns that govern how you see yourself, how you interpret the objective realities of the world around you, and how you choose to interact with those realities.

Renowned American poet Maya Angelou captured the importance of this internal support system when she said, "If you don't like something, change it. If you can't change it, change your attitudes."

Each of us acts in the world and interprets that world differently based on our unique mental and emotional makeup. We constantly recreate the objective reality of this world based on our own perceptions of it. To develop the self-confident, empowered "I" so necessary for success, you must discover and overcome the prejudices about yourself and the world around you that dwell within your mind. We call this process of change *reinventing your attitudes.*

"Our eyes do not simply pick up information from an outside world and relay it to our brains," write Margaret Wheatley and Myron Kellner-Rogers in *A Simpler Way*:

> *Information relayed from the outside through the eye accounts for only 20 percent of what we use to create a perception. At least 80 percent of the information that the brain works with is information already in the brain. We each create our own worlds by what we choose to notice, creating a world of distinctions that makes sense to us. We then "see" the world through this self we have created. Information from the external world is a minor influence.* [1]

Becoming aware of your internal biases and training yourself to interpret people, events, and ideas with as little filtering as possible will improve not only your job performance but also the way the world perceives you. When you train yourself to interpret people, events, and ideas with a minimum of filtering, you will take action more boldly and make decisions with more clarity and objectivity.

In this chapter, we focus on helping you reinvent four mental attitudes that handicap women in particular. In our fifty-plus combined years of managing and coaching both men and women, we can tell you that these attitudes rarely appear in men but occur with frightening regularity in managerial women. They are far more than just nasty little habits. They are saboteurs that will undermine even your mightiest efforts to build a successful career:

- *Victim orientation:* This pitfall is rooted in a viewpoint that is negative, powerless, and other-directed. It affects how you see your entire life, including your own actions and their consequences. You see external circumstances and other people as the causes of whatever happens to you. "Poor me," and "How could this happen to me?" are two hints that a victim orientation is in control.
- *Limiting self-beliefs:* This concept deals with how you see yourself based on your misguided perceptions of fears and ineptness. You see more weaknesses—more "missings"—than are really there, and you fail to recognize or acknowledge the strengths that you already possess.
- *Rigid mind-set:* A rigid mind-set is the filter through which you judge the world around you, based exclusively on your stubborn adherence to your own existing knowledge base and its total irrefutability. You hold your own "already knowing" as absolute truth, and you stridently resist any attempts to change or challenge that truth. The emotionally charged "I'm right and you're wrong" attitude toward others and their ideas is the telling symptom of a rigid mind-set.
- *Revering status quo:* This refers to your instinctive, subconscious belief that what is, is right and must therefore be maintained, protected, and reinforced. It is a "system think" that locks you into old, routine patterns of action. You automatically support "the way it's always been done," rather than constantly searching for improvements so that the proverbial "it" could be done better (faster, cheaper, easier, etc.).

These four mental attitudes are at the core of what Wheatley and Kellner-Rogers describe as "seeing the world through the self we have created." The influence of these attitudes on our perceptions of reality is so ingrained within each of us that we usually fail to recognize it.

Nancy's experience with the CEO of a national health-care company is a vivid example of the debilitating power of just one of these barriers. After completing a successful training program for this company, Nancy had continued to maintain a friendly relationship with Leanne Martin, the CEO. One day, she left a telephone message for Leanne. Three days passed and Leanne had not called—highly unusual behavior for this efficient woman who had always been diligent about returning Nancy's phone calls. Nancy assumed that Leanne was simply overwhelmed with work, so she called and left a second message.

Several weeks later, Nancy still had not heard from Leanne. She kept reassuring herself that there was a logical explanation, and she placed a third call. Once again Leanne failed to return it. At this point, Nancy's long-held, deeply seated limiting self-belief began to nag at her psyche: *I'm not really as expert a consultant as I'm portraying myself to be.*

This belief was the catalyst for a whole range of questions and wild theories that took root in Nancy's mind. As the days passed while she awaited Leanne's phone call, these little roots of self-doubt grew into full-grown forests:

> "I must have done something that made Leanne mad. Maybe she's not happy with my last consulting report."
> "My recommendations must not have worked and she doesn't want to have anything to do with me again."
> "She must have found somebody who will do a better job, and she doesn't want to tell me."

Nancy's mind ran wild with imaginings that completely distorted reality. Then they began distorting her actions. The next time Leanne's name appeared on Nancy's daily contact planner, she decided not to call. When another health-care-related company requested Nancy's references for a potential assignment, she left Leanne's name off the list. This pattern continued until the day Leanne finally called and left a message for Nancy. She apologized for not returning Nancy's calls: "I've been traveling like a fiend and just now found three ancient messages from you in an inside pocket of my briefcase. You must have thought I'd flipped out completely!"

No . . . it was Nancy who had done the flipping out. She had been victimized by her limiting self-belief that she really was not a top-notch consultant. As a result, her brain had falsely interpreted an event and she had acted on that interpretation as though it were reality. This had caused Nancy to change her behavior, which almost cost her not only a valuable client but also a good friend.

That second health-care-related company didn't select Nancy for the assignment. Would they be on her client roster today if she had used Leanne Martin's name as a reference? She'll never know.

Nancy's story shows how much damage can be done when just one of these mental barriers begins taking control. Imagine how stuck a person would become if multiple barriers were operating (which is most often the case). These attitudes are habitual, negative patterns of interpreting yourself and the world around you. They are debilitating because they distort reality and block you from taking the actions necessary to achieve the successful career you desire. Once you are aware of how they operate in your own life, you can begin to break up these negative mental habits and replace them with positive ones that create the foundation for your future success.

One of the exercises in our A Woman's Way of Leadership professional development program always creates an "Aha!" shift for participants when they realize just how powerfully their internal attitudes influence their interpretation of the world around them. Here's the first half of the exercise. We will ask you to complete the second half later in this chapter.

On a piece of paper, make a list of the major barriers that are preventing you from achieving more success in your career. To help you get started, here are some examples that other women have shared with us in the seminars:

- I don't have enough education; don't have an MBA.
- I don't have enough experience in certain disciplines (management, technical skills, finance, new business, etc.).
- My boss won't let me take on new responsibilities.
- I'm afraid to change jobs, take a promotion, fail.
- Top management is all men who are not willing to promote women to high levels.
- My reputation is that I'm stubborn because I don't give in to unreasonable requests of my boss.

Once you've completed your list, set it aside, forget about it for a while, and continue reading this chapter.

Mental Barrier #1: Victim Orientation

Victim orientation is the most pervasive of the four mental barriers for all people and one of the most ubiquitous for women. Much of Nancy's coaching and Candy's management of other women has dealt with this issue. It would appear that women have been struggling to rise above the glass ceiling in corporate America for so long that they have begun to think of themselves as victims—and they are behaving that way, as well.

Measuring every event that happens to you through the eyes of a victim is a debilitating drag on your long-term advancement and personal career growth. When you look at your life through a victim's eyes, you see everything as occurring *to* you. You see external circumstances and other people as the cause of whatever happens. "They" are in control, and you are not. You see yourself as powerless. And so you become what you see: someone who reacts, rather than someone who causes a reaction. This kind of thinking is self-destructive and false. It will keep you from the very life you desire.

As with every other mental barrier, victim orientation first shows up as an internal conversation: your mind chattering ceaselessly, talking to no one else but you. But with this particular barrier, the internal chatter quickly appears in your conversations in the external world. Here are just a few verbal examples that suggest the presence of a victim orientation:

- "I can't change things."
- "This mess I'm in is his/her/their fault."
- "If only he/she/they/it would _____, my problems would go away."
- "My boss won't let me."

Looking through the eyes of a victim is like using the filter on a camera to manipulate the picture's true image. This filter attaches false motivations to others and false meanings to events. Anthony Robbins, one of the first popularizers of neurolinguistic programming, described this dynamic in *Awaken the Giant Within*: "You see, it's never the environment, it's never the events of our lives, but the *meaning* we attach to the events—how we interpret them—that shapes who we are today and who we'll become tomorrow."[2]

Robin Cartland, an operations manager for a manufacturing company, experienced a dramatic shift in the results she could achieve by simply changing her filter. Robin was frustrated that she was not able to hire additional staff, and she was immersed in a victim's mentality: "It's all the president's fault! No matter what I do, he won't approve the hires I want."

The president had organized the company around the principle of a lean permanent staff. Cadres of temporary workers were regularly hired during peak production periods. Robin believed that this practice placed an unreasonable burden on the permanent employees due to the amount of attention required to hire, process, manage, train, and physically support an ever-changing pool of temporary workers. But the president had repeatedly turned down her requests for him to convert some freelance positions to permanent staff.

When she began coaching with Nancy, Robin was a confirmed victim, saying she "couldn't do anything," "it was always going to be this way," and "nothing would change his mind."

Nancy challenged Robin to talk to the president one more time and to stop focusing on her own goals. Instead, Nancy advised her to justify her request based on the president's goals and priorities. His key measurement was profitability, so Robin based her rationale on the cost of lost productivity from full-time staff, and the cost of constantly paying new temporary workers while they were being trained. For the first time, she approached her boss with the mind-set of an executive who was responsible for the well-being of the company, rather than the victim who was being mistreated by management.

"Why didn't you share all of this with me sooner?" was the president's response.

This time, he approved Robin's request to hire additional full-time staff. Once she stopped blaming him for rejecting her recommendation and took responsibility for finding a new sales approach that aligned with his financial goals, she got the results she desired.

Just like Robin Cartland, you choose the meaning you attach to the goings-on in the world around you. You can choose to be a victim who reacts, or you can choose to be an owner who causes a reaction in your company—and a successful outcome for yourself.

To transform a victim mentality into a dynamic, supportive mind-set, follow this three-step process:

1. *Develop an empowering motto.* Repeat this motto three or four times at the beginning of each day and again whenever you sense your inner victim trying to surface. This is a sort of internal brainwashing technique to convince yourself of your true worth and abilities. Something as simple as "I am the one with all of the power," or "I have all of the power to create results" will work just fine in transforming your internal voice from victim to booster.

2. *Change the language of your internal "chatter" and your external speaking.* Anytime you think or say "I can't . . . I wish . . . ," force yourself to change this language to "I can . . . I will." Be vigilant about making this shift until this more positive language occurs automatically, both inside your head and in your external speech. Once you have a more supportive thinking/language pattern in place, the shift to more powerful actions is a natural next step. And

this is soon followed by a shift in how the outside world perceives you.

3. *Finally and forever give up your attachment to "why me?" questions.* These questions can only reinforce your own powerlessness with reasons and rationales. Instead of asking yourself "why?" ask yourself "what?": "What can I do differently to change the situation or outcome so that I get what I want?" By staying focused on "what," you are directing yourself to find the solution and then move into action to achieve it.

Mental Barrier #2: Limiting Self-Beliefs

Limiting self-beliefs deal with how you see yourself—the person you think you know deep inside—with all of your fears and perceived ineptness. They are limiting because they reflect something far less than the reality of who you actually are. You judge yourself negatively; you think of yourself as having more failings, more flaws, more "missings," and fewer strengths, fewer talents. Your internal belief system is telling you one thing about yourself, while the truth is often something entirely different—and far better!

Limiting self-beliefs are usually easy to see in others but far more elusive to find in ourselves. For it is one thing to identify a limiting self-belief and quite another to recognize it as a false perception—to realize that you are better than you believe you are. This challenge is magnified by the fact that many of these negative self-perceptions have been ingrained in our psyches since childhood. They are deep-seated historical convictions that we hold about ourselves.

As very young children, we are blessed with *unlimited* self-beliefs in ourselves and our abilities: we learn to walk, talk, read, and write; in short, we repeatedly tackle the unknown and overcome it. But as we grow and undergo the socialization and education processes in our families, our schools, and our neighborhoods, we begin to accept the external world's assessments of us as Truth. What our teachers, parents, and bosses tell us about our talents (or lack of them) becomes what we think of ourselves. As we internalize these external assessments, we lose our belief in self, which is the foundation for our self-confidence. This process is particularly stringent on girls, and particularly relentless in a coeducational environment in which studies have documented that teachers—male and female—unconsciously demonstrate preference for their male students. The self-concept that you are "less than" becomes a fait accompli if you are a girl.

One clue that a limiting self-belief is operating in your life is your reaction to compliments. If you consistently answer with "Thank you, BUT . . ." and then proceed to say something about yourself that either diminishes or negates the compliment, a limiting self-belief is most likely hard at work on your psyche.

Just as with the victim mentality, the clues to uncovering a limiting self-belief can be found in your internal mind "chatter" as well as your external language. Here are just a few examples:

- "I've never been any good at _____."
- "No matter how hard I try, I just can't _____."
- "I wish I were better at _____."
- "I'm really _____ (lazy, dumb, slow, shy)."

If you allow these negative self-beliefs to take root, they will become truly constricting forces in your career and your life. When your internal beliefs are at cross-purposes with your external performance, eventually your performance will decline, as your subconscious struggles to bring reality into alignment with your negative mental perceptions of yourself.

Candy saw this debilitating dynamic in action with Susan, a young account supervisor, during a new business presentation. Susan had consistently shown command of her material and delivered many exceptional presentations to her existing clients. Yet she perceived herself as a poor presenter in new business situations. Just before the final presentation was to be delivered to a prospective client, Candy noticed that Susan was visibly nervous. She attempted to reassure Susan about the strengths of her skills, but Susan reiterated her own conviction that she was a poor presenter in new business meetings in which the individuals in the audience were relative strangers to her.

Can you guess what happened?

Yep. Susan delivered an abominable performance—stumbling through the points, stumped by simple questions, and stiff as a board to boot! Her limiting self-belief won out over her true capabilities . . . because she let it.

Just because a belief is deeply grounded in past experiences or perceptions does not make it a fact. Even if it was accurate at some point in your life, it doesn't have to be the reality of who you are today and tomorrow. Only by first confronting your limiting self-beliefs will you then be able to open yourself up to accept the truth of your full talents and capabilities. When you choose to let go of these beliefs and accept the fullness of your gifts, you will achieve the successful career you have envisioned.

The limiting self-belief that almost prevented Nancy from realizing her dreams for her own life was her belief that she was lazy. For years, friends and colleagues had encouraged her to become a business consultant. They were convinced that this field complemented her strengths, knowledge base, and personality. The idea excited her, but she kept resisting. Nancy just knew that if she went into business for herself, she would fail because she was lazy. Her family had always called her lazy. Her past and current actions confirmed this belief in her mind: she liked nothing better than to sit at the beach for hours staring off into the ocean or to curl up in her room all day reading a great book. Nancy imagined herself taking off day after day just to laze away the hours—and failing to generate enough business to make a living. Her entire work history contradicted her "lazy" belief, yet still she held onto it. It was her deep, dark, little secret.

"I really think I do my best work when I'm in a structured corporate environment," Nancy would tell her friends whenever the entrepreneur discussion came up. "I'm just more comfortable when the job is already clearly defined and my work hours are structured."

Finally, after listening to Nancy's rationale for several months, her closest friend confronted her. "I just don't get it," Kieta said. "You keep hanging on to this structure idea. But the entire time I've known you, you've worked in organizations you claim to love, yet you're always fighting to get out of the structure. You've never just done the job they gave you. You're always making waves by asking for some new responsibility or fighting to get some new project started."

"So what! That's only a small part of what you have to do to succeed in a large organization," Nancy answered. She still didn't get the point that Kieta was making.

"Maybe," Kieta said, "but that's also exactly what you do if you're a successful entrepreneur."

Nancy still resisted, so Kieta convinced her to make a list of her strengths and weaknesses as an independent businesswoman. Here it is:

Strengths	*Weaknesses*
Creative problem solver	Not detail-oriented
Quick learner/excellent memory	Not politically astute
Strategic thinker/looks at big picture	Lazy worker/undisciplined with time
Persuasive communicator	
Strong team builder	
Decisive, nurturing manager	
Strong analytical skills	

Nancy noticed first (and with a sigh of relief) that the strengths outnumbered the weaknesses. This did not surprise Kieta, but she was downright shocked when she spotted *lazy*. She reminded Nancy of all that she had accomplished in her work over the ten years that they had been friends. Nancy still refused to budge. So Kieta gave her a homework assignment: keep a record of her daily activities at work for the next week. At the end of that week, Kieta sat down with Nancy and divided the activities into those that were directed by others (boss, coworkers, and so on) and those that Nancy had initiated on her own. Kieta pointed to the self-initiated list: "Look at how much is there! Most managers wouldn't have half that stuff done. This is not the list of a lazy person. It belongs to a successful entrepreneur. And that entrepreneur is you, Nancy."

For the first time, Nancy saw the full measure of who she was: a hardworking, self-motivated, *entrepreneurial* leader.

Once Nancy started her own business and realized the success she could create, she finally acknowledged how false and limiting this one, single self-belief had been. In accepting Kieta's homework challenge, Nancy was forced to confront her belief and to look at herself through more objective eyes. Once she abandoned her "lazy" limiting self-belief, she set herself free to achieve the life she had always envisioned.

The key to overcoming your own limiting self-beliefs is to either abandon them or transform them. Rather than remind yourself of the "missings," you must begin to proactively look for ways to, as they say, "accentuate the positive and eliminate the negative" in your thinking as well as in your speech:

"I am very good at _____."
"When I try hard, I can _____."
"I am capable of _____."
"Thank you for the compliment!" (I deserve it.)

In learning to fill in the blanks for these statements (and repeating them to yourself several times a day), you are redesigning the internal feedback system that supported you when you were a young child. You are, once again, learning to look to yourself—rather than listening to others—for your sense of who you are and what talents you possess.

This redesigning process is simple, but it requires diligence if you are to succeed. Particularly when the outside world offers you its negative opinions or assessments, you must break your habit of automatic acceptance. Instead, examine this external feedback using your own internal knowledge, and make a conscious decision whether to accept it or reject it.

If you adopt these practices as daily regimens, they will start you on the pathway to rebuilding your unlimited self-beliefs, your power, and your confidence to tackle any challenge and overcome any barrier—just as you did when you were a small child.

Mental Barrier #3: Rigid Mind-Set

Rigid mind-set, the third mental barrier, has to do with the knowledge that you hold to be true—so true, in fact, as to be irrefutable, unchangeable, and unchallengeable. A rigid mind-set is simply a lazy way of thinking, and it shows up even in the smartest of people. It is the primary enemy of creativity and innovation, those things that are the lifeblood of American business and the keys to satisfaction and joy for individual employees. Albert Einstein understood the restrictive power of a rigid mind-set when he said, "No problem can be solved from the same consciousness that created it. We must learn to see the world anew."

A rigid mind-set is an attitude of automatically rejecting new ideas, new information, or new ways of behaving that are contrary to your "already knowing" and experience. It keeps your mind closed to people and ideas that challenge what you have always believed to be absolute (and therefore, irrefutable) truths about the world around you. When an employee offers you a recommendation that directly contradicts the idea that is already in place in your own mind, you suffer from a rigid mind-set if you have any of the following reactions:

- *An instantaneous, negative, emotional response:* You feel angry, frustrated, even disrespected. You feel that your authority or expertise is being challenged.
- *An "I'm right (and you're wrong)" response:* You automatically dismiss the idea because you are so sure that the choice you have already made is the only right choice or clearly the best choice.
- *A stuck-in-the-same-place reaction:* Adopting the new idea would require you to make so many other changes (organizational, processes, etc.) that you aren't willing to even consider it.

All three of these responses are typically preceded by a physical "gut reaction." It can be a feeling of tightness or constriction in your stomach, your shoulders, your chest, or even your forehead. This is your early warning system of a rigid mind-set.

It's awfully tempting in business to be lured by the comforts of a rigid mentality. It enables you to retreat to the safety of being right; it allows you to make faster decisions because you eliminate discussion and exploration. In the short term it requires less effort. But in the long run it produces less powerful results.

For Kristin, a top-level financial executive at a major insurance company, this rigid adherence to being right was so habitual that she never even recognized its presence. She had begun coaching with Nancy to resolve some performance issues with several of her subordinates in the company. According to Kristin, they were processing the work much more slowly than their counterparts in similar functions at other companies. Their absenteeism was high, and when they did come to work, their attitudes ranged from negative to mildly hostile.

Nancy listened carefully to Kristin's assessments and got an "Aha!": What Kristin had identified as a people breakdown was actually a system breakdown. About 80 percent of their work depended on customized computer processing programs and the intranet linkage between departments. Cumbersome computer programming issues were very likely the source of the employee performance problems.

Nancy was encouraged because a system problem was usually much easier to solve than a people problem. Nancy spent the next month getting an in-depth understanding of the insurance-claims processing systems. Then she scheduled a meeting to share her thoughts for improvements with Kristin.

What a shock! To every one of Nancy's suggestions, Kristin instantly responded with a polite but rigid "No!" before Nancy could even finish expressing her complete thought. Kristin was stubbornly holding on to her initial "right" conclusion: this was a people problem, not a system breakdown.

Recognizing the rigid mind-set, Nancy kept suggesting changes with gentler "OK, but what if . . . ?" questions. The force of Kristin's "No!"s felt to Nancy like a series of dull punches to the gut.

After two hours, Nancy challenged Kristin, "If it isn't a systems problem, then who do you need to replace—and who would you hire— to fix it?" This was the question that finally gave Kristin her "Aha!" She realized that even if she replaced every employee, the problem would remain. Once Kristin opened her mind and began looking for the system breakdowns, she implemented three key changes in claims processing. Voilá! The performance problems with the individual employees simply disappeared.

The real lesson for Kristin was to see the devastating force of a "No!" when it arises from the emotional, judgmental space of a rigid mind-set. As Kristin's coach, Nancy was being paid to hang in there until she had helped Kristin achieve her goals. But would one of Kristin's employees have withstood a steady stream of "No!" answers long enough to get to a "Yes"? Would a subordinate have risked repeatedly being "wrong" in the quest to get his or her new idea considered? Not likely.

To be an effective leader at any level of your organization, you must consciously break down your natural tendency of seeing your way as right and everyone else's ideas as wrong by looking first for the possibilities (and not the problems) that may exist in each new idea or suggestion. Exploring every idea with the thought that it may contain a breakthrough (rather than looking first for why it won't work) is the mind-set of true leadership, no matter where you are in the hierarchy of management. An outstanding leader is an innovator who is willing to move beyond rigid mind-sets and consciously choose to transcend her habitual way of responding to people, information, and circumstances. The leader's mind is open to exploring new theories, new pathways, and new territories. When the leader is a *possibility thinker*, she creates an environment in which creative ideas can flourish.

The first step to overcoming a rigid mind-set is to become aware of it. The second (and third, and fourth, and fifth) step is simple: remind your mind to remain objective. Pay attention to that instinctive gut reaction to a person or idea. This is your first signal that a rigid mind-set is intervening to block you from something new. When it happens, take a breath and quell any desire to react swiftly. Do nothing for a moment. Think *possibility*, and allow your mind to listen openly, ask plenty of exploratory questions, and objectively evaluate the merits of this person or idea. When you learn to listen first, look for possibility second, question and evaluate third, and reject only as your last step, you are breaking out of a rigid mind-set and into the space of an innovative and inspiring leader.

Mental Barrier #4: Revering Status Quo

Revering status quo has to do with the actions you *don't* take because of your pervasive belief that "if it ain't broke, don't fix it," or "it's always been done this way." It's that little voice on the inside that keeps you—and your organization—small, because it holds you both exactly where you are today. It may sound like a rigid mind-set, but it is quite different. A rigid mind-set is about giving honor and primacy to yourself ("I'm right"), whereas revering status quo is an attitude that gives honor and primacy to some established, external process, person, or system ("It's right"). This is an automatic acceptance of the way things are without thought for how they might be improved.

Revering status quo is a mental barrier because it keeps you stuck in the known and comfortable and holds you back from initiating any actions that are new or different. It is risk-averse and fear-based. And if you live your life by it, you will fail to rise to the challenges and opportunities that define the difference between a safe, mediocre career and a dynamic, exceptional one—between merely managing and leading!

Women seem to have a special reverence for the status quo. In fact, for us it even has a special name: the Good Girl Syndrome. We relate to the rules and regulations and to those above us on the corporate hierarchy much as a little girl relates to her parents. When she challenges authority, the usual result is punishment. So we support the status quo that our company's senior management has established. In our efforts to be accepted by the predominantly male cultures in which we work, we are "good girls."

In your job performance, this Good Girl Syndrome is what keeps you working within the lines, fulfilling your responsibilities or completing projects exactly as they were given to you. It keeps you from looking outside of the boundaries to see what extra measure of performance you can deliver. In short, it keeps you from excelling.

The Good Girl Syndrome slows your professional growth and career progress precisely because you place more value on being in agreement with your superiors than on searching for new and better ideas that will benefit your company—and your career. In corporate America, the pathway to top leadership is often achieved by the contrarian—the employee who finds a new path, a different way, sometimes even an opposite direction and ends up moving the company ahead.

Christopher Columbus was a contrarian who believed the world was round. At the time, all empirical evidence pointed to a flat world. But Queen Isabella of Spain was the leader who opened her mind to a new possibility and provided the money and resources to make his discoveries possible.

Author and organization development guru David Whyte captured the value of this contrarian perspective in his book, *The Heart Aroused*:

> *Ironically, we bring more vitality into our organizations when we refuse to make their goals the measure of our success and start to ask about the greater goals they might serve, and when we stop looking to them as parents who will supply necessities we can only obtain when we wrestle directly with our own destiny.*[3]

Bringing this unique perspective to your work will enable you to create a job that offers you growth opportunities and expands the possibilities for your company.

This contrarian point of view paid big dividends for Lillian Andrews. She was an executive vice president responsible for corporate PR and investor communications in a large bank that had recently decentralized its advertising functions. Lillian's boss, the president of this Fortune 500 company, had made the final decision to eliminate corporate advertising based on his conviction that it was not delivering concrete results for the bank.

Lillian reviewed the bank's consumer research and realized that several critical measures had declined steadily and significantly since the advertising had been decentralized. She believed that the lack of a strong corporate-image campaign was a key factor in the decline. She developed a bold recommendation to reinstate a corporate ad campaign and corporate control of the advertising function, even though this was in direct conflict with her boss's beliefs and with his earlier decision.

What happened? Her boss approved her recommendation. Why? Because she saturated her rationale with facts and framed her argument around a goal that her boss believed in: improving the bank's bottom line. Keeping the bank above all competitors on several key consumer scores was one of his most important strategic objectives. She simply showed him how a central corporate advertising function was the best tool. She achieved a major expansion in the scope of her job when her boss reinstated the corporate advertising function and placed it—and a $25 million budget—under her control. In her willingness to be a contrarian and challenge the status quo, Lillian won. So did her boss, and so did her company.

If Lillian, instead, had been a "good girl" who revered the status quo, just think about where she and her company would be now. She would be in her same old job, and her company would be in the same, small place in the minds of consumers. *Status quo*, by definition, is about keeping everything exactly the way it is. But if your competition continues moving forward while you remain in the same spot, both you and your company fall farther and farther behind.

One of Candy's coworkers often jokingly told the story of the buggy whip manufacturer. At one point in time he produced most of the buggy whips sold in the eastern half of the United States, and he made a handsome profit. Then the car was invented and the buggy whip market began to shrink. His competitors began switching over their manufacturing to service the car industry. But he was still making money on buggy whips, so he stayed with the status quo. And he did make money on every single buggy whip he sold. Even the very last one!

Like the buggy whip example, status quo scenarios are often both tragic and funny, once they are revealed and challenged.

Early in Nancy's career, when she was director of human resources at a large law firm, the status quo took on the image of an old-fashioned safe, located just outside her office. Historically, every time an attorney wanted a document, the safe had to be opened by the human resources director. It mattered not if she was having a delicate, confidential meeting with an employee; she was to respond immediately whenever an attorney knocked. Nancy questioned this practice and was told, "This is the way it's always been done." Nancy pointed out the lost productivity for herself as well as the attorneys and suggested opening the safe at the beginning of the day and closing it at the end. "No." She suggested giving keys to each attorney or to the secretaries. "No" was always the answer.

Nancy spent three years in that firm. She probably got up two or three times each day to open and close that safe, about half an hour of unproductive work every day for three years. Revering status quo wasn't merely frustrating to Nancy, it was costly to the company.

To overcome a "revering status quo" mentality, you need to retrain your mind to be an instinctive challenger rather than an automatic acceptor. This requires a conscious commitment on your part to build a habit of inquisitiveness. And you'll probably need a good dose of courage because choosing an anti–status quo solution involves a certain level of risk in this status quo–oriented world. You will often be the "lone wolf in the wilderness" in your corporation. If your courage begins to wane, just remember that lone wolves are usually the winners in today's wilder, more competitive corporate environments.

Training yourself to seek out the anti–status quo requires you to reorient your "good girl" perspective. Instead of working to be *good*, you want to look for ways to be *better*: Better than your peers. Better than your boss expects you to be. Better than your own last effort.

So how do you find those ways to be better? Well, here are a few practical tools:

- *Ask for help and ask for explanations.* Don't get stuck in the mind-set that you should be figuring everything out for yourself. Others in and out of your company have a wealth of experience and information that can guide you into that *better* space.
- *Always be on the lookout for opportunities and improvements.* The first step to finding new opportunities and solutions to problems is to keep your mind constantly alert and searching for them.
- *Be willing to offer ideas and solutions.* This step takes courage because management will probably say no far more often than yes.

When this happens, you must avoid falling prey to the victim mentality. Remind yourself that their "no" is not aimed at you, it's aimed at your idea. Circumstances change, so today's "no" could turn into tomorrow's "yes." Your mission is simply to keep offering.

If you consistently use these tools in your job performance, and if you consistently keep these *better* criteria as your benchmarks, we can promise you that you won't be a "good girl" anymore.

You'll be *better*.

Now it's time to complete the second half of the assignment that you began earlier in this chapter. Pull out the list of "barriers to success" that you created. Go through each item and decide if it is, in fact, a manifestation of one (or more) of these four mental barriers. For example, if we look at our sample list near the beginning of this chapter, here's what we would say:

- All of the "not enough" barriers are manifestations of either a victim mentality or limiting self-beliefs.
- All of the "afraid of" barriers are limiting self-beliefs or revering status quo.
- The "boss won't let me" barrier is a victim mentality.
- The "management is men, and they won't promote women" barrier is a victim mentality.
- The "reputation as stubborn" barrier is a rigid mind-set.

In our A Woman's Way of Leadership programs, once the women realize that 90 percent to 100 percent of the barriers that they originally identified as external are actually self-created by one or more of these four mental attitudes, an audible gasp emerges from every woman in the room. It's a huge "Aha!" when these women realize the degree to which their own attitudes have colored their perceptions of the external world—and their subsequent performance in it. You see, these attitudes either created a barrier where none really existed or magnified a small difficulty into such a large barrier that it seemed impossible to overcome.

When a woman realizes that she has complete power to make any barrier small (and therefore, easy to leap over) simply by how she thinks about it, her "Aha!" represents a gasp of both realization and relief. In reality, nothing stands between her and her dreams.

Once you learn to use the power of your attitudes to minimize rather than magnify an external barrier, you have given yourself the necessary internal support system to realize your goals, because you now have eyes that see, a mind that understands, and a heart that is open to accept the abundance of opportunities around you. You have set yourself free to achieve all of your dreams and possibilities because you see *more* rather than *less* in yourself, in others, and in every position you hold in the organization. You'll find that the road to achieving your Activating Vision is more comfortable, more fun, and more fulfilling!

CHAPTER 5

REINVENTING YOUR JOB

BUILDING THE EXPANDED 100% JOB

Dance Lesson #5: If you want a job that is more challenging and brings you more joy, create it yourself. No one else can do it for you.

Highly successful people are often called lucky by the rest of the world. But Ben Franklin was right when he said, "Luck is nothing more than preparation meeting opportunity."

If you have finished the various exercises in the previous chapters, your internal preparation is complete. But let's do a quick check-in to make sure you've created the key pieces:

- The big picture: Activating Vision, Heart's Purpose, and Defining Values
- A specific plan: context-driven Destination Goals
- Internal attitudes: transforming mental barriers into mental boosters

Do you still have work to do in any of these areas? Then we suggest you make a commitment to complete them by the time you've finished reading this chapter. Why is this so important? Because Ben Franklin was right: you can't take full advantage of your *outside* opportunities until you're prepared on the *inside*.

With these pieces in place, you have completed the process of reinventing your future: You have a crystal clear idea of where you're going.

You've also completed the process of reinventing your attitudes: You've built the internal support system that will help you achieve your new future with ease. You are now ready to actually step onto the dance floor—to begin interacting anew with the business world that surrounds you today. And since the single most dominant piece of your professional present is your current job, this is precisely where you will begin.

In this chapter, you will learn to reinvent your present: You will examine your current job from a new perspective and custom-fit it to match your particular talents, goals, and passions. This may be the last place you'd think of as your first opportunity. But if you are like the one out of four U.S. workers who is neither satisfied nor happy in his or her current position, the initial step to achieve more challenge, satisfaction, and joy from your work is not to change jobs. It is to look at the one you have through new eyes—the eyes of an owner rather than someone who is just loitering in the position.

To fully understand the significance of this shift, think of your job as if it were a house. After all, you live in a job just as you live in a house. In making the move from renter to homeowner, your perspectives and priorities shift. You no longer think of the property simply as something to use, without thought of upkeep or repairs. Now it's *yours*. If you're unhappy with something, you don't stand by, waiting for someone else to notice. You fix it yourself! And as a smart homeowner, you add to the value of your investment by improving the property.

When you take ownership of any job, the same attitude applies. You make changes in it so that it will be a comfortable fit with your personality, talents, and goals. If you're skeptical of this notion of customizing, changing, and improving a job, look at someone who has recently taken a new position in your company. After a few months, compare that person to his or her predecessor. Does the performance of the job look exactly the same for both people? Of course not. The job description merely sets the basic standard. Each individual performs that job in his or her own way by applying a unique set of talents to achieve excellence.

Understanding this principle is critical for women. Typically, we are "by the book" job performers. We keep ourselves in a small, well-defined box, single-mindedly concentrating on fulfilling every aspect of the job description. Instead, we should be using it as a guideline and then overlaying our true talents and desires to perform our responsibilities in a way that is both differentiated and excellent.

Even if your job seems just fine as it is, as an owner you always look for ways to make it better and ways *it* can make *you* better. You add value to it. And it, in turn, adds value to you. If something isn't working, you don't stand around waiting for somebody else to solve it; you take responsibility for improving it yourself.

The trick is to know how. That's where our Expanded 100% Job concept will show you the way. In this chapter, we will give you the knowledge and practical tools to grow your current position into an Expanded 100% Job, one that combines your current job description with additional special projects and responsibilities to provide you with more joy, challenge, and growth opportunities. The Expanded 100% Job will develop your skill sets and accelerate your career advancement. But above all, it will feed your passions and fill your days with fun.

An Expanded 100% Job that is closely aligned with your values and expertise will be a success magnet for your future. In enabling you to fully use your talents and demonstrate your larger potential in your organization, the Expanded 100% Job puts you on the fast track for promotion. More important, influential people and opportunities will be drawn to you. So your work will do more than increase your feelings of self-fulfillment and satisfaction; it will require less effort and be more fun.

These feelings have eluded many women in corporate America because their positions do not represent a level of challenge equal to their skills, and they are acutely aware of the shortfall. For years, surveys have documented the undervaluation and underutilization of women in corporate organizations. Dr. Judy B. Rosener, author of *America's Competitive Secret: Utilizing Women as a Management Strategy*, asked male and female professionals what the term *underutilized* meant to them:

> *They said that underutilization means "not being challenged, motivated, or empowered," "not being used," "being assigned roles that don't fit one's skills," "not being required to perform tasks*

that take advantage of or build on one's education, experience, and ability."[1]

Women have far more than simply an opportunity to expand the scope and parameters of their jobs in corporate America. They have a craving to use all of their skills so they can fully contribute to their companies.

Before spending the time and energy it takes to create an Expanded 100% Job, make sure you're in an environment that will support your efforts rather than resist them. Building an Expanded 100% Job is a process of creation, which is difficult enough (and risky enough) even in the best of circumstances. If you are also fighting to fit into a corporate culture that is not a natural match for your personality and values, this creation process will be thwarted at every turn. So before you begin creating, do some assessing of your corporate culture. At the end of this assessment, you may find that your unhappiness or dissatisfaction with your current position is a culture problem rather than a specific job or boss problem. In this situation, choosing a new company is most often a better career-building decision. Let us explain why.

The Influence of Company Culture

Culture is one of the primary defining characteristics of any company. To help you understand the true impact of culture in an organization, let's look at it within the larger context of a country and its citizens. The culture expresses and elevates a nation's unique value system; it binds the citizens together into a cohesive group; it even affects their collective personality and goals. Culture, then, is more than just an influence upon the people; it is an archetype that simultaneously expresses and defines the limits of acceptability for their attitudes and behaviors. And just as it reinforces and rewards those who adhere to it, a culture separates and punishes those who don't.

Pretend for just a moment that you are a young, professional American woman who moves to Japan. You came from a country that values individuality and self-expression and where women populate the managerial ranks of almost every industry. You enter a country that values teams over individuals and group harmony over self-expression and where women are, even today, restricted primarily to administrative, secretarial, or other subordinate roles in business.

After incessant rounds of interviews for managerial jobs and a steady string of polite rejections, you finally accept a lower-level position. You begin contributing many ideas for improvements, which are implemented. You receive high ratings on your reviews, yet you remain in the same position, watching in frustration as every man at your level is eventually promoted.

So, is something lacking in your talents and skill sets? Or are you simply out of sync with Japan's culture? The culture is not wrong and neither are you. The two of you are just different. This difference causes you to work harder than you should and to be rewarded with less than you expect. And as this occurs, you are feeling increasingly frustrated, angry, and exhausted. Constantly struggling to fit in, and yet never being completely able to, drains your energy, your self-esteem, and your self-confidence. You think the problem is you. It's not!

A company's culture is just as fixed and stubborn as a country's. Its values are just as powerful and pervasive. And if those values do not match your own, the company's culture will surely change you long before you can change it. It will blunt your satisfaction with your work and stunt your promotability in the organization.

A company's culture is, on the other hand, tougher to spot than a country's. When you live in Japan, it's easy to identify the cultural differences as the source of your struggles. But because you are not as attuned to the role of culture in your company, you often fail to recognize it as the root of your difficulties. You may not even realize that you're in a mismatched culture. The natural conclusion, when you begin to work harder and achieve even less, is to believe that *you* are the problem. And the culture—as represented by the judgments of management, bosses, and peers—confirms this assessment. So you begin struggling to change yourself in order to succeed. The danger is that you end up out of sync with more than the company's culture; you end up becoming out of sync with yourself. This is how the culture chips away at your identity and self-confidence until you become disempowered in both your thinking and your actions.

It is possible to be out of alignment with your corporate culture and still be successful. However, your success will come with an added dose of struggle because you are constantly swimming upstream.

When Lorraine Richards made the decision to move from her hard-charging position in one of New York's leading investment banking firms to become chief investment officer of a government pension fund, she was prepared for surprises. But the biggest shock of all was the difficulty—and the rejection—she encountered solely as a result of the cultural mismatch with her own personality and management style. Even as a child, Lorraine was a classic type A personality: aggressive, achievement-driven, and intense. As an adult, this level of intensity made her the ideal investment banker. She rose quickly, made tons of money, and worked day and night for fifteen years to do it.

About two years after giving birth to her second child and continuing to maintain her day-and-night schedule at work, Lorraine began looking for a lower-stress environment that would enable her to spend more time with her family. The chief investment officer position fulfilled her criteria completely: a nine-to-five job in a slower-paced government organization. She would be managing a large group of employees and overseeing the investment decision-making process of more than $1 billion of funds under management.

Lorraine was in the new job for about three nanoseconds when she encountered her first conflict. She was determined to improve the fund's investment performance significantly within her initial year. So at her first staff meeting she began firing questions and challenges at each of her direct reports. One by one they withered under her attack. Most of them had been employed in the company for ten or more years, and what they liked most about their work was its security and predictability. They weren't hard-chargers . . . and neither was their culture.

While her subordinates were feeling their own fears and frustrations, Lorraine was feeling hers. At every step she felt like Sisyphus, pushing that boulder up the side of a mountain. She wanted fast; they delivered slow. She wanted results; they dwelled on process. She pushed for new ideas; they clung to the old.

Lorraine had been beating her head against this cultural wall for about three months (and her employees had delivered a steady stream of complaints to human resources) when the HR manager decided to speak with the CEO. The topic: Lorraine. The conclusion: "Maybe we made a mistake in hiring her. She's just not a 'people person.'"

Ironically, Lorraine *was* a "people person." As an investment banker, her ability to manage and motivate her subordinates had been a strength, and she garnered tremendous loyalty from her group. She expected a high level of personal accountability and productivity from her people. Her investment banking subordinates found this expectation empowering. But employees in the soft, secure culture of a government organization interpreted this same demand as hard-nosed and uncaring.

The important lesson here is that Lorraine wasn't wrong and neither was the company. They were simply different. One of them would have to change. Guess which one!

So why did Lorraine choose to stay? Her decision-making process is a textbook example of the power of Defining Values. Once she had her second child, Lorraine's Defining Value for *family* became more important than her value for *career growth/personal wealth*. While the calm, nonconfrontational culture of her new company was at odds with her preference for a dynamic, high-intensity workplace, it was the key factor enabling her to combine a high-level job with her (now) primary value for family. So she made a conscious choice to adapt.

Over the next six months, Lorraine entered an intensive coaching program with Nancy. Her central challenge was to "tone herself down." Her efforts covered a broad spectrum: speaking more slowly, asking questions in a less aggressive manner, listening, and most important, changing her expectations and lowering her demands. She had to pick fewer battles and fight them less aggressively, reward small improvements and stop demanding large gains.

"I expect that I'll continue to struggle with these things as long as I work here," Lorraine says now. "I just get more charged up in that whole stressed-out, frenetic, investment banking environment. But right now I want a job that gives me time to spend with my family. So I'm looking at this as a learning experience. If I can make it there [investment banking], *and* make it here, I can make it anywhere."

A company culture is embodied and expressed in the core values that are shared by the employees and the behavior styles and patterns that dominate the organization. These values and behaviors persist even though employees constantly come and go. And even when dynamic, high-level people like Lorraine challenge the culture, most often the culture wins.

The culture of a company is rarely a spoken, explicitly defined factor. Instead, it is revealed implicitly, in whom the company hires and which of their behaviors and achievements are rewarded or penalized by the organization's management. As an individual, you can't dramatically change a culture unless you're the president or CEO. Even then, it's hard! So if you want to achieve success without all of the added stress and struggle, join a company with a culture that matches not only your Defining Values, but your personality and preferred style of behavior as well. To find it, you will need to become a "cultural detective," constantly looking for clues as part of your interviewing process.

The first step to finding a good fit is to learn what works for you. This can be discovered only through introspection and self-assessment. Think about your most ingrained personality traits and behaviors. These are the parts of you that, if you had to change them, would result in your feeling less yourself. Think about the Defining Values you identified for yourself in Chapter 2. Think about the work environment that is most comfortable and fun for you. These are the characteristics you will search for in a company. Since culture is so unchangeable, it should be the deal maker or the deal breaker in your decision to join an organization. You can't possibly transform yourself enough to create a perfect fit where it doesn't already exist on some level. But if you do choose to enter an organization that is only a partial cultural match, as Lorraine did, you'll want to clearly understand those areas where adaptation is a necessary prerequisite to your success.

Candy was twenty-five when she learned the power of culture. It was at that time that she made her first job change, from Needham, Harper

& Steers in Chicago to a large West Coast advertising agency based in San Francisco. NH&S was a creativity-driven agency and Candy had spent two-and-a-half happy years there. Yet she yearned to return to the winter warmth of California. During her job search, she sought to join a marketing-driven agency, believing that her account management skills might develop faster in this environment. She was also just plain curious to learn firsthand how these two types of agencies were different.

Candy's new company was one of the strongest marketing agencies on the West Coast. She quickly experienced a cultural mismatch on almost every dimension. Candy's highest personal priority was to deliver outstanding creative work to her clients. This was what she had loved most about her work at NH&S. But the San Francisco agency was so focused on marketing that their creative work was usually mediocre.

Candy was a collaborative, team-oriented manager. Her new agency was a dictatorial environment in which the account person reigned supreme. Candy had a quick wit, and laughter was a critical ingredient in her daily happiness. This agency had a serious, no-nonsense work environment where laughers were considered to be loafers.

After nine months of struggle, Candy made the decision to resign in about ninety seconds. It happened when she received a phone call from a previous boss, who asked her a single, critical question: "Are you happy there?" She stopped dead in her tracks. You see, like most women, she had been working so hard trying to fit into an antithetical culture that she had never even thought about her own happiness. "No, I'm miserable!" was her answer.

Candy had fallen into a typical female pattern. When she found herself in the wrong culture, she believed that the "missing" was inside her rather than outside in the culture. Because women are community-driven, their first thought is to work harder to be accepted by an unaccepting culture. When this fails—and it usually does—the woman will blame herself in some way for the failure

That same day Candy flew to Los Angeles to interview for a new job. Three weeks later she started working as an account executive at Doyle Dane Bernbach Advertising in Los Angeles. Physically, DDB was the shabbiest advertising agency she had ever seen. The desks were a vintage World War II gunmetal gray, and the carpet was occasionally covered with duct tape to mask the rips. But three cultural factors governed her decision to join DDB:

1. Delivering great creative work had been the agency's core value since it was founded in the 1950s, and the advertising they produced demonstrated that value.
2. It was an open, collaborative company. As Candy walked through the hallways during her interviews, she frequently saw people in small team meetings, loudly discussing business issues.
3. The people working there were having lots of fun. They were smiling, and she heard lots of laughter; even her interview with the president was casual, relaxed, and full of fun and humor.

Candy worked—and thrived—at DDB Los Angeles from 1980 until her retirement in 1998. She had found her cultural soul mate, and this was a key factor supporting her career progress and eventual rise to comanaging director and chief operating officer.

Uncovering the true culture of an organization takes commitment, but it will make a dramatic difference in your career. If you join a company that fits with your own Defining Values and cultural preferences, you will stay longer, rise higher, be happier, expend less effort, and experience less stress. The benefits of cultural fit were validated by a recent study of accounting firms, reported in *Fortune* magazine. The study found that "new employees whose personalities suited the firm's culture were about 20 percent less likely to leave their jobs in the first three years than those whose values-sorting test results suggested a poor fit. They also performed better and were more satisfied with their work."[2] It is, quite simply, easier to succeed if you're in the right culture.

Because women are intrinsically relationship-oriented and strong communicators, they are often attracted to corporate cultures that possess these same qualities. Such process-driven cultures will surely value these women, but they may not promote them to the most senior ranks—particularly if men dominate senior management. Because process and relationship skills are qualitative criteria, the opportunities for "disqualification" are broad and undefined. This puts the female minority at a distinct disadvantage when they are being judged for fit by the close-knit male majority in the executive offices.

If a top management position is what you seek, a results-driven culture offers you the best chance to reach your goal, for two reasons. First, while managers can be process-oriented and survive, leaders cannot. At the core of leadership is the ability to deliver results—to employees, to customers, and to stockholders. Second, since most companies' top management ranks are still male-dominated, the proverbial Old Boys' network is unavoidably in place. It may be painfully apparent, or it may be so subtle that you doubt it's even there. Just know that it is. Your best chance of joining these ranks comes from your ability to deliver results in combination with their core value of rewarding results. It's a quantitative criterion that transcends gender. It's your ticket to the dance!

To find a corporation that feels like home, you must train yourself to observe a company's culture and physically sense it within the walls. Look for the clues that reveal how the company treats its employees and how the employees relate to each other:

- Is space distribution based on power (private offices, varying sizes), or community (more open, shared spaces)?
- What feeling do you get from the reception areas (conservative, creative, sophisticated, down-to-earth)?
- How are individual offices decorated (with one main theme or individual creative imprints)?
- What feeling do you get from the common areas, such as lunchrooms and conference rooms (formal, informal, fun, serious, loud, quiet)?
- When you read the annual report and other company-wide newsletters or memos, what priorities are reinforced, what leadership values are applauded, how (and why) are employees acknowledged?

While you are observing and feeling the physical space, also take a close look at the people. Go beyond the impression of the employees who actually interview you. Their job is to show you only the good side of themselves and their organization. If you want a true sense of the company, observe the people who are not observing you:

- How does the receptionist relate to visitors (formally, informally)?
- Do you see many friendly exchanges in the hallways, or does it appear that most communication goes on behind closed doors?
- Do you see groups of employees eating lunch together? Are they open and friendly with each other or quiet and reserved? How do they treat you?
- How are the people dressed (formal business, business casual, jeans)?

Whenever the opportunity arises, you must probe at every opening and ask questions of employees, former employees, and outside vendors. Following are some culture-revealing questions to use in your own search:

- How does the company measure its success?
- What qualities do the successful employees in the company demonstrate? What qualities do unsuccessful employees have in common?
- Are certain personality or behavior traits especially honored or rewarded in the organization? Are certain traits especially penalized?
- How well represented are women in senior management? Are these women individuals, or simply cookie-cutter images of their male counterparts?
- How are women at different levels of the organization treated?
- What issue(s) caused the company to fire a recent employee?
- What reasons do former employees give for leaving the company?

As you hear the answers, listen closely to the corporate stories and folklore that are revealed and the deeper meanings they carry. Were any of the heroes in these stories heroines? What values, behaviors, or personality traits are admired in these stories? Are they different for women versus men?

As you assemble these pieces of the puzzle called culture, remind yourself that this is the one time when optimism is your enemy. It takes a lot more than a positive attitude to change a corporate culture. If you do choose to join a company that is not a perfect fit, choose wisely. Know what you'll need to change about yourself, and think about whether these changes are worth the effort. And if you find yourself in a cultural mismatch that is either truly unworkable or just plain not worth it, stop struggling! The most constructive use of your optimism is to move yourself and your skills into a new job and a new company.

Creating Your Expanded 100% Job

Once you are in the right company culture, your next step toward a new work life filled with challenge, satisfaction, and joy is creating your Expanded 100% Job. This is a process of custom-designing your job to meet your own needs and goals as well as your company's. You are the only person in the entire organization who can create your ideal job, because you are the only one who knows what would make your work ideal.

The first step in building your Expanded 100% Job is to see your current position in a broader context and from an "ownership" perspective. We will help you look beyond what it *is* to what it can *become*. We will give you practical tools to help you identify the possibilities, the challenges, and the joys that have always been there, just waiting for you to grab them. So instead of passively hoping for your company or your boss to hand-feed you a special project or a new assignment, you can take charge of locating these opportunities and taking ownership of them yourself.

This process involves identifying what you want and then being assumptive about getting it. All too often in business, women either wait patiently to be recognized or rewarded (the Good Girl Syndrome), or they ask permission before expanding even an inch outside of their established responsibilities. If the recognition and rewards aren't bestowed on them or if the permission isn't granted, then they complain that they are underutilized or undervalued. Would a man be this passive? No. He would simply assume that he deserves the reward, ignore the fact that he might need permission, and take ownership of the new responsibility or project as though it had already been officially given to him. This is one of the ways men get ahead . . . and women stay behind.

What you must be really clear about as you reach for the Expanded 100% Job is that no one else knows or even thinks about what you do all day long. Your superiors may be measuring your performance against a couple of big projects or client relations or hitting certain numbers, but rarely is anyone paying attention to your moment-to-moment, day-to-day activities. Not even your boss! This absence of attention gives you the freedom to design what works for you. You can create the job that fits your skills, interests, and passions perfectly. To do it, you will use four building blocks:

1. *Your existing job.* This describes the most basic, universal requirements of your position that are the common denominators for all individuals in that particular job, regardless of who they are, what special talents they possess or lack, or how their particular assignments may differ.

2. *The job description for the next position you want to hold.* Like your current job description, this one also covers the basics. But in this case, "the basics" are exactly the clues you need to determine how to prepare yourself for promotion.

3. *Your boss's understanding of your responsibilities and his or her definition of 100 percent.* This tells you how much or how little your boss understands about what you actually do every day. But more important, you will learn exactly how he or she will evaluate your performance.

4. *Your expansion list of projects and responsibilities.* You will develop this list, based on your goals, your desires, and your unique talents. It is the secret weapon that transforms any position into a job that you love. It will help you earn greater recognition from your superiors and step onto an accelerated career path.

Now let's start expanding your job. Start with a blank sheet of paper, divide it into quarters, and label it as indicated below:

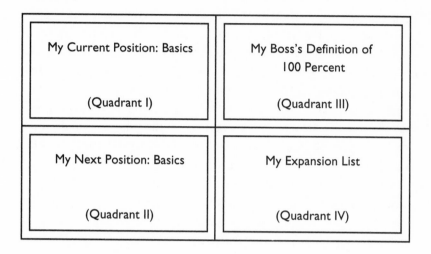

My Current Position: Basics (Quadrant I)	My Boss's Definition of 100 Percent (Quadrant III)
My Next Position: Basics (Quadrant II)	My Expansion List (Quadrant IV)

The next three sections of this chapter will help you work through each of these quadrants.

Quadrants I and II: The Power—and the Limitations—of the Job Description

Do you truly know what your core job responsibilities are? Have you ever seen an actual job description for your position? If your answer is no, then your first step should be to ask for one. Don't be surprised if it is outdated, obsolete, or even nonexistent. One of the fast-disappearing features in today's ever-changing corporate landscape is the job description. With the increasing pace of merging, acquiring, downsizing, and reorganizing, the work of creating or updating job descriptions is often left undone. The void that is created by its obsolescence or absence offers tremendous latitude for you to stretch your position in new directions that will develop your skills and appeal to your passions.

Let's assume that an updated job description already exists. Do you realize the power you have to take ownership of this description and expand it to become exactly the job you want? Remind yourself first that it outlines only the most basic responsibilities and performance requirements that must be delivered by everyone who holds this position, regardless of how exceptional (or unexceptional) they are. The truth is, each individual has unique strengths that make him or her capable of handling more projects and responsibilities than just the basics. But most individuals don't even think about what more they want in their jobs. They accept life within their little box without thinking about how they might reach beyond it to satisfy their true desires. They don't realize the power they have to expand beyond the limited boundaries of their existing job descriptions, the fun they'll have doing it, and the kudos they will receive from management.

Getting from the basic description to the Expanded 100% Job description is much like building your favorite bologna sandwich. You start with two slices of bologna and two pieces of bread. Technically, this is a complete (100 percent) sandwich. It's edible, but like the basic job description, it's not very fulfilling—to your taste buds or your stomach. So you start adding your favorite ingredients. First, you smear on some mayonnaise and mustard, then a couple of slices of red onion, maybe some tomato and lettuce, and a big, thick slice of Swiss cheese. This new sandwich is still just 100 percent of one sandwich, but it's bigger, tastier, and more fulfilling because you've expanded it to fit your individual taste preferences and appetite. It's an Expanded 100% sandwich.

From now on, every time you look at your basic job description, remind yourself that it's just a bunch of baloney! It's up to you to add the special ingredients that will turn it into more.

When Rachel was promoted to manager in her accounting firm, she learned firsthand how spotty the job descriptions were. The one that existed for her position was fifteen years old, and she found an entire collection of job descriptions for each level of management beneath her.

Rachel's first step was to create the job description for her new position. At the time, nobody had coined the term *Expanded 100% Job*, but that was exactly what Rachel was doing, as she worked with her boss to construct the set of projects and responsibilities that she wanted to own.

Included were certain employee development programs and new business functions. Grooming and growing employees had always been one of her passions, and she knew that her new-business development skills were critical if she wanted to get promoted to partner.

The second step in expanding the boundaries of your job is to look at the description for the job you want next (Quadrant II). It tells you the basic skill sets and experience requirements for the next position. With a little ingenuity you can insert projects and responsibilities into your current job that will build the key skill sets and experience to qualify you for promotion. Here's an example (we've changed the names to make it a bit more fun to follow):

Betty and Bill are both management supervisors in their advertising agency. Each is responsible for managing all activities on one large, multimillion-dollar account. Each is eager to be promoted to group management supervisor (GMS). Betty gets the job description for the GMS position and sees that two key responsibilities of this position are managing multiple client accounts and partnering with the chief financial officer (CFO) to negotiate client contracts. Neither she nor Bill has this experience. So while Bill is happily running his single piece of business, Betty expands the boundaries of her existing job by requesting an additional client. She is given a small piece of business from a new client. Then she works side by side with the CFO, "shadowing" him every step of the way as he negotiates the contract with this client.

A few months later, one of the group management supervisors suddenly resigns. Who will get the promotion, Betty or Bill?

In our story Betty does, of course, because she already has experience in two key areas required for the GMS position, not to mention the additional vote of confidence from the CFO, who now has a positive mentoring relationship with Betty.

Admittedly, this is a simplistic scenario. We all know that in most situations like this one, Bill will have some unique strengths of his own, which will make the decision more of a horse race. But if Betty is smart, she will have assessed Bill's strengths long ago and used the job description as a tool to help her determine which skills and experiences she needed to beat Bill.

Quadrant III: Understanding Your Boss's Definition of 100 Percent

Besides you, your boss is the single most critical person who will impact your career growth. He or she will be the first person management will consult regarding your promotability. So your goal should be to constantly perform at a level that exceeds your boss's expectations. You can only do that if you know what doing 100 percent of your job means *to your boss*. Most corporate employees believe they know, yet it is surprising how few actually ask their boss the question, "If I were performing 100 percent of the job, what would it look like to you?"

Chances are, it's been years since your boss took a look at the actual job description for your position. So when you initiate an honest, in-depth dialogue, you will come to understand two fascinating things. First, you will learn your boss's expectations of a job well done—the measuring stick he or she is using to evaluate your performance. Invariably that stick will be quite different from the one you think your boss is using. Second, you will learn how much (or more likely, how little) your boss really knows of the actual projects and responsibilities of your position.

One of the earliest participants in our A Woman's Way of Leadership professional development program, Janet Whitby, called us in astonishment—and anger—after she had this conversation with her boss at a major aerospace company. Janet was like most female managers in her belief that the basic requirements of her job were so demanding that there was no time left to perform the added projects and responsibilities of an Expanded 100% Job. She expected her boss to confirm her beliefs by giving her a long and detailed list of his expectations.

"I couldn't believe it!" she told Nancy. "All he said was, 'Build a great team.' He didn't mention a single other project or area of responsibility. Not a single specific."

Nancy explained to Janet that, instead of feeling angry because her boss didn't understand—or seem to care about—all of the specifics of her work, Janet should be thrilled! All she had to do was deliver on one criterion and her boss would give her a top performance evaluation. This gave Janet the latitude to decide which of her basic responsibilities she would keep, delegate, and even eliminate. She had almost total freedom to build exactly what she wanted in her Expanded 100% Job!

When you realize that your boss is measuring you on far fewer criteria, or just different criteria, than you expected, don't think your boss is wrong for his or her lack of knowledge of what you do. Instead, appreciate the true gift that your boss has just handed to you. This is precisely the opening you want. It gives you plenty of room to develop your *expansion list*: the special projects and responsibilities that will enable you to fully utilize your talents, develop your skills, and follow your passions.

In an ideal world, you would go into this discussion with a blank slate so you could learn what was uppermost in your boss's understanding of your job and priorities for your work. But some bosses are better at giving feedback than input. So be prepared with a few prompts to help your boss get started. Here are a few examples of conversation openers:

- "I thought it would be a good idea to get your thoughts about my job responsibilities and priorities so I can be sure I'm fulfilling all of your expectations."
- "Over the next six to twelve months, what do you want me to accomplish, so you can feel good about giving me a top rating on my performance review?"
- "What do I need to learn/experience/accomplish for you to recommend promoting me to [the desired position]? What skills do I need to develop?"

Once your boss has begun sharing his or her thoughts, you can ask some more specific questions, if you need to, for clarification. Try to avoid questions that can be answered with a simple yes or no. You'll get more information with open-ended prompts, like these:

- "What should I be spending most of my time on?"
- "What do you think my top priorities should be?"
- "What are the most important problems/issues/opportunities that you want me to work on?"

After you've had this discussion, your most important follow-up step will be to close the loop: create a new, single-page job description based on your boss's input and any agreements you made in the meeting. Show it to your boss to make sure that you have accurately translated the responsibilities, priorities, and performance criteria that your boss will be using to evaluate you. Written lists also force accountability—for you and for your boss. As you build this new job description, keep your ultimate goal in mind: to have enough room left to devote some time to your expansion list of projects and responsibilities.

Quadrant IV: Your Expansion List

Your expansion list is the final building block of your Expanded 100% Job description. It contains the special ingredients that will enable you to live up to your full potential, contribute to your company, and experience joy and satisfaction from your work. It will include high-value, long-term projects that you've uncovered, even though they have not yet appeared as even the tiniest blips on your boss's radar screen.

Successful executives in business don't wait around for expanded work assignments to be handed to them. They think like owners: they volunteer for new opportunities; they search out key problems and solve them. You won't find them sitting in the back room, dead-ended on a project unrelated to the company's strategic objectives or their own future. They proactively manage their careers toward their vision of success for themselves.

Your expansion list should be developed with these criteria in mind if you, too, are striving to become a successful executive and achieve your envisioned future:

- *Benefits the company:* solve a problem or take advantage of an opportunity
- *Builds your skills:* prove your readiness for the next promotion
- *Aligns you with movers and shakers:* build the relationships that will advance your career
- *Appeals to your passions:* rejuvenate your energy and enthusiasm and demonstrate your ability for innovation and excellence

Every item on your expansion list should fulfill this last criterion before all others. Working on your passions is precisely what keeps you passionate about your work. It keeps you engaged, energized, and constantly moving forward. It keeps the fun in your days and success in your future.

So what added-value activities would you like to take on? What projects are you enthusiastic about? In all probability, the project that is most exciting to you will not be one that your boss or your company has even identified, because you can often see what they can't. Japanese quality expert Sidney Yoshida demonstrated this point when his research group asked a cross-section of people in a large factory to list all significant problems known to them. When the list was completed, only 4 percent of the problems—the tip of the iceberg—were known to the factory's top managers.

This "iceberg of ignorance" exists in virtually all large companies.[3] It represents a tremendous opportunity for you to identify and own projects that will make dynamic contributions to your company—and to your career.

Nancy identified a small piece of this iceberg of ignorance and merged it with her passion for employee development when she became the manager of a small division of a large accounting firm. As she studied her division's employees, it became clear that some development programs were needed to build critical skills. Yet she knew that corporate management had little regard—and an even smaller budget—for this area. So she started a training program without asking permission from senior management, using her own discretionary budget for her division. To keep the initial costs down, Nancy structured the development programs using internal personnel as trainers and consultants.

Soon, other division managers heard about the programs and asked if their people could attend. With success now under her belt, Nancy marched into her boss's office and requested his official blessing for an ongoing development budget. And she got it. Over time, this program became a banner of success attached to Nancy's name throughout the organization and opened the doors to other interesting projects for her.

When Nancy left two years later, the company had made a long-term commitment to employee training. Her particular programs had expanded regionally, her résumé was richer, and her management skills were stronger because she had identified a piece of the iceberg and had taken a risk to solve the problem. She didn't wait for somebody else to fix it. Instead, Nancy took ownership of the job and did it. She didn't ask for permission, she just assumed the position. Nancy won, and so did her company.

In this chapter, we've asked you to undertake several analytical exercises to diagnose your corporate culture and construct your Expanded 100% Job. But in the end these exercises amount to naught unless you are willing to get into action. Now it's time to take one last look at the job you have constructed and ask yourself one question: "Do I have better than a 50 percent chance of fulfilling this job description?"

If you truly believe that your chances for success are below 50 percent, have no fear. Just do a little redesigning. First, look at the bottom two quadrants (II and IV) and decide what to eliminate. Your single criterion should be leverage. Keep only those projects and responsibilities that offer you the best chance of proving yourself at a new level or in a new area. These activities are key to your ability to achieve a higher profile—and a higher "rating"—in the eyes of management.

Quadrants I and III are "untouchable" because they determine your basic job requirements. Fulfilling the items in these two quadrants is critical if you want an outstanding performance evaluation. On the flip side, failing on these basics translates into poor performance in your current position. But even in these top two quadrants you have choices: you can choose to handle these responsibilities yourself or delegate them to a subordinate and then manage their execution. By delegating you give yourself time to focus on the projects that you truly enjoy and those that will add value to the organization and get you the next promotion.

Why is 50 percent the magic number? Because to grow, you have to establish a gap that requires you to stretch to get over it. The amount of stretch should be challenging—large enough that you will have to reach far outside of your existing skill sets. When you begin a new job with a 50 percent stretch factor, you will be forced to extend yourself well beyond your current comfort zone of skills and responsibilities.

This is key for you to master the new position and continue to move forward on your career pathway.

In our coaching experience, women are particularly uncomfortable playing in this 50/50 arena where the chances of success and failure are equal. Men, on the other hand, gravitate toward it. They seem to know that risk is a necessary ingredient to their career growth, while women still rely on perfection as their pathway to success. So while men are accepting those stretch assignments that enable them to make big career leaps, women want to feel certain about their abilities to perform at the next level before they accept a promotion. In choosing safety, they keep themselves on a slower career path.

Creating an Expanded 100% Job that puts you into this 50 percent world ensures that you remain on an accelerated career pathway, because in constantly stretching toward new skills and responsibilities, you are on a continuous growth curve. Just remember, if you're not at least a little bit scared, you're not stretching far enough and you're not growing fast enough. So play the game. Take some risks. Stop waiting; stop asking; start doing. Because Ben Franklin was right. Executives who "have it all" aren't just lucky; they're prepared. If you use the tools we've discussed in this chapter to expand your responsibilities and your skill sets and to better understand your corporate culture, you can be just as "lucky" as they are.

CHAPTER 6

REINVENTING YOUR SKILL SETS
EXTENDING YOUR PROMOTABILITY

Dance Lesson #6: An ongoing commitment to growing, learning, and self-improvement is a key differentiator between executives who remain upwardly mobile and executives who become obsolete.

Once upon a time, a bright young engineer named Paula was about two years into what she planned to be a brilliant career in a Fortune 100 high-technology company. She had read the first five chapters of our book, so her long-term planning foundations were in place. She was clear about her Defining Values and her Heart's Purpose, she had an Activating Vision, and she'd built a pathway of Destination Goals to get there. She'd also reinvented her attitudes, so she was experiencing an entirely new level of fulfillment and joy in her Expanded 100% Job as a software designer, along with the unflagging support of her boss. Confident that she would achieve her dreams effortlessly (just as we promised her), she charged forth.

Paula quickly established a reputation as the most productive, elegant designer in the division. Her combination of creativity and detail-orientation fueled her success. Soon, she was promoted to manager of her design group. She was good at this too. Her technical expertise enabled her to help the group solve just about any problem. She was promoted a couple more times, and she eventually became the manager of a small but growing division. It was a huge step up for her into a complex world of politics, production, and profits: multiple department managers jockeying for priority, revenues that had to be achieved, budgets to develop and monitor, and other division managers competing with her for management's attention and the next promotion.

Paula hardly knew where to start first, so she decided to rely on her strengths: creative design, problem solving, and technical expertise.

Can you guess what happened next? Paula failed.

What she needed, once she reached this critical position in her career pathway, was not to rely on her old skill sets but to develop new ones. She needed to expand and reorganize her skill sets to meet the more complex responsibilities of her new job. We call this process *reinventing your skill sets*. And before we tell you what it is and how to do it, we want to reassure you about what it isn't. It is not about changing your Defining Values or your sparkling personality. It is not about denying who you are. Rather, it is about enlarging what you can do and who you can be, thus increasing your effectiveness and your value to your subordinates, peers, superiors, and company.

Just as your career follows a progression, so should your skill sets. To continue moving up, you must continue to "trade up" from lower-level technical and detail skills to the higher-level (but softer) leadership skills such as communication, delegation, empowerment, and vision building. The critical importance of these skills has been documented by Morgan W. McCall and Michael M. Lombardo in their book *Off the Track*. They studied hundreds of managers who had been terminated and found that 75 percent of them were deficient on people skills! They were poor listeners, they tended to avoid conflict or view it negatively, and they could give criticism but were unable to accept it from others.[1]

Reinventing your skill sets is a pivotal practice if you truly want control of your career progress. It is also a rigorous process because it requires you to redefine your strengths and weaknesses in the context of each new position. Ultimately, your success at reinventing your skill sets depends on your own strength of character. Can you assess yourself honestly? Can you accept criticism and suggestions from others? Can you take the risk of relegating your old familiar skills to a smaller place in your arsenal? Do you have the courage to develop a critical new leadership skill that may be uncomfortable for you? Do you have the persistence to keep working on it until you can count it as a new strength? This territory is only for the brave. In making these choices, you will energize your career and reinvigorate your spirit.

Improving and reorganizing your skills is an ongoing process, but developing the new skills that characterize your reinvented skill sets is a periodic process that occurs at four specific junctions in your career progress. These are "watershed positions"; they mark dramatic turning points in your responsibilities and, consequently, in the skill sets required to be successful.

1. *Switching from doer to manager.* This is your first real management job—the first time you must motivate, direct, and evaluate the work of others. Until this point, your success has been a direct result of your own work—your own *doing*. Now, the game has changed and you face a new challenge: you will be judged on your ability to get results from others. This first managerial position involves supervising people who perform the same kind of work that you once did, so you can still rely on your technical knowledge as a strength. But to succeed as their manager, you will need to develop your abilities to communicate clearly, delegate, and manage the work of the team. As these begin to take the forefront in your arsenal of skills, you have taken the first step in reinventing your skill sets.

2. *Switching from manager to manager of multiple functions.* You are now beyond the boundaries of your technical expertise. For the first time, you are managing people who perform a variety of different functions, and most of it is work that is unfamiliar to you. Perhaps you rose through the ranks of marketing, and you are now the product manager responsible for leading a multiple-disciplined team of marketing, sales, research, and product development people. You can no longer rely on your technical knowledge as a primary asset. To succeed you must use a broader array of strengths: communication, delegation, long-term planning, team building, revenue delivery, and budget management.

3. *Switching from manager of multiple functions to leader of managers of multiple functions.* This is the first position when you are

no longer in direct control of any doers. Now, you manage people who, in turn, manage groups of doers. Perhaps you are a division manager or a group product manager. You manage a variety of different department managers, and they, in turn, manage individuals in their department. Your success in this position will be determined by your ability to judge managerial talent; you must hire, coordinate, motivate, and guide that talent. You no longer directly manage production workflow. Instead, you set the vision and sort priorities so your subordinates can manage it. As a leader, your job is to provide direction, inspiration, and a clear result to pursue. Then you must trust in their abilities and expertise.

At this junction, your energies are also partially focused up and out, as you represent your division or product group to your company's top management and to prospects, vendors, and various business partners outside your company. This dual in-and-out/up-and-down focus requires a major reinvention of your skill sets if you are to succeed. You will need a larger variety of skills, and they will be higher-level functions: communication, listening, networking, vision building, long-term financial planning, organizational structures, salesmanship, negotiation, mentoring, and the ability to empower others, just to name a few.

It was precisely at this point that Paula derailed herself. Rather than face the rigors of reinventing her skill sets, she chose the comfort of her existing repertoire, which was actually the riskiest choice she could have made.

Of the four turning-point positions, your adjustment to this one and the next will be the most demanding. Your prime value in this position lies in your role as leader and resource to your various managers. You will have days, for example, spent entirely in meetings, making decisions, listening to new ideas, or giving advice to help a manager solve a problem. You may feel, on these days, that you didn't get anything done. But you did! You made it possible for all of those in your division to get their jobs done. This, after all, is a central piece of your role as their leader.

4. *Switching from leader of managers of multiple functions to leader of leaders.* This is a watershed position that few in corpo-

rate America achieve. Those who breathe this rarified air are CEOs, chairmen of the board, and presidents of large, multinational companies—the Jack Welches and Bill Gateses of the world. They are great communicators: visionary, inspiring, and empowering. They are great risk-takers. They are extraordinary relationship and image builders, both within their companies and to a variety of external audiences. And to be all of these things, they are patient, probing listeners.

Reinventing your skill sets is a planned and purposeful process of preparing yourself for promotion into one of these four positions. It involves your analytical skills, your learning abilities, and your willingness to grow. For women in particular, this last area is the most difficult part of the assignment. We tend to cling to what we know, to what makes us comfortable, to what we do well. Our typical reaction when we hit one of these turning-point positions is simply to do more of what we've been doing rather than learn the subtler skills required to excel in our new responsibilities. Then the inevitable happens: our careers stagnate. We're not dancing anymore; we're dead on the dance floor! The following is corporate senior vice president Maureen Craig's description of the special challenges that women face in this area:

> *What I've noticed time and time again is that women get promoted to the $60,000–$70,000 jobs because they're good at detail. To get above that, you need to look at the big picture. . . . Men go into the workforce assuming that they're the macro guy. Women go in assuming that their job is to get copies done properly. This has held up at every single place I've worked.*

Learning to look at the big picture is merely one of the skills that you will learn through this process of reinventing your skill sets. Now that you have a clear understanding of the four turning-point positions, when new skills must take precedence over old, let's take a look at the process that will help you actually identify and develop the necessary skills for each of these four positions.

The Reinvention Process

The steps you will take in the process of reinventing your skill sets can only be successful if they flow from a single philosophical foundation: your own deep, internal commitment to learning and growing. In *The Age of Unreason*, social philosopher Charles Handy writes of the central role of education in our careers:

> *If changing is really learning, if effective organizations need more and more intelligent people, if careers are shorter and more changeable, above all, if more people need to be more self-sufficient for more of their lives, then education has to become the single most important investment that any person can make in their own destiny.*[2]

This commitment to learning comes naturally when we first leave academia and enter the ranks of business, tightly clutching our diplomas as proof of our hard-earned education. But over time and with each promotion, the part of learning that involves study and contemplation becomes lost—and forgotten.

Early in our careers, it is what we *do* that is rewarded rather than what we *learn*. So we plunge into work, doing as much as we can, driving relentlessly toward ever-larger results. This new mantra—learn by doing—fulfills us and earns us promotions . . . for a while. Believing that this is the only education required to fuel our career growth, we become so busy *doing* that we, in fact, create a self-fulfilling prophesy: learning by doing becomes our only methodology for attaining new knowledge.

The four turning points that we described earlier are precisely the times when you can no longer rely only on a learning-by-doing philosophy. To acquire the skill sets you need to be successful in these new venues, you must incorporate *study and contemplation* into your learning regimen.

To successfully reinvent your skill sets, you must search for *outside* knowledge. It comes from books, from articles in newspapers and periodicals, from seminars and speeches at conventions, from talking to experts, and from observing others who are already performing brilliantly in the position that you aspire to reach. You read, you observe, you study, you contemplate, and then you apply. The flow of this process is illustrated in this figure:

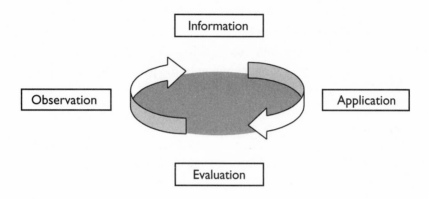

The circular pattern reflects the continuous nature of this process. It is, truly, a lifetime commitment. Now let's look at each step in more detail.

Observe and Evaluate Others

To learn how to excel in the next turning-point position, first find people who are already outstanding at the job. Watch them, and even interview them, to determine what makes them so good. You will want to:

- Identify the key characteristics of the most effective managers versus the least effective. This observation and evaluation process should focus on both the technical side of the position and the soft skills. When exploring the attitudes, behaviors, and skill sets that your company values, ask these questions:
  - How do the leaders communicate to the organization?
  - With whom do they interact on a regular basis (upward, outward, and across organizational divisions/offices)?
  - How do they work with subordinates?

- What reputation do they have throughout the organization?
- How do they manage their day-to-day calendar? How, where, with whom do they spend their time?
- What are their central "deliverables" (profit margin, gross revenues, new client acquisitions, large client relationships/ retentions, new-product development)?

- Use the information you've gathered to develop a list of critical strengths associated with exceptional performance and a parallel list of weaknesses that are common to the poor performers. These will become the basis for your new skills list.

Observe and Evaluate Yourself

Developing an honest, objective understanding of our own strengths and weaknesses is a particular challenge for women. We tend to be overly critical of ourselves. In addition, we often personalize corrective criticism by seeing it as a statement of who we are, rather than simply accepting it as a comment about what we do. Men rarely take criticism so personally. As a result, they use it as input to stimulate improvement. This critical mental distinction in how we receive and subsequently respond to criticism leads to slower performance growth for women versus men.

It is imperative that you be open to receiving evaluations from your superiors, peers, and subordinates. These external viewpoints in combination with your own self-assessment ensure that you are accurately and completely evaluating your strengths and weaknesses. This is the foundation from which you will construct your new skills list.

Develop a New Skills List

Use the information and insights from the previous steps to build your new skills list. Your list should include:

- ***Central strengths of the outstanding performers.*** It is mandatory that you become expert in these skill areas.

- *Weaknesses shared by the poor performers.* Identify which of these (if any) you possess. Do not try to transform a weakness into a strength, for this is usually impossible. It will drain you and divert your efforts from other, more important skill-building areas. Your strategy, instead, should be to manage your weakness and hire those who can provide you with the type of support required to compensate for it.
- *New skills that are unique and high-leverage.* These skills are unique to you (versus your competitors), and they offer some tangible, added value to your organization. Typically, if you are in a male-dominated management structure, one or more of your feminine-based skills will fall into this category. They are the competitive advantage that will enable you to distinguish yourself from your peers. Use them!

Creating your new skills list is all about leveraging your efforts. No senior executive is able to achieve mastery in 100 percent of the skills required for the job. Your smartest (and most effortless) strategy is to follow the principle of Renaissance Italian economist Vilfredo Pareto: 20 percent of your efforts produce 80 percent of your results. First, you need to determine which skills on your new skills list will be the most instrumental in your success. It is on these skills, then, that you must spend the first 20 percent of your efforts in reinventing your skill sets.

Read and Reflect

Reading business-related books and other materials should be an ongoing activity. These are critical sources of new information and insights in a whole variety of areas, such as team building, negotiating, public speaking, leadership, marketing, sales, financial management, organizational structure—the list goes on and on. Whatever strengths you need to build, you can be sure that at least half a dozen excellent books are sitting on the bookstore shelves (or at the warehouse of some Internet site) just waiting to help you.

Apply and Refine

To grow your new skills, you must practice! Use them in the real world. Then hold yourself to a training process of regular evaluation and refinement to ensure that over time your proficiency improves. A key ingredient in the evaluation should be an ongoing external feedback loop. This feedback can come from your boss, your mentor, or your clients. It can be informal, but it should be explicit. And the responsibility of initiating these conversations on a regular basis belongs to you. Without this internal and external support, you will simply repeat the same behaviors and, therefore, be stuck at the same level of expertise.

Once in senior management, you may be tempted to "rest on your laurels" because you've achieved mastery in your desired skill sets, and new learning will occur more rarely now that so much accumulated knowledge and experience is behind you. This attitude is no less than arrogance, and it is the death knell to a dynamic future for you and your company. Hold on to this belief and you will soon be the proverbial old dog—unwilling and unable to learn any new tricks.

Danniela Wickloff, known as Danny to friend and foe alike, was president of an underperforming company. The organization had faced bankruptcy earlier in its history, but Danny brought the business back through sheer willpower (and the replacement of several managers). While it was precisely Danny's controlling qualities that had saved her company, she now faced a new predicament: she had strong players in each key management position, chomping at the bit to assume more authority and own more responsibility. They wanted to be empowered, not controlled. Danny faced losing them if she continued with "business as usual."

At Nancy's urging, Danny agreed to attend a series of all-day business seminars. Nancy hoped Danny would realize how her controlling behaviors were crippling her management team and limiting the growth of the company.

Returning from the first day, Danny was one unhappy student-executive: "It was a complete waste of my time! I spent eight hours listening to the leader talk about concepts that I already knew." When challenged, she grudgingly admitted, "Well, there were a couple of new ideas." However, she still judged the seminar a failure.

Danny had calculated the value of the session based on the quantity of learning rather than the quality. Yet one of the new ideas was a big-leverage concept: share goal-setting with managers and empower them to take control of achieving their own results. She tried it. And this single, little idea made a tremendous difference in the morale of her senior managers and in her company's financial performance the following year.

Danny never returned to the course. Just how much growth potential—for herself, and her company—did she lose because of her arrogant approach to time and learning? We'll never know. But we do know that her most senior, most valued manager quit a year later, frustrated over his own career stagnation at the hands of this controlling boss.

Danny is a living, breathing example of someone who is rigidly stuck with a finite knowledge set. As the president of a small company, Danny had hit one of those critical turning-point positions. For the first time, she was no longer a multifunction manager. She was a leader of multifunction managers. She simply couldn't see the relevance of empowerment (rather than control) to the success of her staff and the growth of her company.

As you become a more senior and experienced executive, the pearls of new knowledge are rarer and more difficult to find. So you must be more vigilant in your hunt to find them. Even a small pearl can have a dramatic effect, because your seniority gives you the power to leverage new knowledge dramatically across the entire organization. By sharing it and by demonstrating it yourself you open the space of innovative ideas and professional growth for every employee in the company.

It is interesting to compare Danniela Wickloff's attitude toward learning with DDB Worldwide's chairperson. Keith Reinhard was a model executive for seeking out new knowledge and ideas and spreading them throughout the company to encourage this kind of learning in others. Candy still remembers the articles she received from Keith, and the books on art and creativity that arrived periodically, always with a personal note attached. He also sent a weekly memo to every employee in the company. Titled "Any Wednesday," these memos were his venue for sharing information, insights, and ideas with the entire worldwide organization. The topics were far ranging, from creativity and teamwork to a list of the ten best American fiction novels of the twentieth century. Through these actions, he demonstrated the value of continuous learning. Is it any wonder that he rose from copywriter to chair of the third largest advertising agency in the world?

Keith Reinhard exemplified the philosophy that no matter how good you are or where you are in your career, you still have something to learn. As a top executive, he also purposefully passed on the best of his learning and the wisdom of his experience to others in the organization. In this way, he took an active role in encouraging them to grow their knowledge and expertise so they could continue advancing in their careers. He set the philosophical foundation for every employee in the company to reinvent his or her skill sets.

How Wave Jumping Can Speed Your Career Progress

The steps involved in reinventing your skill sets are simple and straightforward. But understanding the timing of the process makes the difference between the success and failure of your efforts. It is an advance preparation process that will help you prepare yourself not just for the four turning-point positions but for every promotion or job change. Through this process you will become familiar (and even get some practice) with the skill set of the next position, before you actually take that job.

But it is one thing to prepare for a new job and quite another to actually take it. In our years of coaching, we have observed a significant difference between men and women in how they approach career advancement. Bluntly stated, men will leap while women prefer to linger.

Beth Berke, executive vice president and chief administrative officer at Sony Pictures, sees this reluctance to stretch as a central barrier that women must overcome if they want to rise higher in their companies:

When you offer a man and a woman with similar competencies and work history a risky, challenging, big-step career project, the man will jump up and say, "I'm the man for the job! When do I start?" But the woman will start diagnosing the job and express her uncertainty if she doesn't think she's 100 percent qualified. That nervous hesitation harms women's careers. Where's the growth opportunity if you're already 100 percent qualified for the job?

You can easily move up within your company every bit as fast (and probably more successfully) as that guy down the hall if you learn the art of *wave jumping.* Just think of your career progress as a series of waves. Each promotion or major job or career change is the crest. To reach each crest, you've got to work your way up the learning and experience curve on the front side of the wave. Your goal is to leap from your crest to an equal or higher position on the next wave so that your swim up to that pinnacle will be shorter and require less effort. This process is illustrated in the graph below.

In this aquatic career metaphor, we find three kinds of professionals:

- **Water treaders:** either those who can't swim up to the crest or those who, once there, slide back into the wave. These people are in over their heads. They are failing to build the skills they need to conquer

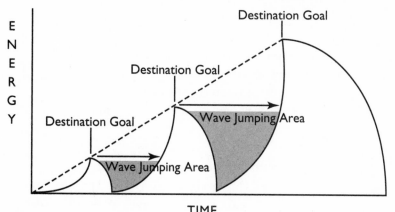

Time/Energy saved by wave-jumping

the crest, but they continue to struggle. Eventually, they either drown (get fired), or swim ashore and find a calmer pond (another career or another company) where they can succeed.

- *Crest sitters:* those who remain solidly on the crest of their wave. Some crest sitters have consciously chosen not to move onto the next wave. But others are simply stuck, for one reason or another. The longer they sit, the more expertise and comfort they build within that position . . . but the slower they progress in their careers. Most outstanding professional women fall into this group. With no long-term career plan in place, they must linger on each crest until they figure out where they want to go next. Many are the perfectionists that Beth Berke described, who believe that they must have 100 percent mastery of their current job and be 100 percent qualified for the next one before they are willing to step onto the next wave. Whether they are being held back by perfectionism or the lack of a long-term goal or both, they are stuck in a stop-and-start pattern that naturally results in a career path with more struggle and slower progress.
- *Wave jumpers:* those who make the leap onto the next wave while they are still relatively new occupants of the crest of their current wave. Most career-driven professional men are in this group. Unlike crest sitters, these men tend to hold a macro view of themselves and their career from their very first day on the job. They believe that they are top-management material, and this current job is but a brief stop on their way up the corporate ladder. This confident self-image and their envisioned future in top management creates an almost instinctive urge to wave jump. Although each crest represents a destination for most women, it is merely a "short stop on the way to the top" for most men. They don't have time to become perfect; they simply need proficiency before they're willing to raise their hands and jump up to the next job.

If you are a crest sitter, the good news is that, in reading this book, you have already learned the concepts that will transform you into an expert wave jumper. An Activating Vision and Destination Goals are the keys to keeping yourself in forward movement because they provide you with a macro viewpoint that will pull you forward in your career—ever toward the next wave. On the other hand, a revering status quo mind-set and limiting self-beliefs are the internal attitudes that you'll want to work on transforming, as they are the source of the perfectionist beliefs and behaviors and the "unworthy" self-perceptions that are keeping you stuck on your crest. Once you stop trying to be a "good girl" and begin acknowledging your strengths (rather than single-mindedly focusing on your weaknesses) your confidence will soar and you will become more comfortable taking the risk of jumping to the next wave.

Confidence is a prerequisite and a constant companion for a wave jumper. In the risky world of business, nothing carries a 100 percent certainty. Success is not an all-or-nothing proposition. When a superior offers you a stretch assignment, if you are confident that you can do more than 50 percent of the job, take it! This is your opportunity to leap across to the next (bigger) wave instead of starting at the bottom. Trust that you will succeed, because you have so carefully constructed all of the internal foundations to support you in these times of risk. You know where you're headed, and you have the confidence, positive attitudes, and learning process in place to help you get there.

Will you still make mistakes? Sure, you will! But it is by living through and learning from mistakes that we achieve exponential growth in both knowledge and wisdom. And *that* is the stuff of leadership

The Reinvention Process: A Sample of Tools and Resources

Your ability to acquire outside knowledge is fundamental to the process of reinventing your skill sets. This knowledge comes in a variety of shapes and from a broad range of sources. It can be secondary information and insights from seminars, business books, or even classic literature. It can be expert opinion or experience. It can be lessons shared within various support groups. It can be primary feedback from standard evaluation tools such as the Myers-Briggs Type Indicator or a 360-degree management assessment, or from coaches and mentors. In the pages that follow, we offer you a small sample of tools and resources.

Consider this merely your starter pack—the tip of an information ice-berg that is just waiting for you to start chipping away.

As you review the different options, look for two or three that offer the most leverage for your personal situation and needs. Which of these can help you build the new skills that you've identified in your rein-vention process? Which of them can support your transformation into a wave jumper?

Information About Your Own Organization and Industry

Reading everything available about your company and its competitors should become a career-long obsession. From the resources we've listed on the following pages, you will glean vital information about your company's financial performance, goals, and values; about the outside world's assessment of your industry, your organization, and your com-petitors; and about your top management's triumphs and, more impor-tant, their problems.

- Annual reports of your company and key competitors: This is absolutely mandatory, regardless of where you are in your career development. Learning to understand the financial reports is also a critical element in your education.
- Trade publications: Read two regularly; finding out which ones your CEO or company president reads is a good starting point.
- General business newspapers: This category includes the *Wall Street Journal* and the business section of your local newspaper.
- General business magazines: *Fortune*, *Forbes Magazine*, *Business Week*, *FastCompany*, and *Harvard Business Review* are all good resources.
- Business journals: *Journal of Marketing*, *Journal of Marketing Research*, and others; search through these periodically for in-depth articles on new developments in business or in your particular discipline.

If you are in a junior or middle management position, you may feel that the various general business publications and journals are not relevant to your current situation. Perhaps. But remember, you want to keep part of your focus on where you're going. And each of these publications is highly relevant to your career destination. When you read articles about successful leaders in *Fortune*, *Forbes Magazine*, or *Business Week*, you are discovering the qualities of outstanding leadership. When you read the story of a successful entrepreneur, you are learning something about managing a company through a high-growth phase of its life cycle. These publications will give you information, stimulate your thinking, and trigger your ideas.

This list of resources may look daunting, but once you become familiar with the format and content of each publication, locating the pertinent information will be easy. You should regularly read at least one publication in each category—though not necessarily from cover to cover. Simply scan the table of contents for articles of interest to you. Rip them out and read them on a timely basis (that is, before the next issue of the publication).

Business Books

Many senior-level executives are regular readers of the publications listed above, but it is shocking how few of them read business books. Nancy remembers one study that found that only 1 percent of corporate presidents had read one book a year in their area of expertise! This same piece of research also found a correlation between the number of books read and the salaries of these senior executives.

Do you think the book readers made more money because they were actually more knowledgeable? Nancy did, and this conclusion produced a significant shift in her own learning strategy. She thought reading books would be an effortless way to grow her salary and her career. So she set a goal of reading one business book every quarter. After the first four or five books, she didn't see much difference in her income, but she continued reading nevertheless.

Then one day she went into the most important meeting of her business life. The corporate boardroom was filled to capacity. Nancy was the most junior executive there—and the only woman. She still remembers looking into the mirror on the wall and seeing this lone young woman among a sea of gray-haired men. Naturally, she was intimidated.

The negotiations became hot and heavy. The group was log-jammed on one particularly knotty issue, and the meeting was about to implode, when a feminine voice spoke up to share a compromise idea. It was accepted! Nancy was the hero (oops, we mean heroine)!

Later, Nancy realized that her breakthrough idea had emerged from three books she had read in the past few months. The ideas had lain dormant, germinating in her subconscious, when miraculously they gelled together to pop out just when she most needed them.

Nancy has since been reading three business books every month, and this reading has repeatedly paid off for her. Many people who are revered as role models and examples of tremendous success are also committed to reading:

- It has always been a passion in Oprah Winfrey's life, and through her book club she shared that passion with millions of fans.
- Steve Forbes made a commitment to read fifty pages a day when he was thirteen, and today he is still devoted to that practice.
- Bill Gates doesn't have an MBA, but being an avid reader has been instrumental in his ability to grow his management skills as fast as he has grown his company.

If you have neither the time nor the inclination to read, technology now gives you an alternative: Books on Tape. You can buy them in many bookstores or rent them monthly either online at www.bookson tape.com or by calling 1-800-88-BOOKS.

Vocabulary Programs

In 1897, long before he became one of the greatest statesmen of the twentieth century, Winston Churchill said: "Of all the talents bestowed upon men, none is so precious as the gift of oratory. . . . Abandoned by his party, betrayed by his friends, stripped of his offices, whoever can command this power is still formidable."[3]

Expanding your vocabulary ranks right up there with reading as a basic, ongoing requirement for professional growth. A broad, varied vocabulary enhances the power, quality, color, and sophistication of your communication style. But most important, it enables you to be accurate, express nuances precisely, and avoid any inadvertent ambiguity that can lead to confusion or misinterpretation. A sophisticated vocabulary enables you to express the complex as simply and directly as possible. Is it any wonder that over the years, studies have shown that possessing a large vocabulary is a precursor of professional success?

Unfortunately for most of us, our vocabulary-building years ended the day we graduated from college and stopped reading books with a higher-level text that included words we didn't understand. The typical American adult uses between 2,000 and 10,000 words. Yet a typical English dictionary contains more than 500,000 words! We're using less than 2 percent of our communication arsenal!

Learning just a few hundred words each year will create a dramatic communication advantage for you over your peers. These words can come randomly from books or other reading, or you can do something really original and actually look through the dictionary, starting with the *A*s! If you prefer a more intensive learning tool, contact Verbal Advantage, a company that specializes in vocabulary programs on tape. You can reach them at www.verbaladvantage.com or by phone at 1-800-999-RSVP.

As you work toward developing an enriched vocabulary, beware of the industry jargon game. Far too many budding junior executives fall into this trap, particularly in their written correspondence, loading up on jargon when it isn't necessary. Your goal is to achieve precision and impact with your communication, not needless complexity and confusion.

Personality Traits Assessment

Your core personality traits have a fundamental impact on your thinking and behavior. Understanding yourself at this level, and then understanding how others perceive you, gives you critical insights for developing more effective management and communication skills. A Myers-Briggs Type Indicator (MBTI), the most widely used personality inventory in the world, will reveal your preferences in four different dimensions:

1. *Extraversion—Introversion:* where do you prefer to spend your time and attention?
2. *Sensing—Intuition:* how do you prefer to receive information?
3. *Thinking—Feeling:* how do you make decisions?
4. *Judging—Perceiving:* how do you interact with the outside world?

Based on your answers to a battery of questions, the MBTI will assign you one value in each of these four dimensions. Normally, an MBTI must be administered by trained, certified professionals. But you can get acquainted with this tool by reading Craig R. Hickman's book *Mind of a Manager, Soul of a Leader*. He gives an excellent overview of the MBTI, including a breakdown of the personality types and a "shorthand adaptation" of the actual assessment instrument. Another shorthand version of the test is available on the Internet at www.personality page.com.

You can also give the MBTI to your subordinates. Sharing your personality types creates the groundwork for understanding individual differences and the role of conflicting preferences and needs. The results are more-open lines of communication, and a harmonious, synergetic work environment where the group achieves higher productivity.

The MBTI assessment opened the door for a new level of understanding at one company where we facilitated a team-building workshop. The test revealed that everyone in the group was an *F* (Feeling) personality type, except Pamela. Her *T* (Thinking) profile was the antithesis of the rest of the group, making her a true lone ranger. She was the maverick who valued theoretical principles, policies, and being right, while the rest of the group valued intimacy, supportiveness, and seeing issues from diverse perspectives. The others expressed differences of opinion with a persuasive, harmonious orientation. But not Pamela. She jumped feetfirst into every issue with laserlike analyses and totally logical language. Although Pamela was often the one to offer the most ingenious idea or solution, she was never "heard." The strong "Feeling" trait of the others caused them to interpret her blunt, incisive comments as personal attacks. To them, she was ruthless and impersonal. The result was a tension-laden environment where meetings involved more dissensions than solutions.

When we revealed these personality differences to the group, they experienced a collective "Aha!" and it felt like a buzzing neon light had been switched on in the room. Instantly, they understood why Pamela was always the critical voice and what value her contrarian point of view brought to their discussions. They realized that her differences of opinion were not automatically wrong. Pamela, in turn, began to understand that she did not have to always be right to be valued by the group. She also realized that a small dose of sensitivity in her communication would produce a major gain in her persuasive powers with her *F* colleagues. In future meetings, she would continue being a *T* and they would continue as *F*s, but with this new level of understanding, each would be more open to receiving the information and viewpoints being shared by the other. They could abandon their arguments and instead commit their collective efforts to searching out better solutions.

Time Management Assessment

The concept of time is unique and quite precious when you spend a minute to think about it. Well, that minute is gone now! You can never get it back to "spend" again, and unlike money, you can't earn more to replace what you've spent.

Every senior executive's most precious resource is time. Getting the most possible work done each day with the least possible effort is an essential ingredient for your survival. If you want career success, you must also be sure that you are getting the *right* things done.

Most people with a time problem are actually accomplishing less because they have failed to correctly assess what they do with their time. We have coached many executives on this issue, and once they started recording where they spent their time, each of them was shocked to learn how much of every day he or she devoted to the trivial.

To improve your own time management habits, first find a philosophy that feels right for you. Books and seminars abound on this subject. We suggest two books that provide both information and diagnostic exercises: *Time Management for Teams*, by Merrill E. and Donna N. Douglass, has an excellent time assessment questionnaire to help you identify your "Time Management Temperament"—your instinctive pattern of responding to specific business challenges. And Franklin Quest CEO Hyrum W. Smith's book *The 10 Natural Laws of Successful Time and Life Management* introduces the concept of creating empty time for yourself, rather than simply filling your newfound time with more "To Dos."

Once you've found a compatible philosophy, work on developing a new set of time management habits. It will take at least a month, and it will require your diligence in setting daily goals and tracking yourself. Otherwise, you will find that the urgent will always displace other tasks—including those that are actually more important. To bolster your commitment, consider scheduling a specific meeting with yourself each week for planning. Treat this meeting with the same level of importance as any management meeting because that's exactly what it is!

Conflict Resolution Assessment

Conflict is as natural and necessary an ingredient in corporate America as learning is in leadership. Successfully negotiating through conflict is a critical skill for success in most companies' senior management ranks.

When strong egos openly butt heads, the situation becomes tense, stressful, and even painful for everyone involved. Conflicts that get out of control are counterproductive to creativity as well as productivity. In this emotionally charged environment, each of us has an instinctive style of responding. The more stressful the situation, the more we hunker down into the style that is most comfortable for us.

Understanding your own natural response and learning how to provide what is needed to solve a conflict, rather than relying on what is comfortable, is an essential ingredient for effective conflict resolution. *The Team-Building Source Book* by Steven L. Phillips and Robin L. Elledge offers an assessment instrument that challenges you to explore and identify your preferred style of conflict resolution by forcing you to choose a response to various scenarios.

We recently witnessed a "double demonstration" of erroneous conflict-resolution styles at one of our client companies. The two executives involved managed completely different divisions of the business. Joe was a classic avoider. When two groups in his division launched into conflict, he ignored it . . . and ignored it . . . and ignored it. Eventually, it festered from a small "situation" to a permanent state of war. Ellen, on the other hand, absolutely craved conflict. The high she derived from solving conflicts was so addictive that she actually stirred the pot just so she could solve the problem. Her division didn't have a single war, just hundreds of little battles.

In both cases, the consequences were dire. Productivity and profitability fell in both divisions. When the company president finally learned of the problems, he took immediate steps to solve the various conflicts. He fired both division managers.

As a senior executive, acknowledging your own conflict resolution style and acquiring a variety of approaches enhances your effectiveness and value to your company, improves the morale and productivity of your subordinates, leads to a better financial bottom line . . . and can make the difference between succeeding in your job and having to search for another one.

Management Behavior Assessment

The higher you rise in management, the more difficult it is to get the kind of discriminating criticism and objective feedback that will help you improve your own skills and behaviors. Subordinates are usually reluctant to tell you anything negative for fear of reprisals. You are powerful, after all, and you can fire them—even if they're right! They may accurately reinforce your strengths, but they cannot be trusted to candidly identify your weaknesses. Your superiors, too, will spend less time assessing your abilities and developing your skills. You are no longer in a position where they feel the need to proactively mentor you or guide your decision making.

At this stage, unless you reach out for input, you will be trapped in your existing skill set, and your career progress will stall. You must create appropriate communication tools for your subordinates to honestly (and anonymously) evaluate your performance and for your superiors to thoroughly critique you.

Such a solution is the 360-degree management assessment, a standardized developmental feedback questionnaire that is completed by a group of your subordinates, peers, and superiors, and provides confidentiality for all of them. The 360 also has the ability to compare your scores to a set of norms for each attribute. A follow-up coaching component then helps you evaluate those areas in which improvement offers you the most significant leverage for your career advancement.

Your company may already offer a 360 feedback instrument. If not, your human resources professionals can help you identify several consultants who perform this assessment. Keep in mind that the one you select will not only administer the questionnaire but also give you advice and counsel on areas for improvement.

Coaches and Mentors

Coaches and mentors are the two most personal and potentially most aggressive support systems to help you through the process of reinventing your skill sets. They are similar, yet there is a subtle, important distinction between them.

The mentor relationship is rooted in the concept of apprenticeship: an experienced senior craftsman passes on his (for most often, it was a *he*) personal storehouse of knowledge to the apprentice and then promotes the apprentice's career by opening doors to future opportunities. Today, a mentor primarily functions within the corporate environment, advising younger, less-seasoned employees. The mentor's role is to help the employee achieve success within the organization, thereby serving the needs of the corporation. Conversely, a coach is an outside resource who partners with an employee to help him or her achieve fulfillment and success—no matter where that leads.

Coaching and mentoring are not mutually exclusive pursuits. Each method can be effective in assisting you on the path toward your Activating Vision. If you use the two together, even better! The velocity of your journey increases because you are putting more wind in your sails.

Mentoring is all about making it within your specific organization. Because of this, mentoring is an essential ingredient for career success. According to University of Southern California Business School professor and award-winning author Warren Bennis:

> *I know of no leader in any era who hasn't had at least one mentor: a teacher who found things in him he didn't know were there, a parent, a senior associate who showed him the way to be, or in some cases, not to be, or demanded more from him than he knew he had to give.*[4]

For women, mentoring is particularly important because we don't naturally know all of the rules of the game in male-dominated corporate America. Your (usually male) mentor can educate you on the subtleties and make your trip up the corporate ladder swifter and easier. Because once you know the rules, you can make intelligent, informed choices about which of them you will—and will not—follow as you play the game.

Working with both male and female mentors is recommended whenever possible. A man will help you understand the politics and success pathways of the organization; a woman can forewarn you of specific gender-based challenges within your company and steer you through them. You get the added knowledge and wisdom of their dual perspectives, and you get the benefit of two management relationships that will support your advancement within the company.

These days, only a handful of progressive companies have formal mentoring programs in place. More typically the relationship you build with your mentor is unofficial and takes place in an unstructured, catch-as-catch-can environment. So if you want a great mentor, you've got to do the catching! You must take responsibility for identifying and securing the mentor you want rather than passively waiting to be selected. Following are some of the qualities to look for in your mentor:

- Someone with an interest and ability to guide your career progress
- Someone who is successful within your company—well-connected and well-respected by top management

- Someone who confronts issues openly, directly, and early with women as well as men
- Someone you respect and trust

You want open and honest two-way communication with your mentor because you will depend on him or her to share knowledge on the political landscape of your company and offer you advice on what works and what doesn't. Finally, you want a mentor who sees the glass as half full, rather than half empty. Only with this mentality of generosity can there be an openhanded transfer of wisdom.

Coaching, on the other hand, is based on a formal relationship with someone outside the organization. It can cover extended periods of an executive's development or be very short-term with a specific task as the focus. The two of you make a mutual commitment to meet for an agreed-upon period of time (usually weekly or biweekly) to accomplish concrete developmental objectives.

Your coach's primary concern is *your* fulfillment and success, not your company's. A coach is a master at understanding the process of developmental learning and creating an emotional environment in which it can occur. He or she partners with you to achieve your Activating Vision and inspires you to reach further than you think you can. Then your coach holds you accountable to this greater standard. The coaching process is focused on uncovering your potential and improving the outcome of your actions. The coach helps you remove any mental blinders and behavior barriers that are preventing you from having it all.

Here are some of the qualities to look for in a coach:

- Someone who understands the human barriers that keep people from achieving results
- Someone who places a high value on committed action and creating results
- Someone with a deep knowledge of the workings of corporate America and a talent for finding creative solutions
- Someone with a professional track record that demonstrates his or her own commitment to personal growth and learning
- Someone who speaks the truth to you, even when it might hurt

Frequently, successful executives bring in coaches to help them through unusual career problems or opportunities—to help them reinvent their skill sets. We've coached executives through the transition from senior manager to president of the company and from senior manager to entrepreneur. We've also known executives who have hired coaches to help them learn to work with their board, interview for a new job, write a big speech, and even learn "royal" table manners for an upcoming dinner with the queen. Because coaching is a customized process, its scope ranges from the painstakingly small to the frighteningly monumental.

Instead of thinking about yourself as an isolated individual body, floating in a sea of opportunities and problems, start thinking of yourself as linked to any knowledge you need. Challenge yourself by asking, "What am I struggling to learn? Is there a coach out there who has already done it?"

To find an impartial coach who is unconnected to a specific methodology, contact either the International Coach Federation (www.coach federation.org") or the Professional Coaches and Mentors Association in California (www.pcmaonline.com).

The Reinvention Process: A Sample of Support Groups

The process of reinventing your skill sets is a highly individualized pursuit. In addition to the preceding tools and resources, a variety of organizations are available to provide you with not only information but, more important, a group environment that supports you through the challenges of reinvention.

Industry Organizations

Most large industries have national trade associations or local chapters. Typically, they provide information, referral services, and many other resources to their member companies and the individuals who work in them. For example, in the advertising industry, Candy had access to the American Association of Advertising Agencies (4As), the American

Advertising Federation (AAF), and her local Advertising Club. These groups provide a variety of research, information, and training materials, as well as opportunities for members to attend networking events, roundtable discussions, and major symposiums.

Industry organizations—and the various events they sponsor—also provide a tremendous networking opportunity for you. You will meet people from other companies and executives from all levels of management. The relationships you build within these organizations will, over time, help you with everything from information and advice to job opportunities and career advancement.

Professional Women's Organizations

Many women-only support groups are emerging. Some are industry specific, while others are functionally based, cutting across industries. These groups provide many of the same resources as industry organizations, although their gender-centric orientation allows them to tailor their services to women's needs.

One of the primary values of these support groups is the networking opportunities they foster. Just as the Old Boys' network has historically represented a special sort of mutual aid society for our male peers, these new professional women's organizations can mature into our own mutual aid society—the *New Women's network*.

The special need—and the special nature—of women-helping-women networks is eloquently described by inspirational author Marianne Williamson:

> *If women succeed only in isolated cases, the professional world will continue to be unsure ground for women in general. We must take the communion of women very seriously at this time and do all we can do to support other women in reaching for the stars. There cannot be too many glorious women. There cannot be too many queens. There cannot be too much success.*[5]

Studies have proved that women's networking groups can dramatically boost the professional performance of their members. We canvassed a group of senior corporate women who, speaking to us individually, each expressed the need for women to receive supplemental support to advance their careers. Yet they themselves were reluctant to associate with any women-only group in their organizations. How unfortunate that so many are resistant to participating in these same-gender networking activities! Receiving this kind of special support or attention seemed to them an admission that they were somehow underprivileged or had special needs—an anathema label to these achievement-driven, highly successful women.

Stanlee Phelps and Nancy Austin, authors of *The Assertive Woman*, interviewed hundreds of female professionals and found this same reluctance about joining women's support groups. The authors believe (as we do) that this prejudice serves only to hold women back in their careers:

> *[A]sk a professional woman if she participates in all-women educational or special interest groups today and she'll likely tell you, "Oh, no. I outgrew all that years ago. Women's groups are passé." Women's groups may be good for an evening's entertainment, but we reserve our respect for the co-ed variety. In our haste to avoid being labeled "troublemakers" or "radical feminists," we have cut ourselves off from a powerful source of information and support from organizations and programs that have moved mountains for many.[6]*

Customized Support Groups

Creating a small, customized group provides a more intimate alternative for supporting your goals. You can choose not only the number and type of people for the group but also the frequency of meeting and the parameters of interaction. These groups can run the gamut from passive and social to aggressive and "strictly business."

Several years ago, Nancy and a close friend formed Partners in Creation. It has ten members, both male and female, who support one another in achieving a variety of professional and personal goals. The group meets monthly for dinner and conversation. Each member discusses his or her successes, challenges, and breakdowns during that month, and requests specific spiritual, emotional, and intellectual support from the rest of the group for the upcoming thirty days.

The members commit to being honest and loving and bringing the full force of their individual knowledge to the discussion. A healthy, confrontational environment is established, so the pot of creativity is constantly stirring. Since the start of Partners in Creation, three of its members have moved into jobs that they love and which take them toward their Activating Visions. Two others were encouraged to take larger risks in their own businesses. One couple adopted two children, and another couple's troubled marriage was reinvigorated.

Through their experiences together, the group has learned that there is creativity in numbers, power in vulnerability, and healing in being loved. The quality of each member's life is richer, more abundant, and definitely more connected to his or her Heart's Purpose and Activating Vision.

If you want to accelerate your career progress and reach a high-level position before you retire, the concepts we've shared in this chapter will help you. Become adept at reinventing your skill sets and you will be more prepared to handle the new responsibilities of each turning-point position. You will also be more self-confident—the key ingredient that enables you to say yes when a big career opportunity knocks. Become a skilled wave jumper and you will begin reaching before you hear anybody knocking! Take advantage of the tools and resources that can support you, and your progress will be faster and easier.

The ultimate benefit of these concepts is the power of choice: You get to choose how fast and how far you go in your career. You are no longer limited by your attitudes or your skill sets, by your fears of failure or the smallness of your dreams. You no longer have to accept the random table scraps your company may toss your way. Instead, you can feast on a main course of challenge and high achievement. You get to have it all!

So go forth, reinvent, and start jumping!

CHAPTER 7

REINVENTING YOUR RELATIONSHIPS
EXPANDING YOUR CAREER CONNECTIONS

Dance Lesson #7: The easiest way to advance your career, especially if you want to reach a top management position, is to ask for a little help from your friends. And the more friends you have, the more help you'll get.

If you've been a full-time professional for at least five years, you have probably been bested for at least one promotion by that proverbial guy down the hall. Remember him from the last chapter? He's the guy whose expertise was no better than yours, and neither was his productivity. Nevertheless, he got the promotion and you got left behind.

How did he do that?

He did it because somebody said yes to him. And that "yes" was an unavoidable "no" to you. Business is, after all, a human endeavor. Whether you want to get promoted, join a new company, or change careers, *who* you know will be every bit as powerful as *what* you know in your quest to achieve your goals.

Let's test this premise by comparing the job-search efforts of Jenny and John, two young advertising account executives who want to find a better paying job in another ad agency. They polish up their résumés and contact the same executive search firm to represent them. Jenny has incredible analytical skills (she's actually quite a bit smarter than John), but John has spent the last three years building a network of contacts in the five largest agencies in the city—people he will now call to investigate the possibilities of joining their agencies.

Who do you think has the best chance of getting the new job? John, of course! Jenny may be smart, but John is street-smart. Since 70 percent of all jobs are found through networking, the odds are definitely on his side.

Jenny is our prototype for millions of professional women: a lone ranger who relies on only herself and insists that every career step be earned through work rather than aided through relationships. She may even believe that using relationships to advance her career is a sort of cheating.

There is nothing innately wrong with this hard-work approach. It's just a lot more difficult! Women who choose this path are shutting themselves off from one of their greatest feminine strengths: a natural affinity for relationship building.

Throughout our childhood and school years, peer interactions dominate our female world. Our relationships are personal and feeling-based in nature. Our goal is friendship, not advancement. When we enter the professional business world, we are confronted by an entirely foreign system: a world in which relationships are thinking-based and hierarchical. Friendships still exist in this world, but advancement is a prime driver of those relationships. We judge this new category of human connections as cold, calculating, and downright dishonest. Rather than adapt to this new world and include thinking-based, advancement-oriented relationships within our broader repertoire, we choose to stay out of the game. This choice costs us dearly. Without the benefit of these relationships, our careers advance more slowly, and we diminish our measure of joy along the way.

In this chapter, we will show you how to integrate your feeling-based instincts for relationship building with the thinking-based mode of the work environment to create an entirely new world of possibilities for your business relationships, both within and outside the walls of your company. This more integrated framework will enable you to repair relationships that have gone askew and create new relationships that you never thought possible.

The first step toward this new perspective on relationship building is to understand where you are today by playing the Promotion Game. It's quite simple, really. Here's the question: Who will have to say yes for me to be promoted to the next position in my company? On a single sheet of paper write the names and titles of every person who would have to say yes, then match up those names with the generic positions we've mapped in the schematic below. If you have a name that doesn't fit one of our generic categories, create a space for it. This schematic will be your frame of reference for the discussion that follows.

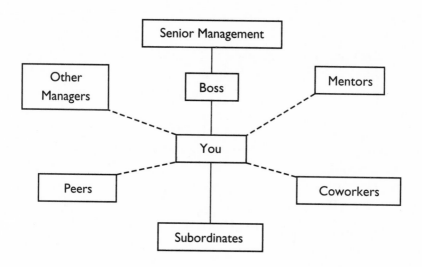

Building a Supportive Boss: Creating a Positive Relationship

We don't have to know you or your company or your next promotion slot to know that not only should your boss be on the schematic, he or she should be at the very center of it. For in the Promotion Game—any Promotion Game—your boss is the hub of the approval wheel.

Besides you, your boss is the single most important person who controls when, how, and where your career will take you within your company. Your boss can choose to give you a positive review or a negative one. Your boss can choose to either diminish your job responsibilities or expand them. Your boss can choose to build your reputation in the company or destroy it. In short, your boss can either champion your career advancement or thwart it.

If you doubt the career-building power of a positive relationship with your boss, just look around at the people who are clearly on the fast track to the higher ranks of management in your company. Are they the most intelligent or the most knowledgeable? Not always (maybe not ever). But they almost always are the smartest when it comes to creating positive relationships with their superiors. Fast trackers know that if they support their boss, their boss will support them.

"Uh, what about a boss like mine, who isn't so great?" you're probably thinking. "He (or she) doesn't deserve my support."

That's exactly where the fast tracker flies right past you on the career pathway. While you are judging your boss for deficiency and inadvertently (or purposefully) creating a negative relationship, fast trackers know that a positive, supportive relationship with a less-than-great boss is their ticket to the next promotion.

The career opportunity represented by a "less than" boss occurs far more often than you might think. To find out exactly how prevalent a "less than" boss has already been in your career, just complete this simple, three-step exercise:

1. Write down the names of every boss to whom you have reported directly.
2. Make a check mark next to the names of the bosses you thought were truly great.
3. Turn your figures into a fraction: the number of great bosses on top and the total number of bosses on the bottom.

Every woman who has participated in our professional development program has completed this exercise. Typically, they rate about one out of every three or four bosses as great. Which means that 65 percent to 75 percent of these women's superiors have been "less than" bosses!

The size of this figure seems almost too staggering to believe. But remember, our measurement of our bosses' excellence is based not on some standardized, accepted scale of greatness but on the most subjective grading scale of all: our opinion. Each of us has our own preferences, internal biases, and criteria for judging our bosses on the great-ness scale. So one person's "less than" boss could be another person's greatest ever. (And once you begin managing others, you will surely be someone's "less than" boss.)

Bosses are human and therefore imperfect, so it's easy to identify areas that are deficient or missing in them. Women often unwittingly lock themselves into a pattern of measuring bosses by what is missing, rather than what is present, in their skill sets and knowledge. When you are constantly searching for weaknesses and "missings" in your boss, it is inevitable that you will find exactly what you are looking for. The more you find, the more "less than" your boss becomes—and the more you get to feel superior.

These comparisons will never get you where you want to go in this life. When you compare yourself to the boss and begin feeling supe-rior, you unwittingly produce a growing reservoir of resentment and negative judgments. These unavoidably spill over into a negative rela-tionship, even though no negative words or conversations may ever occur between you and your boss. Such is the power—and the uncon-trollable nature—of that primitive, nonverbal part of us.

Research has proved that nonverbal communication has tremendous power: only 7 percent of our communication occurs through the actual words we speak; 38 percent is through our tone of voice; and a major-ity 55 percent is with facial expressions, postures, and gestures. So we actually communicate far more through our unspoken thoughts and feelings than through the spoken word. If unchecked, this unconscious negative energy can build to tsunami-like intensity.

If you have any such negative thoughts about your boss rattling away in your head, you can be sure that they are showing up subconsciously in your behavior and damaging your relationship with your boss. Ulti-mately, these negative thoughts and feelings will handicap your career progress. Your boss may not know exactly what you are thinking, but at some level, he or she develops a *shadow sense* about your willingness to play on the team and support his or her agenda. And that *shadow sense* won't be positive.

While men seem to instinctively build relationships with their "less than" bosses, many women we've coached seem determined to torpedo themselves, and their career hopes and dreams, over this issue. As women, we've struggled so diligently to be perfect in our own jobs that we make the mistake of expecting our bosses to do the same. We often begin to play a self-defeating game of comparing our knowledge, technical expertise, and skill to theirs. This is based on the false premise that a boss's skills must equal or exceed our own if he or she is to deserve the position above us and our respect and cooperation.

This "matched skills" scenario is a recipe for disaster for bosses as well as the women reporting to them. These bosses have not reinvented their skill sets to meet the new requirements and responsibilities of the higher position. Eventually, they will become mediocre at best and a failure in the position at worst. And if your boss's skills and strengths match your own, where is your opportunity to learn and grow?

Ironically, "less than" bosses are a great career opportunity if you can learn to support them rather than sabotage them. You may view your boss as "less than" precisely because his or her weak skills are your strengths. Learning to contribute your talents to support your boss's efforts and appreciate his or her strengths so you can develop them within your own skill set is the recipe for a winning relationship with your boss and a winning career for you.

In making a conscious decision to support a "less than" boss and learn from that person, you are converting a challenge into a triumph. Executive coach and management consultant Ira Chaleff explains in his book, *The Courageous Follower*, why supporting a weak boss is both your responsibility and your duty:

> *When the most capable person is not the leader, a courageous follower faces several challenges. Most important is to deal with our own feelings about the matter. We often find it difficult to work for someone who is slower than we are, who fails to fully and rapidly grasp situations confronting the organization. Rather than feeling intimidated by their position, we may have difficulty masking our disdain. There may be bitterness if we hoped for the number one position ourselves. . . . As difficult as it may be in this situation, our guiding principle should remain service to the organization.[1]*

The unspoken message in Chaleff's principles is that it is not your right nor your obligation to point out to upper management your boss's weaknesses or inadequacies. You have three choices: leave the company, request a new boss, or support your boss so he or she can succeed in his or her responsibilities for the company. The first two choices will almost certainly reflect more negatively on you than on your boss. The third choice sets the stage for a "win-win-win" situation: when your boss succeeds, the company benefits; when you help your boss succeed, your boss will want you to benefit as well.

Counseling women on how to improve their relationships with their bosses is one of the most frequent issues we encounter in our A Woman's Way of Leadership professional development program. Consider Marion Halleck's relationship with the senior partner of her financial investment company. Marion was a senior advisor for individual clients with at least $500,000 to invest. Her boss, Jon, was making her life miserable by questioning her every expense, the amount of time she spent out of the office, even the value of the three new clients she'd brought into the firm in the past year. When Marion spoke about Jon, she focused on only his weaknesses: a mania for minutiae, poor new-business performance, and perfectionist tendencies that slowed down the timetables of major projects. She had fallen into the trap of focusing on what was missing, while failing to see the strengths that had earned Jon the promotion into a more senior position.

Marion expected us to endorse her decision to leave the firm. Instead, we asked her why she thought Jon, who was about two years her junior, had been made a managing partner. What strengths did he have? Marion sat silently for about two minutes, looking somewhat bewildered. She admitted to us later that she had never really spent any time thinking about Jon's strengths. Looking for what was there, instead of what was missing, was a first for her.

To make it a little easier, we asked her to give us three positives about Jon. She gave us four. He was a whiz at analyzing investment opportunities, he enjoyed managing the firm's back-room operations (an activity most other partners detested), he always had a complete grasp of the details on any account, and he was remarkably even-tempered. During the course of the conversation, Marion realized that she had a lot to learn from Jon.

We asked Marion to spend the next month doing two things differently. First, we asked her to constantly measure Jon for his strengths and show her appreciation once in a while. Second, we asked her to schedule an appointment once a week to update Jon on her accounts and activities and seek his advice. This would answer his questions before he asked them, satisfy his need to have a complete grasp of the details, and give Marion a chance to learn from Jon.

Marion called us a month later to tell us how much happier she was, with her job and with her boss. Jon had even stopped challenging her expenses and her whereabouts. A positive, trusting relationship was beginning to grow. It created the foundation Marion needed to be successful at the next step—enlisting Jon's support for her Expanded 100% responsibilities.

Just like Marion, you have all of the power to transform your relationship with a "less than" boss. Just follow these four easy steps:

1. ***Think team.*** Remember that you and your boss work together to form a more complete whole. Your boss's skill sets should not match your own if he or she has been successfully reinventing them to fulfill the higher level of responsibility. In fact, the more complementary your skill sets, the stronger a whole you will be. The "less than" areas of expertise that you see in your boss represent your opportunities to be a strong contributor in support of him or her. If your boss possesses strengths that are your weaknesses, these are your opportunities to observe, learn, and expand your own skill sets.

2. ***Think positive.*** Discipline yourself to replace negative comparisons with positive thinking patterns. If you find yourself ruminating about what's missing in your boss, spend the next month doing nothing but looking for the expertise and other added-value qualities that your boss brings to the picture. Look for what's there, not what's missing. When you start measuring for the positives in your boss, he or she will soon begin measuring for the same in you. The result? A mutually respectful, supportive relationship.

3. *Think like the boss.* Take a lesson from the Native Americans: walk a mile in your boss's shoes. Once you understand your boss's goals, the external pressures and challenges your boss faces, and his or her internal attitudes and preferred work styles, you can begin to align yourself with him or her as a partner. Here are a few questions you should seek to answer:
   - What are the key business goals that your boss must achieve?
   - What are your boss's personal career goals?
   - What work issues and challenges does he or she worry about most?
   - What fears, hopes, and expectations might your boss have about you?
   - What behavioral styles make your boss most comfortable and most uncomfortable?

4. *Speak and show your support.* If you want to achieve a true transformation of your relationship with your "less than" boss, you must demonstrate your support explicitly in both your language and your actions. One of our professional development program participants even went so far as to sit down with her boss and ask him, "What can I do to give you more help in achieving your business goals for our group?" Her boss answered her, and as soon as she began following through with the specifics he had discussed, he promoted her! Several months later he told her that she was the first person who had ever asked him this question, and he was impressed by it.

Building a supportive boss is all about building yourself into a supportive follower. Once you prove yourself to the boss—once he or she realizes that you are fully committed to the team and his or her goals—your boss will return that commitment to you. Now he or she will be receptive to your requests, supportive of your efforts to build an Expanded 100% Job, and the champion of your career goals.

At this point, your challenge is to take the next step and initiate a dialogue between you and your boss, in which you openly and honestly ask for what you want. For many women, this is the scary part. They will either delay this conversation or deny it to themselves completely because it is uncomfortable. Then, when they don't get what they want (because the boss never knew they wanted it), they become resentful and end up marching into the boss's office and demanding their due. No wonder they are so often disappointed!

The ancient Roman statesman Seneca said, "It is not because things are difficult that we do not dare; it is because we do not dare that things are difficult." If you want to propel your career forward, you must replace your tendency to delay with a tendency to dare. Stop waiting for the gift of a raise or a promotion or an expansion of your responsibilities. Instead, make a rational and respectful case for what you want and give your boss the opportunity to say yes! If your rationale is designed to support your company's objectives and your boss's goals, how could your boss possibly say no? For professional women who are reluctant to rely on relationships for advancement, perhaps this is the most daring act of all—allowing your boss to support you.

One of Nancy's coaching clients, the director of corporate communications for an international Fortune 500 company, was given a major increase in responsibilities when she finally dared to go to her boss and ask for it. Despite her senior position within the company, Katherine was dissatisfied with her job. Charity work was her personal passion. Her goal was to spend roughly five more years in a corporate environment and then join a charitable organization. She learned that her own company channeled millions of dollars to a variety of charitable community organizations, but no single person was responsible for the overall disbursement of funds. When her boss had a free moment, she raised the opportunity for the company to gain more visibility through strategically focused charitable donations. She asked to be on his consideration list if he decided to assign someone this responsibility.

A month later Katherine's boss called and told her that he'd decided to give her the new responsibility. This would never have happened if she had not first raised the subject, and in a way that spoke to the company's goals and appealed to her boss's managerial style. Katherine knew that her boss was paternalistic. He needed to feel like the giver of gifts and bestower of blessings. She simply couched her request in a way that would enable him to fulfill this need—to "bless" her with this new responsibility.

This piece of an Expanded 100% Job will do more than help Katherine make the necessary contacts to enter the charity arena five years from now. It will give her company "more bang for the buck" from their charitable contributions.

Once your boss has agreed to support you in expanding your responsibilities and authority, you must continue to earn that support every day. Keep your boss informed of what you are doing, how you are doing, and what help you need from him or her to do it better. Reciprocate as well by periodically asking your boss what more you could be doing to support his or her efforts. Over time, as your boss's projects (and yours) become successes, you will find that your boss is not merely a supporter but also an advocate who pushes you and your career forward.

Whether you are seeking to enlarge your current position by creating an Expanded 100% Job, like Katherine, or advance your career a notch by securing a promotion to a higher position, it will be far easier if your boss chooses to help. And regardless of how secure or insecure, or how smart or stupid your boss is, he or she will base that choice not solely on the quality of your work but also on the quality of your relationship. And it is you—not your boss—who controls this variable.

Expanding and Supporting Your Career Network

Networking is that all-important skill of making connections and building your business relationships outward and upward. It provides you with supporters who will stand up for you in the boardroom and spread the good news about your abilities to those decision makers with whom you have little or no personal contact.

We consistently find in our coaching that one of the vast chasms between women and men is their degree of comfort with networking. It arises from the instinctive difference between women and men on the thinking/feeling and hierarchy/peer aspects of relationship building. Precisely because career advancement is a root motive for networking, most men take to it like ducks to water. They understand that the contacts they make through networking are some of the resources they will use to move ahead on their career pathways. And they understand that this is a legitimate part of playing the game called business. Women, on the other hand, often view networking as an illegitimate way to move around the business game board—a disingenuous form of relationship building, based on selfish motives and false feelings. Almost unanimously, the women we have coached say they would rather be promoted based on their work than their connections.

This is extraordinarily naive thinking! Your career progress depends every bit as much on the breadth and quality of your relationships as on the quality of your work. In fact, the more advanced your level of management, the more important your network becomes as a career resource for you, as well as a business resource for your company. Those golf outings and industry conventions may look like boondoggles to you, as you sit in your little middle-management office and work the day and night away. But you can bet that your top management (and your male peers) are systematically using these opportunities to reach out and connect with other executives in a wide range of organizations: companies in your industry, potential clients, vendors, government legislators, investment bankers, investment analysts, and so on.

Now let's look at a more immediate situation: the difference that networking can make to a middle manager's promotional pathway. Just imagine yourself as president of a large company. A senior position opens up within your organization and you are given three names for the position. All of the candidates are qualified and have approximately equal tenure within the company. But there is a difference that doesn't show up on the written reports: One candidate (we'll call him Tom) had sent you a note, congratulating you on a recent speech; he also played a round of golf with you a year ago, after which he made an appointment to get your advice on an important career decision. Finally, he has authored several trade-paper articles, which he also sent to you. He attached a note to one of these articles, politely acknowledging that his conclusions differed from those he understood you to hold on the topic.

As a result of Tom's efforts, you know him better than the other two candidates—Dick and Mary. You know that Tom takes advantage of opportunities to develop management contacts and that he is an honest, straightforward communicator who is unafraid to disagree—respectfully—with senior management. Dick and Mary may also have these skills, but they didn't demonstrate them to you. Tom did. So he wins!

In this example, all three executives have equal expertise and experience, although that rarely occurs in real life. What does occur with clocklike regularity is the tie-breaking power of networking.

By the time you reach middle management, you are competing for the next promotion with peers who are every bit as qualified as you are. At this point the strong networker has a clear advantage, just as Tom did, because she has demonstrated her capabilities and potential. But even more important, the strong networker has created relationships with more executives who will say yes to her promotion.

It is possible for women to become powerful networkers. In fact, you can use your natural tendency to seek connection and intimacy to actually distinguish your networking activities and relationships from those of your male colleagues. Far too many of these colleagues are "needy networkers"—selecting targets and building relationships based solely on the "what can I get" principle. They constantly put their own needs above those of the people in their network. These "needy networkers" are the source of women's distaste for and distrust of networking. All we have to do is use our feminine preference for nurturing to beat them at this game of relationship-building—and to feel more comfortable with ourselves in the process. Powerful networking is not based on need, it is based on nurturing. When we consciously use our natural instinct to support others, we create not only connection but also true closeness in our networking relationships. We become like magnets, attracting others who desire to experience these deeper, emotional bonds. As a female networker, you also create a more personal (although still professional) level of interaction than a man would typically develop.

Shelly Lazarus, the CEO of Ogilvy & Mather Advertising, exemplifies many of the nurturing, relationship-building attitudes and behaviors we've discussed. She is a powerful networker, yet she does not view herself or her activities in this context.

"I never think consciously about networking. . . . I don't do it to achieve any specific outcome. I just do it to maintain a relationship with someone I like and have respect for," she says. For Shelly Lazarus, networking isn't work at all; it is sheer joy: "I really have met the most amazing people during the course of my career . . . people who I loved working with, and respected. Just because they leave, you can still maintain a relationship with them. . . . These relationships give me an enormous amount of pleasure."

While managing a large financial account at DDB in Los Angeles, Candy saw the burst of pride that Shelly's communications brought to those lucky enough to be on the receiving end of her messages. The ad agency had launched a new campaign for a client, and about a week after the initial full-page ad appeared in the *Wall Street Journal*, the senior client who had approved the campaign rushed into Candy's office, waving the ad and a small note, like an excited schoolboy. "Just look at this!" he said, thrusting the notecard proudly into her hands.

Shelly Lazarus's name was embossed at the top, and below it was a handwritten message complimenting him on a very "smart" campaign and an agency that was doing a terrific job.

The senior client had worked with Shelly many years before. Her short, congratulatory note was, for him, a special acknowledgment of his expertise and a job well done. But even more important, it was a sign of personal friendship and genuine caring.

Shelly's note had no ulterior motive, no specific business goal. In fact, she would probably wince if we dared to call this networking. For her, it is simply staying in touch. This is precisely the source of its effectiveness: genuine thoughts and feelings are behind every note and every telephone call. She is a natural nurturer, and she would tell you that she, in turn, is nurtured by these relationships.

Now, imagine that one day in the future, this financial client becomes the president of a large company. They fire their ad agency and must find another. How likely is it that he will put Shelly Lazarus's agency, Ogilvy & Mather, on the list of candidates?

About 100 percent.

This is a woman's way of networking. It's strategically smart in that it is selective about who's in the network, and it's softer and more integrated in terms of providing both rational and emotional support. With this dual foundation, you are far more powerful at building deep, long-lasting, reciprocal relationships.

Your starting point for networking, then, is simply to allow yourself to rely on your nurturing instincts. Your activities will have nothing to do with *getting* and everything to do with *giving*, nothing to do with *needing* and everything to do with *nurturing*. We've coined a three-pronged pseudonym to help you maintain this supportive focus in your networking activities: Yes, I C.A.N.

- **C** *stands for* **Connect:** Your orientation is not merely about contacting people in your network; it is about connecting yourself with them and connecting them with one another. Authors Donna Fisher and Sandy Vilas describe this process as links in their book, *Power Networking*:

    Networking is making links from people we know to people they know, in an organized way, for a specific purpose, while remaining committed to doing our part and expecting nothing in return.[2]

    If you operate from a "how can I help you" framework, you will constantly be looking for opportunities in which you can help someone in your network, as well as times when two people in your network can help each other. You provide both direct and indirect nurturing. Does Joe have a problem or opportunity that Jill is particularly experienced with? If so, tell Joe about Jill, and invite him to call on her for help. Then give Jill a call to let her know Joe may be contacting her. Over time, as you become known for your interest and expertise in helping people connect with others, you become a connection-building hub. People in your network will begin seeking you out for help, connections, and advice. And when you, in turn, need these things from them, they will be only too happy to return the favors.

- **A** *stands for* **Acknowledge:** This is a particularly positive and powerful networking practice with individuals who are in higher management positions. Rarely does the president of a company encounter anyone who makes a point of patting him or her on the back (and not asking for anything in return!). So when someone does, the president appreciates this rare and wonderful gift. If you see a news article that is particularly informative or even flattering about someone you know, send it with a note to the people who would be interested. When someone gives a speech that you find insightful or inspiring, let him or her know what you liked about it. If your expressions of acknowledgment are genuine—based on your true thoughts and feelings rather than simply what the receiver might want to hear—you will do far more than create a connection; you will distinguish yourself as honest and unafraid to express your thoughts and opinions.

- **N** *stands for* **Nurture:** This feminine-based instinct is a natural asset for professional women. Yet we so often turn away from it in our networking. Let's use it and stand out! If people in your network are having difficulty, give them your support. It could be as simple as a card or a phone call to lift their spirits, or as complicated as volunteering your time and expertise to help them solve a problem. You can brand your nurturing style by applying three simple "tune-in" principles:

  1. *Tune in to the other person's timetable.* Nurture the individuals in your network when *they* need it rather than when you do. Communicate when it's most convenient or advantageous for them rather than for you.

  2. *Tune in to the whole person, not just the business person.* Find out about their families, hobbies, interests, and philanthropic attachments. If they love opera, then invite them to attend. If their children love soccer, invite the family to a professional soccer game.

  3. *Tune in to the broad spectrum of nurturing tools available to you.* Not every contact must be face-to-face, and not every outing has to involve sports. In these high-technology times, you have a wide spectrum of contact tools and entertainment options available. You can call, write a

personal note, send a card, E-mail, even E-mail a greeting card. You can choose from a wide variety of mail-order gifts to commemorate birthdays, births, deaths, and just about everything in between. While you can play golf, you can also invite people to an entire variety of cultural and arts events or to your home for a small get-together.

This Yes, I C.A.N. foundation will ensure that you are a powerful relationship builder, but highly effective networking is also characterized by two left-brain, thinking components: selectivity and system. These ensure that you are selecting the proper individuals for inclusion in your network and maintaining your connections with them.

Start with a strategic focus to identify your networking prospects. Establishing a few criteria for selecting the people you want to incorporate into your network is important for two reasons. First, you work in a high-pressure professional world in which the additional time for networking is a precious resource. And second, your natural feminine nurturing tendencies will be directed toward peers and subordinates, but your networking activities should be primarily directed "up and out" to superiors within your company and to senior executives and peers in the external business environment. These are the connections that will ultimately support your career advancement, and your company's achievement of its business goals. For example, within your company you want to establish a relationship with those key senior executives who are important "yes" votes in your Promotion Game schematic. In the external environment, you will want to identify those organizations and events that offer strong connection opportunities with companies and executives who can contribute to your advancement, your growth in expertise or experience, or your ability to make other important professional connections.

Here, you are playing the Promotion Game, the Career Game, and the larger Game of Life. This is where women wince because it begins to feel like taking rather than giving. This perception couldn't be further from the truth! You are merely being picky with your networking prospects, just as you are picky when you choose your friends. A little strategic focus in the beginning to properly select your network actu-

ally frees you in the long run to spend your time connecting, acknowledging, and nurturing. Being picky simply allows you to give more—
and more freely—to the people you pick!

The next step is to establish specific goals and tracking tools. This
left-brain measurement function will be instrumental in helping you
build a new habit of networking, as well as maintain a large network,
once you have built it. Perhaps you establish three goals to begin building your "up and out" networking habit; for example:

1. Attend at least two networking events a month for the next six
   months. Before attending each event, think about two or three
   specific people you would like to meet or goals you would like to
   achieve in building your own connection skills (for example, meet
   at least five new people who are at a higher level in their
   organizations than you are in your company).
2. Add at least five new people each month to your network, for the
   next six months. You will undoubtedly meet some of these people
   at your networking events. Perhaps you learn of others through
   news articles and take the initiative to contact them. Part of this
   list should include the key senior executives within your own
   company—those who could be important influencers (or even
   "yes" votes) in your Promotion Game.
3. Contact each new person in the network with a Yes, I C.A.N.
   item, once a month for the first three months. This will establish
   a new contact within your network. Over time, however, as your
   network enlarges, the contact schedule for each person can be less
   frequent (once every 60 to 120 days). A computer-based contact
   management system will help you orchestrate this schedule
   effortlessly.

As you embark upon this brave new world of feminine, feeling-based
networking, you will certainly have fears. Focus not on yourself but on
the support you want to give to each person in your network and your
fears will disappear. For who would reject the gift of sincere acknowledgment? Who would view you as weak or needy if you are totally

focused on helping them solve their problem? Who would call you pushy when your every action is nurturing their needs and desires?

The final guideline for feminine-based networking is a reminder to allow yourself to ask for—and accept—nurturing from your network. Just as you enjoy nurturing others, they enjoy nurturing you. Especially when you build a Yes I C.A.N. network, the relationships are based on the desire to support, rather than the obligation to reciprocate. When you deny others in your network the opportunity to support you, you actually damage the bonds that you have created.

Whether you are reinventing a relationship with a boss, rebuilding your bond with a peer or subordinate, or creating an entirely new set of connections with senior management people within your company and in the business world beyond, simply remaining true to the Yes I C.A.N. philosophy in all of your interactions—and allowing that philosophy to flow *to* you as well as *from* you—will bring you tremendous personal satisfaction and much, much more. It will give you a broad-based human support system that makes your life and your work more joyful and, well . . . a lot less work!

You have a limited time to accomplish your goals for your career and your life. Relationships can help you reach the finish line and achieve your dreams a little faster, and they add immeasurably to your sheer enjoyment of the race.

CHAPTER 8

TAPPING INTO THE POWERS OF FEMININE LEADERSHIP

Dance Lesson #8: You possess innate feminine qualities that are powerful and unique characteristics of leadership. When you choose to tap into your true strengths, you will differentiate yourself and become a more valuable leader in your company.

Pharaohs ruled ancient Egypt for thousands of years. They were builders, philosophers, murderers, and tyrants. They were all-powerful, all-knowing, and all male.

Hatshepsut donned the male dress and golden beard of the pharaoh at about age twenty-two and ruled for a quarter century. This was the first pharaoh to keep Egypt at peace. And with peace came an unprecedented age of building and beautification. The 3,500-year-old Deir el Bahari temple and the hundred-foot-high, gold-tipped marble obelisk at Thebes, two miraculous building achievements of the ancient world, still stand today.

Hatshepsut died in 1468 B.C. In death, not even the pharaoh's dress, golden beard, and title of "his majesty" could change the fact that Hatshepsut was a woman. So this pharaoh was laid to rest in the Valley of the Queens.

Only one other woman would ever rule Egypt alone: Cleopatra. Unlike Hatshepsut, Cleopatra recognized the special advantages of her gender. She relied on her feminine strengths to achieve her political and economic objectives. She understood that her true potency was as queen—not king—of Egypt.

Cleopatra enriched Egypt by negotiating treaties, expanding trade, and reducing taxes. Through her relationships with Julius Caesar and Mark Antony she was able to delay Egypt's absorption into the Roman Empire for the entirety of her rule.

The reigns of Hatshepsut and Cleopatra are rich in parallels and contrasts. Both were teenage monarchs, mothers, and legendary beauties with equally legendary intellects. But Hatshepsut masked her femininity beneath the male clothing of a pharaoh, while Cleopatra relied on her womanhood as her greatest strength.

Hatshepsut would pay an eternal price for daring to join the ranks of male leadership. Today, her name is not included in Egypt's official lists of pharaohs. She is neither well-known nor well-honored. On the other hand, Cleopatra—the queen—has been immortalized in books, songs, operas, paintings, films, poems, and sculptures for the past two thousand years.

Perhaps Cleopatra fascinates us because she is such a potent example of a feminine-based leader who triumphed in a masculine-driven world. She showed us that femininity carries added powers for leadership, such as intuition, communication, relationship building, and creativity. To tap into those powers in our own lives, we must stop thinking like Hatshepsut and start thinking like Cleopatra. Instead of working so hard to don a masculine disguise in order to fit into a business world filled with men, we need to allow ourselves to rely on our own innate leadership strengths—our *feminine* strengths.

This "Hatshepsut syndrome" is what first brought Candy and Nancy together, as client and consultant. Candy had hired Nancy to help DDB diagnose a widespread employee morale problem and identify the solutions. After delivering her final report and recommendations, Nancy shared one additional (and very personal) observation with Candy: "This is a testosterone-driven culture. You've completely sacrificed your femininity to rise in management here. Now you're relying almost exclusively on your masculine skill sets. That makes you the same as every other senior executive."

"Well, how else do you think a woman can get ahead here?" Candy asked. "What's so wrong with being the same as the people at the top if that's where I want to go?"

"The people at the top are men, and you're a woman. And your employees need something that these men can't give them," Nancy pointed out. "This is a hard-driving culture. To be more motivated, more productive, and more creative, your employees need a dose of feminine energy. They need some nurturing, and you're the one best suited to provide it. If you do, you'll find a new level of creativity and joy in yourself as well."

Candy remembers being a little incredulous at the thought that she would be a better, more powerful leader in her company if she were more feminine. But somewhere deep within her, a little "Aha!" told her there was some truth to Nancy's advice. She needed to reestablish contact with her right-brain attributes.

"OK, so how do I do it?" she asked.

Nancy remembers feeling a little queasy as she offered up the next advice: "Well, I'd like you to start by taking a weekend course to learn how to tap into your feminine side and balance your masculine and feminine energy. It's taught by a woman named Zanda."

Stone silence filled the room. Candy's face spoke volumes—all negative. Then she said, "*Zanda?* No last name? Just Zanda? Are you kidding? How am I going to get my boss to pay several hundred dollars so I can take a course in feminine energy from somebody who doesn't even have a last name?"

"I'll admit that it sounds a little 'woo-wooee,'" Nancy said. "But after taking the course myself, I feel more centered, more at peace, and more powerful in my actions. Just trust me."

Candy did trust Nancy and took the course. Then she signed up for several more. Over the next four months she spent one weekend a month in the company of other women and men learning about the powers of feminine energy. During the week she began trying some of Zanda's "rituals" to nurture her feminine side: taking baths in the midst of a trio of scented candles, massaging her body with aromatic oils, and burning incense as she dressed for work in the morning.

Over time Candy began to sense a subtle shift impossible to describe accurately in words. She just *felt* it. The perennial tightness in her chest disappeared. It was as if someone had gently pried open her ribcage and let the fresh air flow straight into her heart.

Candy found herself more relaxed, calmer, and less frenetic at work. Not surprisingly, the employees began to find her more accessible. She began communicating with a new sense of ease and effectiveness. Freed from years of unspoken condemnation of that female side of her being, she was able to accept and express the unique value of the feminine qualities within her. They were strengths, not weaknesses, after all! When Candy allowed her female energy to flow, the response was an increase in the flow of energy from everyone around her. Tensions eased. Cooperation increased as people began sharing both their thoughts and their feelings. In honoring her natural, nurturing brand of leadership, Candy had reintroduced a key "missing"—the heart—into the daily lives of her company's employees. She had created an environment in which everyone, female and male, could do the same.

Zanda's "woo-wooee" courses turned out to be the most practical, logical thing Candy could have done to improve employee morale and develop her own leadership position in the company.

Candy's adoption of masculine patterns to succeed in business is typical of many career-driven professional women. To cope with the pressures of their male-dominated business domains, they choose to fit in rather than risk the judgment of inferiority. Bonita Long and Sharon Kahn, authors of *Women, Work, and Coping: A Multidisciplinary Approach to Workplace Stress*, state:

> *Male-positive, female-negative is such a pervasive aspect of our Western public cultures that it is unusual to identify ways in which women differ from men without the assumption being made that women are somehow inferior. Female characteristics and values, such as emotions, intuition, and interdependence, are denied legitimacy and are covertly or actively suppressed.*[1]

Through this process of disconnecting from our true, instinctive, feminine traits to find acceptance (and advancement) within our organizations, we have denied the most powerful part of our beings. No wonder so few of us have risen from middle management, where we are ever more populous, to the top executive ranks. We have forced ourselves to undergo a sort of psychic sex change—to become tough, analytical, rational, and unemotional—thinking that these male traits of leadership would be the key to the top-executive ranks. We believed that if we could just *fit in*, we would succeed. Well, we were wrong. Because true leaders do not worry about fitting in. They stand out and they lead! Those few women who have reached the apex of their organizations are proof of the power of feminine-based leadership. Just look at some of the women in *Fortune* magazine's list of the fifty most powerful women in American business. What differentiates these women from their male counterparts is their reliance on the female qualities of leadership as the foundation of their competitive edge—and their willingness not only to admit it but to flaunt it:

- The intuitive instincts of Joy Covey, former CFO of Amazon.com, who says, "It may not seem logical, but trust me. I know where I'm going. And it's far."[2]
- The relationship-building expertise of Nancy Peretsman, executive vice president and managing director at Allen & Company investment banking firm, which earned her this accolade from Priceline.com founder and chairman Jay Walker: "[Peretsman] is the confidante of about twenty moguls, most of whom probably wouldn't talk to each other except to scream. She's the last of a generation of investment bankers whose power is in their long-term relationships."[3]
- The perception Andrea Jung, Avon chairperson and CEO, has of the nurturing responsibilities that are an inherent part of power, demonstrated when she says: "Power is the privilege to influence. It's an unbelievable responsibility to influence decisions, shareholder value, and most important to me, people's careers and livelihoods."[4]

Is there a lesson to be learned here? You bet! It is the first lesson of leadership: know who you are and where your true strength lies. As women, we possess four such strengths that are strongly based in our right-brain-dominant thinking: creativity, intuition, communication, and relationship building. The last three of these are areas in which we women have an almost hereditary advantage over men, based on generations of practice as the primary nurturers of our families and our communities. In the past, these three feminine qualities have been given little honor in our male-dominated organizations. So in our own efforts to progress, we have relegated them to minor roles in our leadership skill sets. But now that women are such a large population in the American workplace, the pathways to leadership must be expanded to honor the fullness of both the men and the women who travel them.

In this chapter, we will help you rediscover and refine these four feminine leadership qualities. Once you allow them to come to the forefront and become the foundation of your leadership style, you will be a more natural, more powerful, and more distinctive leader in your organization.

We will also help you learn to identify that fine line between strength and weakness in each area. Part of the paradox of leadership is that each skill can be an asset or a stumbling block, depending on your practice of it. Being able to recognize the difference is critical. Just think about it. Being a decisive leader is good, unless it is taken too far and you become autocratic. Being a good listener is an asset, unless it becomes a crutch for delaying a critical decision. Being admired by peers, subordinates, and superiors is a winning quality in today's business world, unless you become a "people pleaser" who is more concerned with friendship than respect.

The challenge of leadership, then, is learning to practice the fine art of living on the edge of *just enough*. Just enough strength, compassion, collaboration, independence, order, chaos. Just enough to assure your success as a leader, your organization's growth and profitability, and your employees of a supportive, enlightened work environment.

Finally, we are not advising you to rely solely on these four feminine-based skills. We will also teach you how to develop two additional skills that are critical if you want to become a high-level leader: risk taking and vision building. Whether consciously or unconsciously, most women shy away from these two areas. Yet at the very core of both is the most uniquely feminine of all leadership traits: *intuition*. This most feminine of skills, then, is the secret key to building your confidence and expertise in the uncertain worlds of risk and vision.

Feminine Leadership Quality #1: Building Rich Working Relationships

The world of business relationships can be simplified into two distinct halves: networking relationships and working relationships. Both are vital to a successful career, but the purposes and the processes of each are about as different as night and day. Here are some examples of the dichotomy:

Networking	*Working*
Optional creation/optional contact	Mandatory creation/mandatory contact
Infrequent contact	Regular/high-frequency contact
No quantitative objectives	Specific, quantitative objectives
No specific roles or expectations	Highly specific roles and expectations

Much of the previous chapter concentrated on the networking world; our discussion in this chapter will center on the more specific world of working relationships. These are the one-on-one relationships between you and your individual superiors, subordinates, peers, clients, vendors, buyers, and so forth. They are also the group relationships that are built among team members and among teams. In today's business environment where teams are so often the only way to solve complex problems, the quality of these relationships can make the difference between success and failure.

Women have a unique sense of what it takes to build rich working relationships, whether they are negotiating with a competitor or cooperating with peers. One CFO of a Fortune 500 company shared the following observation about the difference between women and men in this area:

> *For men, it's a "buddy" type of relationship. Men do this gregarious pat 'em on the back, pump 'em up, get 'em rolling kind of thing. It's not deep. And you wonder whether it's sincere. Women seem to go deeper in their conversations to learn what really matters to one another. It's a more sincere communication.*

Men tend to look at their business relationships in a hierarchical or competitive context, as opportunities to establish power or dominance. This makes it possible to have functional relationships, but not *rich* relationships, because a certain level of trust can never be part of the exchange. Women, however, approach their business relationships in a cooperative context, as opportunities to establish connections. Whether we are communicating across issues, divisions, languages, or cultures, this connection-driven style is ultimately more conducive to long-term relationship building. It encourages a more open, multidirectional flow of information and ideas between buyer and seller, superior and subordinate, peer and peer.

This distinction between women and men may be partially a learned behavior, but its roots lie in the physiological differences in our brains. So it seems we are actually "built" to behave instinctively different. The *Los Angeles Times* article "Breaking the Glass Ceiling: Can Women Reach the Top of America's Largest Corporations?" states:

> *British geneticist Anne Moir . . . cites numerous studies showing, for example, that men have fewer fibers connecting the verbal and emotional areas of the brain, making it more difficult for them to express emotions. . . . Psychological studies indicate that women are more focused on intimacy and making connections with other people, while men are more centered on autonomy, power, and asserting independence.[5]*

Our feminine instinct to seek connection and intimacy in our relationships is advantageous, as long as we are sensitive enough to create *just enough* connection and *just enough* intimacy to achieve the proper depth level. We must also be sensitive to how the relationship is interpreted by the men who are either within it or outside observers. To use your relationship-building skills to your full advantage, you must assess each association not only in terms of its reality but also in terms of how it is perceived by others. Since most business cultures are still male-dominated, that means looking at your relationships from a "man's-eye-view," in the areas described on the following pages.

Remember the Role of Status

Most men view status as a hierarchical-based system. They evaluate their position and power within an organization by looking at where they are in the vertical hierarchy. Given this framework, an upwardly mobile man will focus his attentions on communicating and building relationships with those above him. Women, on the other hand, view status as a more holistic framework. They consequently take a different route in building their power and position within the organization. Theirs is a more broad-based system of connections.

If we were creatures in the wild, men would be the lions, sitting proudly atop the food chain, while women would be the spiders, comfortably supported by the silken threads of a web. Connection is about building the web—creating relationships that are deeper, more varied, and less hierarchical. While women function well in these more egalitarian relationships, men tend to interpret the lack of status cues from a female superior as weakness. Deborah Tannen notes in her book *You Just Don't Understand: Women and Men in Conversation*:

> *Men are more often inclined to focus on the jockeying for status in conversation. . . . Women are more often attuned to the negotiation of connections. . . . Imagine how often women who think they are displaying a positive quality—connection—are misjudged by men who perceive them as revealing a lack of independence, which the men regard as synonymous with incompetence and insecurity.*[6]

Particularly in your business relationships with men, remember the role of status. It gives you a powerful advantage because you can easily combine status signals with your natural connection-driven patterns. This is as simple as learning to place the order, if you are the boss, rather than express a preference or ask for help from a subordinate. When Mary wants John to take on an additional project, notice how much more confident and clear she sounds in the first statement:

> *Placing an order*: "John, I have a new project assignment for you to manage. It's a wonderful opportunity for you to learn."
>
> *Expressing a preference:* "John, I'd really like you to take on this new project assignment."
>
> *Asking for help:* "John, could you take on this new project assignment for me? It would be . . ."

If you tend to speak to your subordinates in the weaker "preference" or "help" formats, simply learning to "place the order" will make a world of difference in your male colleagues' perceptions of your position, power, and competence within the organization. It will also make a world of difference in your ability to get productivity and results from your subordinates.

Understand the Risks of Protection

The connection-seeking pattern of women is one of those areas in which it is so easy to slide over the edge from just enough to too much, particularly when the other half of the equation is a male. Connection covers a vast array of interactions between business associates, from the friendly hello as you are passing each other in the hall to the more infamous trysts and tête-à-têtes. Somewhere in the middle of this array is the connective relationship that falls in the realm of *protection*.

The signs of protection are subtle. It usually involves a man making a decision for you rather than giving you the chance to make it for yourself, believing that he is actually doing you a favor: the boss who meets with your angry client because he wants to save you from being abused verbally in the meeting, the mentor who doesn't tell you about a job opening overseas because he assumes that you wouldn't want to move your family.

Just as women seek connection, men have been trained from childhood to protect women from harm. It is only natural for them to carry this training into the business world—and just as natural for them to regard protectors as superior, and "protectees" as subordinate.

Once you have allowed yourself to be protected by your boss, for example, your peers (and even your subordinates) will view you as less powerful relative to your boss and relative to them.

Andrea Hoffman had been the senior attorney handling all contract work for a large, corporate client. Her client decided to expand its operations to South America. When the client was ready for the legal contract work and needed someone from her firm, Andrea expected to make the trip. But the managing partner assigned it to another attorney, one who hadn't worked with the client for two years. Although Andrea was the expert, the other attorney had a larger advantage: he was a man.

When Andrea learned that she had been passed over, she was seething. She talked to her boss, who told her that he hadn't given her the assignment because of the political unrest in this particular country. He was concerned for her safety, and simply didn't want to put a woman from the firm in physical jeopardy.

Andrea's boss's decision was paternalistic and unchangeable: by not consulting her, he had denied her a voice—and a choice—in the decision. He just made it for her, as if she were a child. In doing so, he denied her a key growth experience and harmed her future promotability. But he failed to understand any of these issues when Andrea discussed them directly with him. It was this last failure that caused Andrea to join another firm. She had no reason to believe that future decisions would be made any differently.

The best way to avoid protection is to actively prevent it before it happens. The minute Andrea heard about that international assignment, she should have spoken to her boss—before he'd reached any decision—and expressed her expectation that she would go and her desire to make the trip, despite any political unrest. He would have either given her the assignment or faced his own true motives in selecting a man for the job.

Protection is a difficult issue because there is no classic "bad guy" who is consciously trying to hurt your career. In fact, the protector usually sees himself as a good guy who really cares for your career and your well-being. But there is a fundamental difference between a mentor and a protector. A mentor will give you advice and counsel but ultimately encourage you to make your own decisions and take your own risks. A protector will give you this same counsel, but when a decision must be made, he makes it for you—often without even consulting you in the process.

Nurture, but Don't Mother

As a woman, the strength of your natural tendency to nurture others can be debilitating to your own career growth if it is overdone in the business domain. Women most often mother their subordinates. And typically, the more we like somebody, the more likely we are to go beyond the *just enough* level of nurturing and unknowingly fall head over heels into mothering mode.

If you are a mothering manager, you come to the rescue with far more than just a helping hand. You give a project to a subordinate, but when you observe that she is having difficulty, you help her by taking part of it back and doing it yourself. Rather than holding her accountable for completion, you take on that responsibility. You do her work, rather than keeping focused on your own. As a result, you create an employee who will be less responsible and more dependent on you in the future, and you add the wrong level of work to your own workload. In this scenario, the employee cannot develop her skills sufficiently to qualify for promotion . . . and neither can you.

The difference between managing and mothering is a critical distinction to master. Managers support their subordinates with guidance and resources as needed; mothers *are* the resource.

Use Collaboration as a Support—Not a Substitute— for Leadership

Collaboration and the creation of successful teams are positive, empowering qualities in any work environment, and women are natural collaborators, often to a fault. Women can enjoy this group dynamic so much that we fail to remember that even in a collaborative group, someone has to be the leader. If you want to move higher in your organization, then *you* want to be that leader. You must constantly demonstrate a willingness to be responsible for results—an attitude that "the buck stops here."

In today's marketplace, it isn't enough to create a collaborative work environment. The leader must also exhibit the ability to make quick (and often controversial) decisions. The unpopular decisions—those not supported by the group—are certainly among the toughest. They require you to tolerate the ambiguity of collaboration and leadership. You can be compassionate and caring yet still make that layoff decision. You can seek consensus, but you must be able to stand alone when your principles mandate it. Solitude is an unavoidable condition of leadership.

Be Friendly, but Don't Become Friends

As a leader, there is a critical difference between being friendly to your subordinates and being friends with them. Because women are so connection-oriented, we all too easily move beyond friendly and into friendship. This can compromise objectivity and authority when the truly tough decisions come along. Even if you are able to remain objective and separate your business decisions from the friendships that they may affect, this style of "friendship management" can create a false perception of favoritism among other employees. Despite your best intentions, perception is reality to your subordinates and other employees.

Sally Giardini, a regional vice president for a financial services company, experienced the downside of "friendship management" firsthand when she was transferred to her company's Texas office to lead a turnaround situation. In fulfilling her mandate to reverse the office's sales and profit declines, Sally would undoubtedly be faced with many difficult decisions, including staff layoffs. But she had never learned the distinction between being a friend and being a manager. So even though the Texas staff viewed her as the enemy, she sought to make friends. And she did find one. John was the group's leading salesperson, and he quickly became Sally's confidante. They were both single, so they often had drinks and dinner together after work. Because John was her only friend in the Texas office, she began depending on his input in her decision making. Her reorganization and layoff plans were created partially as a result of the information John provided on each of his coworkers.

You've probably guessed the rest of the story. As it turned out, much of John's input to Sally was false. Which meant her decisions were faulty. And to make matters worse, the rest of the staff interpreted her relationship with John as far more than simply a friendship. Even if her decisions had been correct, they would have been questionable under these circumstances.

This story has a predictable end. Sally failed to return the Texas office to profitability, so she was fired. Her desire for friends had compromised her ability to manage subordinates (and superiors), undermined her skill at making good decisions, and ultimately damaged her career.

Feminine Leadership Quality #2: Communicating "Whole-istically"

"Whole-istic" communication is a more complete, multidimensional style of interaction. It is about communicating not only the head's thoughts but also the heart's thoughts. It is about not only facts and language and facial expression but also emotion and physical contact (yes, physical contact!) when you talk to people. It is about not only honesty and logic but also empathy and passion. It is not just about talking; it is also about listening with all of these same skills. And women are trained from childhood to do it. We grow up in a world of intimacy and cooperation. Boys grow up in a world of status and competition. While boys were learning about power, hierarchy, and risk taking in their playing experiences, girls were developing their "whole-istic" communication skills through imaginative group play, dolls, and other make-believe games. Even on the competitive playing field, we were attuned to our own wants and needs, as well as those of other girls on the team. We learned to watch for a whole set of nonverbal cues to alert us to someone's unhappiness, fear, anger, or other emotion. Little boys just don't learn those skills. Theirs is an overt world of communications, whereas ours is filled with nuance. Even the physical aspect of boys' communications is a world of high fives, punches in the shoulder, and pats on the butt. Ours is a more intimate world of hand-holding, hugs, and heads touching in secret conversation. We are constantly tuned into the *whole* of communications: verbal, physical (nonverbal), and emotional. This triad works together to create "whole-istic" communication—but only if the giver and the receiver are both tuned in to them.

To truly appreciate and use our strengths in this area, we must first debunk some popular communication myths about women and discover the secrets behind the myths.

Myth: *Women are too emotional in business.*
Secret: *Emotions are one of our strongest business advantages.*

Homo sapiens were a highly emotional species eons before they became verbal. Early humans possessed a unique combination of physical strength, creative intelligence, and emotional response that enabled them to survive the attacks of ferocious predators and the dangers of natural disasters. Emotions are still an elemental—and unavoidable—aspect of our humanity whether we are male or female. But by the time they reach adulthood, men have typically undergone the equivalent of emotional boot camp. They are taught by most adult authority figures to control, mute, or even ignore their emotions. Just look at how we react to the crying of a little boy who runs to the sidelines of his soccer game with a scraped knee, compared to the little girl with the same injury. "Shake it off," are some of the first words out of the adult's mouth for the boy. Not so for the girl. She is comforted and asked how much it hurts. Her emotions are validated and rewarded. His are denigrated and ignored. Is it any wonder that little girls make more emotional adults than little boys?

As adults, we probably feel the same emotions, regardless of our gender. But we women have learned to display our emotions, while men have learned to suppress theirs. We tend to access our emotions more quickly when processing information. But most men will think first and feel later, and they may never actually show what they feel.

Women definitely introduce a new emotional component into the business arena. Since this component is different from the nonemotional norm in the male-dominated organization, the male establishment views almost any show of emotion from a woman as an indication of her inferiority—or of her suitability for a human resources job, rather than a line position in the company. Yet when a man shows the same emotional behaviors, he is lauded for his sensitivity, his caring, his passion, or his concern.

On the flip side of this emotional coin, when a woman shows negative emotions like anger or frustration, she is judged much more harshly than the man who displays the same set of emotional behaviors. In her coaching, Nancy has witnessed this double standard time and again. Nancy was coaching Carrie, a brilliant young manager who was extremely impatient with her subordinates. Occasionally, her impatience would spew forth in an angry outburst ("How can you take so long to finish such a simple project? I need it today! Get out of here, and don't come back until you've got it done!"). Carrie's subordinates had complained to the human resources director, who then hired Nancy to help Carrie overcome this problem.

After Nancy had been working with Carrie for about two weeks, she was walking down the hall toward Carrie's office, when she heard a man shouting in his office. As she passed by, she glanced through the door to see Carrie's boss, red-faced, wagging his finger at an employee as he shouted something about a recent sales fiasco.

Nancy spoke to the human resources director about the boss and was told, "Oh, Bob just gets a little overzealous sometimes. The sales guys love his aggressiveness . . . as long as it's not directed at them!" Needless to say, Nancy realized that Carrie was simply displaying the same behavior that she had observed in her boss. But while her boss was labeled "aggressive," she received the all-too-trite moniker of "bitch."

This double emotional standard operates throughout the emotional spectrum. But it is most damaging to women on the edges of that spectrum. Here's our visual representation of the spectrum in one emotional venue, and how it is interpreted when the "package" in which it is delivered is female versus male:

-4	-3	-2	-I	0	+I	+2	+3	+4

Angry ———— Aggressive ———— Neutral ———— Supportive ———— Loving
"Bitch" ———— "Pushy" ———— (Woman) ———————— "Too Soft"
"Hotheaded" – "Passionate" ———— (Man) ———————— "Warm/Caring"

Dwelling on the left edge of the spectrum earned Carrie the reputation of a "bitch," but when Bob entered the same emotional space, his hotheaded actions were accepted as simply a part of his persona.

More frequently, the contrast occurs on the right edge—the softer emotional side of the spectrum. One of the participants in our A Woman's Way of Leadership program shared her "on the edge" story about a layoff situation in her division of a Fortune 500 company. When the layoff plan was explained to Sally and the other senior managers in an executive planning meeting, she expressed her opinion that the compensation packages were inadequate and the company was not treating these long-time employees decently. She wanted the company to do more in the areas of counseling, retraining, and job placement. The president dismissed Sally's concerns as an overreaction and told her that she was getting too "personally involved" with the situation.

Two weeks later, when the layoffs began, the division's male human resources director told the president that the company could be legally culpable unless it provided retraining and outplacement for these employees, many of whom were twenty-year company veterans. The president approved his request. But more important, in the next executive meeting, he cited the HR director as a positive example of how caring the division's senior managers were.

Sally was thrilled for the exiting employees, but she was irritated that this solution was seen as "too soft" when it came from her lips, and just right when a man expressed the same idea.

After going through our program, Sally told us what she would have done differently, given her new learning about emotional "edges": "I would still have taken the 'too soft' position, because it was the right thing for the company to do," she said. "But I would have added some tougher-sounding rationale so that the president would have seen my point of view as smart, instead of soft. If I'd told him that the training and outplacement costs would be a lot less than a lawsuit from even one disgruntled ex-employee, he probably would have thanked me for the idea!"

The edges of the emotional spectrum are a danger zone for women, but in the middle, we have a distinct advantage in the game of communication. Here, the double emotional standard actually gives you a significant communications advantage over your male colleagues. When you keep your energies in this part of the emotional range, you have more latitude than men to integrate your emotions into your business communications, precisely because the male establishment (and the legal environment) accepts certain midrange displays of emotion more readily from a woman than from a man.

Just think about the power of touch to convey emotions. Think about how restricted men are from using this power, due to their own emotional closure and the current legal environment. In this arena, women have a powerful communication advantage: we are not only more in tune with our emotions, but we are freer to use both talk and touch to communicate those emotions to superiors, peers, and subordinates.

Candy was still a young account executive when she realized that when a conversation included a simple pat on the shoulder, it gave more comfort to a subordinate. Even when she was in "debate mode" with a client, she would automatically use this reassuring touch on an arm or shoulder to maintain a positive emotional connection in the midst of a potentially disconnecting conversation. For Candy, this integration of touch and talk was natural, not manipulative. It occurred because of her own instinctive need to express her emotions through physical gestures. Its positive impact on the receiver was merely a serendipitous side effect. But once she became aware of its power, she made this pairing of talk and touch one of her communication signatures. It gave her a special ability to reassure, comfort, motivate, and negotiate that most men could not duplicate in their own interactions.

Gestures are signals of our emotions, so they speak to our hearts and minds in ways that words cannot. They can motivate us or demotivate us. A leader who fails to connect emotionally with her employees will soon find a workforce dominated by boredom and apathy—and a company dominated by poor performance. Conversely, a leader who taps into the emotional factors of communication can inspire employees to achieve unparalleled heights by building their passion, commitment, and joy. Once the balance between just enough and too much is recognized, emotions become a woman's special asset and a powerful tool in our communication skill sets.

Myth: *Women talk too much and listen too little.*
Secret: *Listening is a key strength of great leaders, and women excel at it.*

"Whole-istic" communication involves not just the giving but also the receiving of messages in their entirety—*in their whole*. It doesn't take a brain surgeon to figure out that whoever does most of the talking in an exchange cannot be doing much receiving.

When Candy was a young management supervisor at DDB, she found herself seated next to Alan Pando, the president of her agency's Los Angeles office, on a three-hour flight headed home from a successful client meeting. There was cause for celebration, so the drinks and conversation were both flowing. At one point, they began talking about bosses and subordinates. Alan jokingly asked her, "When two businesspeople are sitting together in a plane, how can you tell which one is the boss?" She thought of lots of answers: the one in the outside seat, the one with the most expensive watch, the one with the smallest briefcase, the one without a suntan (this was California, after all). It was none of the above.

"I've been watching people in planes for thirty years," he said, "and almost every time, the boss turns out to be the one who does less talking."

Of course, the first thing Candy did was try to remember if she had talked her boss's ear off during the last two hours. And she had! Even though Candy's boss was just talking about airplane conversations, he had given her two critical clues about leadership that remain with her to this day. The first is that true leaders spend more time listening than talking. The second is that the very act of listening itself is a demonstration of power, if it is based in self-confidence rather than subservience.

Listening, then, is yet one more strike against women with management goals—if one accepts the popular belief that we women are a talkative bunch, not just in our personal lives but in our professional lives as well. To this myth, we say, simply, *"au contraire!"* Study after study has shown that when men and women are together, men are the truly talkative half of the species, whether they are in classrooms, meetings, or business discussions:

- A tape-recorded study of seven university faculty meetings showed that men spoke more frequently and longer. The men's turns ranged from eleven to seventeen seconds, compared to the women's, which ranged from three to ten seconds. The women's longest turns were still shorter than the men's shortest turns![7]
- A study of mixed-group conversations showed that men made 97 percent of the interruptions and talked from 58 percent to 92 percent of the time.[8]
- In *Hardball for Women*, authors Pat Heim and Susan K. Golant cite a study on listening skills published in the *Journal of Business Communications*, which stated that only 33 percent of the managers studied were female, but they represented 58 percent of the "good listeners."[9]

This last study also found a strong correlation between a positive work environment and the manager's listening skills: 91 percent of the employees who thought their managers were good listeners also expressed satisfaction with their own jobs. Being a good listener, then, is not a trait confined to the Y chromosome. We double-X chromosomers have it, too. And these studies suggest that we are even better at it than the guys are.

Listening does more than validate and motivate your employees. It improves your own decision making, if you're practicing a certain kind of listening. Numerous studies—statistical, historical, and biographical—show us that great leaders are also *proactive* listeners. They don't listen only when someone seeks them out; they purposefully design situations that encourage subordinates to give input and criticisms, to debate and argue. They use a variety of methods to create an egalitarian environment where the status of an individual (including the leader) has no bearing on the status of his or her ideas. For example, Winston Churchill would appoint an official "contrarian" in key cabinet meetings to argue the opposite of every idea put forth by the rest of the group.

Even though the leader may already have a decision in mind, her key role in creating an open, egalitarian meeting is to question and listen. She is looking for ideas that she may have overlooked, strengths that she didn't see, or weakness that she failed to uncover. She is looking for input to either validate her thinking or point her to a different decision.

As a group director in a large accounting firm, Nancy always prided herself on her ability to listen to her team. Then one of her subordinates revealed the subtle difference between a listening leader, and a *proactive* listening leader.

Nancy routinely called a group meeting of her key direct reports to discuss major decisions before they became set in stone. Nancy relied on the group's input and depended on them to make important contributions in these meetings. It was only after she left the company to start her own consulting firm that she learned how her subordinates really felt about these meetings.

About three years later, Nancy submitted a consulting proposal to Shauna Jackson. She had been one of Nancy's direct reports and had since been promoted several times in the company. Shauna turned Nancy's proposal down and awarded the job to another consultant. In a follow-up phone conversation, Nancy learned that Shauna's memory of those group meetings long ago was quite different from her own: "Well, you called us a team. But in fact, we never could be because you always owned the game!"

Nancy was shocked but managed to hold her tongue and listen to Shauna's explanation: "You always came to the table with nine marbles [knowledge, experience, solutions, and so forth]. The rest of the team, including me, only came to the table with two marbles. So you always owned the game."

Nancy challenged Shauna, saying, "But what if I put out all of my nine marbles and the problem wasn't solved? Then when you added your two marbles, a miraculous solution occurred. Which marble would be more valuable?"

Shauna didn't care. And that was the point. Nancy was the leader of the group, and rather than wait for her subordinates to contribute, she put her "marbles" on the table first. From that point on, the subordinates felt comfortable only reacting to her "marbles," rather than contributing their own. Shauna had just taught Nancy that a leader must be careful to mask her own preferences and reveal her own opinions only after the other people on her team had completely communicated theirs. Her power to be a completely objective, proactive listener was the prerequisite that would encourage her team to contribute 100 percent of their ideas.

Even the most proactive listeners will fail to receive the entire message unless they are also tuned in to the nonverbal cues of the communicator. This ability to supplement your proactive listening with nonverbal listening—to correctly "hear" what is shown in addition to what is said—takes you into the realm of "whole-istic" listening.

Just as emotions have been with us from our earliest moments as Homo sapiens, so has nonverbal communication. Our body language has a 50,000-year evolutionary jump on verbal language. Long before we spoke, we felt and we showed. Today, we have a nonverbal vocabulary of roughly 700,000 gestures, compared to an unabridged English dictionary of 500,000 words (of which the average person uses between 2,000 and 10,000!). So it is no wonder that studies have shown that words represent only about 7 percent of what we communicate, compared with 38 percent from tone of voice and 55 percent from facial expressions, posture, and gestures.

Clearly, no message is completely understood unless you have also "listened" to its nonverbal component. Our nonverbal vocabulary may not differ significantly between men and women, but women may be better attuned to this dimension of communication, simply because we live in it more deeply. From childhood to motherhood, our communication "training" encourages us to zero in on nonverbal cues. As children in group play, we look for signs of unhappiness, frustration, anger, satisfaction, and fear in our friends; as mothers we are constantly working to interpret the signals of our nonspeaking infants and toddlers so that we can fulfill their wants and needs. And just as infants' only cues are nonverbal (unless you count crying as a verbal cue), it is often the nonverbal cues of adults that are the most important to "hear."

Judy Monahan, the long-time marketing director of a privately held company, was a primarily nonverbal communicator. When Judy was upset about something, she became quiet. She never directly expressed her anger or frustration with language. Hers was an adult version of a little girl's pouting. Judy seemed to want someone to notice that she was unhappy and then ask her what was wrong, or better yet, figure out the problem and solve it without ever having a conversation with her. On the other hand, if nobody noticed or took action, eventually Judy would explode in shouts and tears of anger.

For almost ten years, Judy's sales promotion work had been handled by the same small advertising agency in San Francisco. For most of those years, the same account manager, Cynthia Farrell, had been Judy's main contact at the agency. Although Judy was Cynthia's client, the two women had become close personal friends. As a result, Cynthia was highly attuned to Judy's nonverbal pattern of communication. The agency's relationship with Judy was very positive because Cynthia's antennae were always up. The minute she sensed Judy becoming tense, she'd search for the problem that was brewing and solve it before it could fully develop.

Then Cynthia left the agency to take a higher-level job with a competitive firm in Chicago. Judy was justifiably upset, but Cynthia reassured her, "Don't worry. I'm sure Richard [the president of the agency] will put somebody terrific on your business." What Cynthia didn't tell Judy was that she had also suggested to Richard that a woman would probably be more successful in sensing any problems that might be bubbling up to Judy's surface.

Richard didn't know Judy very well, so he ignored Cynthia's advice and assigned one of his up-and-coming managers (translation: a guy) to handle Judy's business. In working with her new male contact, Judy was reserved and terse. He just thought that was the way she was. He never bothered to get to know her socially, and he never asked about how she was feeling. So when she was overly critical of an ad, he took it at face value, rather than understanding that it was Judy's way of yelling for help. He wasn't listening for the real problem that Judy so desperately wanted somebody to detect: she was mad at Richard because he'd given her the wrong person and never even asked her opinion about it. What she really wanted was for Richard to sense her anger, call her to apologize, and assign somebody new (preferably a woman) to handle her account. When after three months he hadn't called her, she finally picked up the phone and called him—to tell him that she was firing the agency.

As a woman, you can use your natural strengths—as Cynthia did— to distinguish yourself from your male colleagues on this dimension of "whole-istic" listening: listen more, listen proactively, and "listen" to the nonverbal piece of the message.

You must also be aware of our natural tendency as women to *let* men dominate business discussions, simply because they are men. We need to understand that the male of the species uses talking as a way to dominate others. To prevent this domination, simply "check in" to make sure your listening comes from an internal sense of self-confidence and power, rather than fear and subservience. And make sure that you fully express your own ideas and opinions.

These two myths about women's emotionality and talkativeness are certainly not the only ones that can sabotage us in business. Spend some time to identify other myths that are held as truths in your company: mothers being less devoted to their careers; people without an MBA being unqualified to rise beyond a certain level; women being unable to perform certain job functions. The list goes on and on. When you identify a myth, look for the secret truth that is hidden behind it. Each secret becomes a new tool to enhance your effectiveness, position, and power within your company.

Feminine Leadership Quality #3: Listening to Your Intuition

The stronger right-brain functions of women give us a sixth sense that is often a key component in truly high-level decision making where the risks are many, the information is spotty, and a singular, simple, "right" solution hardly ever exists. Intuition is a method of knowing without using rational thought or your conscious mind. We are all born with the innate ability to dip into our intuitive style of knowing, but not all of us consciously use it.

Intuition is easy to recognize, because it is something you feel. It is the hair rising on the back of your neck or that small, quiet voice coming from within. It is a hunch, a gut feeling. It emanates not from your linear, sequential left brain, but from your artistic, spatial right brain. So there is no question that intuition feels different from rationally driven thought—it is almost insubstantial in comparison! It is a process of gaining information that is independent of your five physical senses. It speaks insights, thoughts, and ideas that resonate as truth to your soul.

Of all the traits of leadership, intuition is the one most strongly associated with women. This association is so strong that it is often referred to as "feminine intuition" and given very little official sanction, or value, in management ranks. Yet it has been proved to be a highly effective leadership tool for both women and men in business. Douglas Dean of the New Jersey Institute of Technology studied the relationship between intuition and business growth. He found that "80 percent of company executives whose corporate profits more than doubled in the past five years had above average precognitive powers."[10] And Weston Agor of the University of Texas in El Paso found that of the two thousand managers he tested, those at the higher levels consistently scored higher in intuition.[11]

The combination of globalization and advancements in technology and communications has made it both necessary and possible for business to operate at the speed of light twenty-four hours a day. As a result, today's leaders are compelled to be rapid-fire decision makers. Usually there is insufficient data, as well as insufficient time, to complete the formal analyses that will reveal the rational decision. In these situations, an executive's insight—intuition—is the key tool that helps him or her find the best solution.

But it is one thing to arrive at a decision intuitively, and quite another to sell that solution to the mostly male management of your organization. Here, you must use analyses and left-brain rationale as your allies. They provide the logical support for your *intuitive* idea and create the perception that it is really a *logical* idea, after all. Nobody but you has to know that it all started with intuition!

Nancy and Candy have a wealth of subjective stories from clients that validate how important listening to their intuition was to the effective leadership of their organizations:

- One woman's gut kept telling her to sit down and talk with a subordinate, yet she never found time. Three weeks later she received that person's resignation. Could she have saved this employee? Her intuition told her she could. But she didn't listen to it.
- Another woman repeatedly "heard" a new business acquaintance's name in her head and finally called him. Through that call, she ended up being hired for her dream job.
- And another woman interviewed a job candidate for a senior position in the firm and had a persistent, nagging feeling that something wasn't quite right. She ignored the feeling and approved the candidate for hire. Eighteen months later the executive retired after he had a mental breakdown and created havoc in the company.

Learning to listen to your intuition requires you to distinguish between true intuition and other kinds of random internal thoughts. Nancy learned the difference when she met a fourth-generation astrologer from India. She told him that she had difficulty recognizing whether her internal thoughts were intuition or something else. He sat back in his chair, holding his stomach as he laughed. "Oh, yes," he told her, "wild imaginings!"

With those two words he helped Nancy understand the difference. Intuition speaks in a soft, gentle, honoring voice. But when there is an internal "thought battle" taking place, your intuition is not participating. Your always-active mind is simply chattering. Intuition doesn't work that way. It is serene wisdom speaking. It is sure, sincere, and knowing. It *is*, and it doesn't find it necessary to participate in an argument with what *isn't*. If your internal voices are battling, you need to stop, get quiet, allow yourself to be emptied of thoughts, and wait. Intuition reveals itself in calm and silence.

Feminine Leadership Quality #4: Unleashing Your Creativity

Before you can begin to value your own creativity, you must acknowledge that you have it in the first place! In truth, all of life is creative. Just as our physiology equips us with a survival instinct, our psychology equips us with an instinct to create. Author Julia Cameron writes in *The Vein of Gold: A Journey to Your Creative Heart*: "Creativity is our species' natural response to the challenges of human experience."

As small children we are constantly creating: building with blocks, coloring, drawing, finger painting, forming strange shapes from clay, working our way up the levels of a computer game, or figuring out how to climb a tree. Yet by the time we reach adulthood, most of us believe that we're not creative, and we demonstrate that belief with lives that reveal very little innovation, imagination, or dynamism.

Where has all of our creativity gone? Most of us began losing our belief in our own creativity when we started school and were taught that there is a "right" way of doing everything, from eating to reading to playing. We were only praised when we built recognizable structures, colored inside the lines, wrote sentences that were grammatically correct, and crafted poems that always rhymed. In reaching for this praise—and avoiding the figurative knuckle rapping that came when we broke these rules—we stifled our own creativity. We began to simply accept preexisting forms and already-proved solutions rather than look for new ones. We learned to follow the rules. Yet the very essence of creativity is *breaking the rules!*

Recently, while completing an exercise from Julia Cameron's groundbreaking book, *The Artist's Way*, Nancy suddenly recalled the exact incident when she lost confidence in her own creativity. The exercise was to write in detail "old enemies of your creative self-worth." According to Cameron, "It is always necessary to acknowledge creative injuries and grieve them. Otherwise, they become creative scar tissue and block your growth."[12]

Nancy hadn't realized that her creativity had been killed, until she flashed back to the day in kindergarten when everyone in her class had made hot plates from clay. Nancy had always loved bright, vivid colors. So instead of choosing the more acceptable browns and greens, she painted her entire plate in swirls of blue and purple. One look at the teacher's expression of disgust told Nancy that she had done something wrong. Then the teacher showed Nancy's plate to the class as an example of what *not* to do! The little boy sitting next to Nancy, whose work had been highly praised, felt so badly that he gave his hot plate to her.

Nancy took the two plates home and gave them to her mother. Rather than share the painful truth, she simply allowed her mother to think that she had made them both. At every Sunday, Thanksgiving, and Christmas dinner for years, both plates were displayed. Each time was a reminder to Nancy of the teacher's message that she was a poor artist—not creative. Imagine!

Creativity is about imagination and innovative problem solving. It is about ideas, and they are the fuel for growth in any company. Whether you are a midlevel manager or the most senior leader, whether you work in the arts or sciences, in government or business, in manufacturing or service, your ideas and your ability to help others generate ideas are a prime source of your value to your organization.

To be creative—and to build an environment in which others can be creative—requires a special combination of open-mindedness and open-heartedness that allows you to think new ideas, dream new dreams, see new pathways and new possibilities. It depends on your right brain, and we women have a special affinity and comfort with right-brain thinking.

The second requirement of creativity is that you have the courage to follow a dream, even when you are the only one who believes in it. For creativity is not just about ideas; it is about the willingness to risk sharing your ideas with others who may reject them. And it is about the willingness to take action to keep your ideas alive, even when no one except you believes in them. This can be a stumbling block for women. In our efforts to be accepted by the male-dominated business world, we seek to fit in with the group that surrounds us. Yet creativity itself demands that we break the rules, stand out, and allow ourselves to express our unique perceptions and individuality. It requires us to draw on a deeper, more independent place within ourselves.

You must begin by nurturing your own creative embers back to life. Each tip that follows will help you rediscover that special condition of open-mindedness and open-heartedness that "primes the pump" of your creativity.

Forget Boundaries and Rules

Boundaries and rules are the enemies of creativity because they force you into preexisting patterns of thinking. The essence of creativity is exploring outside the boundaries and challenging existing rules. If you are having difficulty coming up with ideas, ask yourself if you are subconsciously assuming any boundaries or following any rules that are restricting your mind's ability to make new combinations and create new ideas.

In our A Woman's Way of Leadership professional development program, we illustrate the power of assumed boundaries by giving participants a simple "connect the numbers" puzzle, shown here. We ask them to find three different ways to connect the numbers consecutively with one continuous line, without lifting their pencil from the paper, without going through any number twice, and without crossing over any lines they've drawn.

1	2	3
4	5	6
7	8	9

Most participants quickly draw the obvious "correct" answer: horizontal line from 1 through 3, slanted line to 4, horizontal line to 5 and 6, slanted line to 7, horizontal line to 8 and 9. Then they get stuck. Very few have given us more than this first solution, yet there are many . . . *if* you can overcome the plethora of boundaries that you assumed existed. Here are just three examples of the solutions, along with the assumed rules that they break:

1. Rip the paper into three pieces, line the numbers up in one long row, and draw one single straight line. (Assumed boundaries: cannot rearrange the numbers; cannot rip the paper.)
2. Draw a line from 1 through 3, then a circular line from three around the box until you are back at 4, then straight from 4 through 6, then a smaller circular line around the bottom of the box from 6 to 7, then straight through 8 and 9. (Assumed boundaries: straight lines only; no lines drawn beyond the edges of the box as defined by the numbers.)
3. Start the line at 9 and work backward to 1. (Assumed boundary: *consecutive* means from smallest to largest.)

The ability of rules, both real and assumed, to completely block our creativity has been demonstrated by British psychologist Peter Watson. Watson conducted an experiment, cited in *Cracking Creativity: The Secrets of Creative Genius* by Michael Michalko, in which Watson would present the subject with three numbers in a sequence (2 4 6):

> *He would then ask subjects to explain the number rule for the sequence and to give other examples of the rule. The subjects could ask as many questions as they wished without penalty. . . . The profound discovery Watson made was that most people process the same information over and over until proven wrong, without searching for alternatives, even when there is no penalty for asking questions. . . . In his hundreds of experiments . . . his subjects didn't even try to find out if there is a simpler—or even another—rule.*[13]

By the way, for those of you who like to get the answers to a puzzle, the numeric rule that Peter Watson was illustrating was the most elemental one of all: that the numbers increase!

To be a creative thinker, you must consciously break out of this "follow the rules" mind-set and train yourself instead to dwell in the world of "what if." Constantly asking yourself a possibility-oriented "what if" question will help you examine problems and opportunities from new and different perspectives, identify the rules that you want to ignore (or break), and process information and relationships in a variety of original ways. You can also try the following exercises to encourage your mind to explore new ways of thinking:

- Ask unusual questions, such as "What would the opposite answer look like?" or "What would the most expensive solution be?"
- Think of the problem metaphorically or in pictures and do the same with the ideas you are developing. For example, if you want to reorganize a division to be more entrepreneurial, you might think of a rambunctious, maverick stallion. ("What if our division were like a wild stallion?") Write down what qualities this stallion would possess and then look at what you can do to create these qualities in your division.
- Try combining dissimilar thoughts or ideas that you think are completely incompatible or opposite. This is a standard method in new product/service ideation sessions: "What if we could make . . ." For example, a snack candy that is sweet and sour; a dinner entrée that is salad and dessert; a cookie that is crunchy and soft; a business division that is both family-oriented and profit-driven.

Shift Your Focus from One Solution to Many

Creative employees operate from a deep belief that every problem has multiple solutions. So they focus first on finding lots of solutions rather than on identifying the single right solution.

The creative teams in an advertising agency prove this premise every day. Ultimately, they will produce only one new advertising campaign for a client. But first they develop perhaps a half-dozen alternatives. Often, it is far more difficult for agency and client teams to choose "the best" of the alternatives than it was to come up with all of the options in the first place.

Whenever you tackle a problem or seek an opportunity, consider setting an idea quota for yourself to spur your creative mind to action. Make it big. This will support your development of a greater diversity of thoughts and ideas. When you direct your mind to look for lots of solutions and stop worrying about finding the "right" answer, you silence your internal critic and allow your mind the freedom and non-judgmental space it needs for idea creation.

Thomas Edison is one of our most potent role models for the development of creative ideas. He was such a prolific inventor that even today he owns the record for the most patents ever registered by a single individual (1,093). Most of those patents never amounted to much (proving that he didn't "self-edit" his ideas). But the few that did—such as the electric light bulb, the phonograph, and the movie camera—changed the quality of life for the entire world.

Allow Your Mind Time for Latent Germination

Many a creative genius will tell you that "forgetting about it" is an essential part of finding the solution, especially if you're feeling stuck on a problem. Nancy takes long walks with her dog, Bear; Candy lights candles and soaks in a hot bath. Albert Einstein used to get ideas when he was shaving; mathematician Henri Poincaré would take a vacation to solve a particularly tough problem.

Candy learned about the "sleeping on it" method from Dave Park, her boss at DDB in Los Angeles. He told her that whenever he had a particularly difficult issue to solve, he would think of that problem at night, just before closing his eyes to sleep, and promise himself that the solution would appear before morning. Invariably, the freshly brewed answer would be right there, in his mind, when he awoke the next day.

Often, concepts and ideas need the gift of time to brew and simmer before they can be fully cooked. Living internally with the problem gives your subconscious mind the opportunity to experiment and play with the idea until it comes into specific, conscious clarity. This is when your creative thoughts are growing and developing. To the outside world, it may appear that nothing is happening. But this deep, internal process is a powerful stage of creation.

Set Deadlines for Your Ideas

Creative thinking is an unstructured place for your mind to live. You can actually help the creative productivity of your mind by giving yourself a deadline for ideas. Having a specific, goal-driven timetable (for example, five ideas in five days) provides an impetus for the ideas and gives you a method to monitor your progress and measure your accomplishments. It can be one chapter a month for a writer, one new client a week for a law firm, one new product introduction a year, and so on.

When your creativity is highly activated, you will find that breakthroughs and results occur at a more rapid—yet easier—pace. You will know that you're in the flow of creativity by how you feel: joyous, alive, and connected to that inner light that glows from deep within your soul.

Using Intuition as a Foundation for Intelligent Risk Taking

The four feminine-based strengths of leadership are a good beginning. However, they alone cannot get you into the very pinnacle of management. To reach this particular height requires a combination of skill sets that are rational and emotional, creative and concrete, left and right brain in origin. Truly great leaders are a blend, then, of feminine and masculine traits. And a core trait of these leaders is their penchant for taking risks.

One of the paradoxes of leadership is that precisely because most large organizations are risk averse, they need leaders who are risk-oriented to direct them. Winston Churchill, for example, was one of the greatest leaders of the twentieth century. He also made some dramatic mistakes during his time as Lord of the Admiralty in World War I. The wisdom he gained from these errors was, ironically, the education that prepared him for greatness as Britain's prime minister during World War II. He once said, "Success is going from failure to failure without loss of enthusiasm."

Most corporate leaders have a lot in common with Churchill. One of the reasons behind their rise through the ranks is that they took more risks than their safety-minded peers, and so naturally, they made more mistakes. As a result, they learned more about themselves and more about making decisions in a complex and uncertain business world. This learning set the stage for them to achieve more successes.

One of the foundations that support risk taking is the personality trait of aggression, and boys are simply born with a larger dose of it than girls. Nancy Chodorow, Ph.D., summarizes her research on this subject in *Feminism and Psychoanalytic Theory*: "Across cultures, one pattern is virtually universal. Boys are more aggressive than girls. Aggression is the one behavior that consistently differentiates boys and girls at all ages."[14]

Risk taking, then, is clearly a masculine-based skill set. And it is further reinforced in boys' experiences in their play, especially in team sports. If they make a mistake, the coach tells them to "shake it off" and get back in the game. They learn that "you win some, you lose some" and that the wisdom gained from diagnosing a loss gives them a better chance of winning the next game. Carrying this attitude into the game of business is a natural transition when these boys grow into men. In comparison, most midmanagement women today have less of a natural proclivity toward risk taking, as well as less actual practice.

This world of "risky business" becomes even more foreign and traumatic when a woman reaches a higher rung of her career ladder and suddenly realizes that she is an aberration. One day, after a key promotion, she walks into a room for a meeting with her new peers. She looks around, and for the first time in her life, she is either the only woman in the group or one of a tiny minority. Suddenly, fitting in becomes a primary goal. While her male peers are busy taking risks, she goes through a period of adjustment. And all too often, part of her adjustment is learning to play it safe by following all of the rules. Inevitably, her progress slows. She is not taking the high-stakes actions required to propel herself forward.

Becoming an intelligent risk taker is a daunting task, but if you want to reach a top leadership position, you must first succeed here. And you have the perfect feminine foundation already in place to build this skill set. That foundation is intuition. Although aggression promotes risk taking, it is intuition that enables top executives to be intelligent about the risks they take.

Today's business environment moves like Superman—faster than a speeding bullet. In the most senior management ranks, few decisions are based on clear-cut issues of black and white, right and wrong choices. To lead in that environment, you must be a smart and intuitive risk taker.

"There is not a single day when I don't wish that I had more time and more information to make decisions," says Oxygen Media founder Geraldine Laybourne. "Usually, the higher the stakes, the greater the ambiguity. That's what's so daunting—and so exciting."[15]

Geraldine learned long ago how to make decisions in ambiguous and uncertain situations. But many women have extreme difficulty in this area. They look for safety (and certainty) in their decisions, so they dither in the "paralysis of analysis" syndrome. They wait . . . and wait . . . and wait to have all of the facts and statistics before making a decision. What these women don't understand is that by waiting, they have made a decision! And many times, this decision—which seems so safe at the time—is the riskiest one they could have chosen.

If you want to become more willing and adept at intelligent risk taking, you can begin by recognizing that the world in which you live is a risk-filled place. Whether you are struggling over a personal decision, a career decision, or a business decision, safety is the exception rather than the rule. And regardless of the venue, you must choose between three types of decisions: the safe decision, the risky decision, or no decision. This last type—no decision—exists only in your imagination. For when you truly examine this option, it will fall not in its own category but in one of the other two. It is either a safe decision or a risky one.

Jill Townsend had been a hard-charging sales director in her Fortune 500 insurance company. Then she got the Big Promotion, from sales director to marketing director of her company's health-care division. Suddenly, she found herself responsible for a multimillion-dollar marketing budget, with very little direct experience in key marketing functions such as consumer promotion and advertising.

Jill had been in her new job about a month when it was time to approve the annual advertising plan—a central piece of the marketing program to achieve the annual goals for consumer enrollment in the health plan. Well, Jill didn't really understand much about advertising media, so she decided *not to decide*. Halfway through the consumer enrollment season, when she realized her mistake, it was too late to implement the $15 million advertising plan.

At the end of the consumer enrollment period, the division had missed its goal by 20 percent—the first shortfall in many years. And what about the $15 million that Jill had "saved"? Its effect on the bottom line was more than cancelled out by the future dollars that would be lost due to the enrollment shortfall.

Jill's "no decision" ended up being the riskiest—and costliest—choice she could possibly have made for both her company and her career. Senior management ensured that she wouldn't be around to make the same choice again. She was demoted and moved back into sales after just eight months as director of marketing.

In today's workplace, rarely, if ever, are all of the facts available—especially as you rise higher in management. With broadened management responsibilities, it is inevitable that you will be making more decisions in areas in which you have no direct expertise or experience. This was how Jill got stuck. Rather than relying on the experts who could give her counsel and then applying her own logic and intuition to make the decision, she froze.

To break out of no-decision mode, first give yourself a deadline for making an actual decision—either the safe or the risky one. Then use your tools and resources as a leader to assess the problem and make your decision:

1. Review all available information and analyses.
2. Collect any new information that is critical to the decision, if you can get it in time to meet your decision deadline.
3. Consult the experts whose knowledge and experience can add to your data.
4. Look for any principles or corporate values that can guide you.
5. Remember the lessons learned from your past experiences.
6. Now, listen to your intuition. Can you hear it? If not, listen harder, until you can hear this soft, subtle voice of inner wisdom. It is one of your most trustworthy guides through uncertainty.
7. Once you've completed this process, make your decision and act with conviction.

Intelligent risk taking means examining and understanding the risk in front of you, facing the unknown, and pushing past your fears. You must step through your trepidation and into the decision, and trust that all will be well on the other side (even though you can expect that, sometimes, it won't be). Intuition is the internal guidepost that gives you that added dose of wisdom in your decision making. If you do make a mistake, learn all you can from it and then move forward with a little more wisdom for the next time.

Laura Ramirez's story demonstrates how frightening risk can be for women and the value of intuition in supporting our ability not merely to take those risks but also to take them intelligently. She was the senior vice president of human resources for a large financial institution that had just hired a heavy-hitting CEO to "turn them around." The new CEO sent out a memo inviting the executive management team to his first planning session. Laura, a long-standing member of this team, was the only one whose name was not on the list. She was also the only woman.

Laura's intuition gave her a simple message: "Be in this meeting as part of the team, or you will lose your power to influence the company's management decisions."

Once she became committed to taking the risk, logic stepped in and helped her chart the course for her actions. She could have chosen to confront the CEO, which would have put her in the position of either making him wrong or asking his permission to attend the meeting. Neither outcome was empowering for her. She knew that her position required and merited her membership on the management team, so she simply walked into the meeting early, sat down right next to the CEO's preordained seat, and began chatting calmly with the other "legitimate" team members. In telling the story, she says, "The tension was thick while everyone waited to see the CEO's reaction. I know they expected him to squish me down to ant size."

The CEO walked in, sat down next to Laura, and did nothing!

Without a word being said, she became a member of the executive team from that day forward. She also earned a double dose of respect from the CEO and the other team members for her courage and class in successfully handling a very delicate situation without making anyone wrong.

Laura had just taken the ultimate career risk: putting her job on the line. But her decision was anchored in her ownership of her position and the principle that her function must be represented on the executive team. Laura's actions were also based on a second principle, that of collaboration rather than confrontation with her boss. Laura knew it was more important for her to be a member of the executive team than it was for her to be "right."

If Laura had ignored her intuition, she would never have committed herself to taking this risk. And she would have paid a steep price for her decision to do nothing.

Using Creativity as a Foundation for Big-Picture Thinking

Big-picture thinking pertains almost exclusively to those who live in the topmost tier of management in their organizations. The midlevel manager's effectiveness in her work tends to depend more on her detail and managerial skills than on her vision ability. But at a certain point in every career, too much detail focus sets the stage for failure rather than continued advancement. Few companies have ever succeeded because the president or CEO was a great detail person. They succeeded because the CEO had a vision—a destination somewhere "out there"—a sweeping view of where the company would be in the future.

For women, being truly visionary is a particular challenge. Just as we don't tend to think big about ourselves and our careers, neither do we tend to think big for our companies. Yet vision building is, like risk taking, a must-have skill set for leadership. And, just as our feminine-based intuition is the foundation for intelligent risk taking, we can tap into the right-brain skill of creativity as our foundation for developing vision as a leadership strength.

Vision is the focal point that exists out in the distance of time. It begins as a purely creative idea that becomes a desire, a dream, and a direction. It is what keeps the company and its individual employees on track, despite the plethora of short-term opportunities and crises that occur daily, tempting all to go off-road, into directions unknown.

Precisely because of this focusing power of vision, the sooner you acquire this leadership skill in building the future of your career and your company, the more powerful you will be. Many of the tools that will help you build creativity can also be applied to big-picture thinking. In addition to those already mentioned, here are a few more logic-based exercises that will give you practice in building this new leadership skill set.

Seek First to Understand the Vision

As a younger employee, you will have few actual vision-building opportunities for your company. But you will have many learning opportunities. Whatever your level within your organization, you will be more successful if you understand what your top management wants to achieve. Start by asking your boss what top management's vision is for the company. If the boss doesn't know, keep asking until you find someone who does. When you actually see your company's official vision statement, ask questions until you're absolutely sure you understand what it means. As soon as you know where the president and CEO want the company to go, you can align your efforts to support theirs.

Understanding the vision is also good practice. Through this exercise you will learn the difference between a strong vision and a flawed one. Knowing this will help you learn how to create a powerful vision yourself, once you are in a top leadership position.

Develop the Vision Habit

We all know how difficult it is to spend quality time planning for the future with the fires of urgency continually licking at our heels. Companies tend to evaluate performance based on specific projects, crisis handling, quarterly profits, and a whole variety of other short-term goals.

During most of your career, your ability to be a visionary thinker will be neither recognized nor rewarded by your company. But if you want a truly high-powered career, if your goal is to end up running any large organization, then your ability to create a vision and motivate your employees to achieve it is a critical qualification for the job. And like any other skill, practice is the only way to develop excellence.

Routinely ask yourself, "What can I do this week that will make a difference in my division and my company five or ten years from now?" This kind of thinking requires a commitment of at least two hours a week so that you can identify the long-term issues and then formulate the vision, goals, and specific actions required to achieve them. This time commitment can be easily abandoned because it only involves you. It's not important to anybody else. But ultimately it will be critical to your career success.

One way to ensure that you keep this two-hour commitment is to schedule it into your week in advance, just as you would schedule any other high-priority meeting. If a true crisis does arise that requires you to cancel this meeting, always reschedule it in the same week. And be sure to write down your thoughts on long-term issues, vision, goals, and specific action steps. This gives you a written record and a tracking device against which to measure your progress.

Finally, remember that you are building a *vision habit*, and like any other habit, it will take time and diligence to develop.

Think So Big It Seems Impossible

The dynamics of a vision-development process for your company are, in many ways, similar to the process you followed in Chapter 2 when you developed your Activating Vision. In both domains, your vision will be about the far-off future, and it will be so big that it seems impossible to achieve. But employees can accomplish remarkable feats when their imaginations are engaged and their energies properly directed. They can transform today's hyperbole into tomorrow's reality. Your job, as their leader, is to give them something big enough and noble enough to be worthy of their devotion.

Perhaps the best example in recent history of a big vision, and the remarkable accomplishment that it inspired, was the way John F.

Kennedy explained the space program to the American people. He did not talk in terms of complex goals or theories but of a single grand achievement—an unprecedented accomplishment in the history of nations: "Someday an American will land on the moon." He effectively translated a huge endeavor—making America the preeminent nation in outer space—into a single visual symbol that every American could understand and get excited about achieving.

At the time Kennedy articulated this vision, its achievement seemed impossible. Yet it was precisely this pairing of a grand symbol with the impossibility of the dream that galvanized Americans to get to work and make it happen.

As soon as you have clearly defined the grand vision for your company—its future destination—your own decision making becomes much clearer because the vision serves as a constant guide. You must always hold fast to the vision, because it provides the key context against which you can judge the wisdom or folly of every decision that is made and every action that is undertaken within your company, starting with your own.

Of all six leadership strengths, intelligent risk taking and big-picture thinking often appear to be the leaders of the pack. When we talk about why leaders are great, their vision-building and risk-taking abilities are frequently the foremost factors in our observations. Is this because visionaries and risk takers are the boldest—the most masculine—expressions of leadership? After all, they must possess aggression and an extra measure of ego (that is, belief in their own ability to succeed in the most uncertain of conditions), which are both male-oriented traits.

But just as most great kings in history were supported by equally outstanding queens, these two leadership skills actually depend on the feminine leadership qualities of intuition and creativity for their very existence. This relationship between the masculine and feminine sides of leadership always comes as a huge "Aha!" to the women in our A Woman's Way of Leadership course when they understand that leadership is, at its very center, a predominantly feminine state of being.

Two Final "Aha!"s About Leadership

Now our leadership conversation comes full-circle, back to the very first exercise you completed in Chapter 1, when you listed three or four off-the-top-of-your-head business leaders and the characteristics that you admired about them. Most of your names were probably male, and a good number of the traits you listed were probably masculine, as well. Yet in this chapter, we have put forth a fundamentally different image of leadership.

Now we would like you to refer to the exercise you completed in Chapter 1, in which you listed three leaders from your own personal experience and then named three characteristics that made each one a great leader. (If you've tossed this list, please take a few minutes to recreate it.)

Virtually every woman who has participated in our leadership program has completed this exercise. Below are the characteristics we collected from fifty women. We have separated them into different categories. If you have additional traits, add them to this list:

Communication and Motivation
Good communicator

Good listener; listens before speaking

Empathetic/understanding; compassionate; caring; supportive

Interested in the "whole self"

Eloquent speaker; speaks into area of relatedness;
    well-spoken/articulate

Inspiring/motivating

Good relationship builder; social; worked well with people; able to
    be on the same level; treated everyone with respect, regardless
    of status; down-to-earth; nonthreatening/supportive in con-
    frontation; not condescending; direct; sincere; made an effort to
    get to know employees and remember them; created trusting
    relationships

Unselfish; giving; generous with time

Positive; optimistic

Team builder; inspired each member of the team; acknowledged employees' contributions

Politically correct; diplomatic

Willing to say "I don't know"

Taught/developed by example; advanced mentoring skills; role model

Calm/reasonable under pressure; level head; even tempered/consistent; easygoing

Charismatic

Good delegator

Believed in me/demanding; allowed me to work independently

Encouraged me to accept risk; challenged my skill set; pushed me toward higher goals

Totally relinquished power and control

Empowered others

Other Leadership Skills
Strategic thinker

Visionary thinker

Creative thinker

Risk taker

Took charge; prioritized; goal-focused

Leadership Character
Ethical

Integrity; honesty

Commanded respect; quiet power

Confident

Assertive; able to be aggressive when necessary

Hard worker; excellent work ethic

Competent; multieducated; well-rounded; knowledgeable;
   intelligent

As you look through these lists, you will notice that at least 75 percent of the traits that we admire about outstanding leaders are in the
communication and motivation category, and several others in the *leadership character* category are also communication-related characteristics.
Here is our first "Aha!": Great leaders can excel in many different areas,
but the one in which they *must* excel is communication.

In addition to understanding the importance of this communication
dimension of leadership, one more dimension is pivotal to completing
the lessons on leadership in this chapter: the *being* versus *doing*
dimension.

For the rank-and-file employees in a company, the "doing" aspects
of their work are foremost in importance if they are to excel in their
jobs. But if you are a leader (or destined to become one), the picture
becomes more complex. The most potent leaders understand that their
power comes not from the specific "doing" tasks that they alone accomplish. It comes from their ability to guide and motivate many others in
the organization. Employees, then, must want to follow their leader.
And we follow our leaders not so much because of what they do but
because of who they are—and what they are—to us.

With this new theory in mind, look back at the leadership list once
more and divide the characteristics into three groups:

1. *Being* traits: for example, "good listener" is a *being* trait because a
   person doesn't *do* good listening; a person either is, or is not, a
   good listener.
2. *Doing* traits: "taught/developed by example" is a *doing* trait
   because it is a specific task that the leader does.

3. *Dual* traits: "team builder" is a *dual* trait, because a leader either is, or is not, a team builder; but he also takes specific actions to build the team.

You have probably assigned at least two-thirds of these characteristics to the *being* category. Several more are *dual* traits. All in all, at least 80 percent of this list of leadership attributes is on the *being* end of the spectrum. "Aha!" If you want to be a great leader, you must be authentic! Being true to yourself is the most basic of requirements if you want others to be true to you as their leader.

If you happen to be female, being authentic means honoring your natural feminine qualities. They are central to who you are, not only as a woman but also as a leader in your organization. So ultimately, for that little round peg to hold onto her structural integrity and her power, all she needs to do is *stay round*. Instead of shaving away parts of herself, she gently shaves the sides of the square hole. Then she can go through to the other side . . . just the way she is.

CHAPTER 9

ENRICHING CONCEPTS FOR YOUR CAREER

Dance Lesson #9: Your career is like a dance marathon. To move through it with power, grace, and energy to spare, take along these six internal dance partners.

Your ability to consistently derive professional growth and personal enrichment from your work is one of the keys to your vitality and longevity in your career. To that end, we will introduce you in this chapter to six Career-Enriching Concepts that will allow you to function in your work life with more mental clarity, decisiveness, and fun. You will experience greater effectiveness with less daily effort and stress. Whether you are a fresh, young manager or a seasoned veteran in top management, these concepts will add value, richness, and texture to your experiences, your actions, and your management style. They can help you go the distance, feeling enriched and invigorated rather than drained and depleted from the experiences of work. Here are the six Career-Enriching Concepts:

1. *Be a cockeyed optimist.* It will empower you to take bigger risks and achieve the impossible. It will make every task easier and every day more fun.
2. *Establish clear boundaries for your identity and your time.* Separating who you are from what you do will enable you to set

boundaries on your time, and put your work in its proper place as just one facet in your multifaceted life.

3. *Be intentional rather than effortful.* Approaching every goal with intention magnifies the power of your efforts. This keeps your mental focus on the end result, so your physical efforts can take you there more directly and effortlessly.

4. *Listen to yourself for approval, not others.* You will make more powerful contributions at work when your actions and decisions become your own. When your self-worth comes not from what the external world thinks of you but from what *you* think of you, your self-esteem will increase, stress will diminish, and more satisfaction will occur from every step you take in the dance that is your career.

5. *Focus your being in the present.* Devoting your single-minded attention to *now* increases your productivity and stimulates your creativity. This focus on the present brings calm into your life. In this mental environment, creative ideas can flow forth.

6. *Accept mistakes in yourself and others, and learn from them.* Mistakes are inevitable in business, and they are beneficial to your career growth if you concentrate on learning from them, rather than assigning blame.

These six Career-Enriching Concepts are energy boosters. They will ease your career journey by helping you choose where to devote your energies and by reducing the amount of effort you must put forth to achieve each result. Like a booster system on a rocket, they will help you arrive at your career destination with as efficient an expenditure of energy as possible. In other words, you get what you want, but with a lot less work. This is why some people seem to work less and achieve more than others.

To understand the relationship among physical effort, energy boosters, and results, think in terms of weights on a two-sided scale. The weight on the right side represents the result that you seek. The weight of the result depends on how difficult it will be to reach that end. To achieve it, you have to put enough weight on the left side of the scale— the *effort* side—to make the result tip up in your favor. If the only factor that you contribute on the left side of the scale is *work*, then this one variable must deliver 100 percent of the weight required to achieve the result on the other side. You can reduce the amount of work required to tip the scale if you add another factor—the small *energy booster* weights that are contributed by using the six Career-Enriching Concepts.

When you develop these six concepts into daily habits, your actual tasks at work may change little, but your experience of work will be transformed as you begin to achieve bigger results with less actual effort. You will feel more emotional satisfaction and less personal sacrifice, more comfort and less hardship, more joy and less struggle.

Career-Enriching Concept #1: Be a Cockeyed Optimist

Did you ever hear the story of the two little farm girls whose father took them into the barn one day, and inside the barn was one gigantic pile of . . . manure? The first little girl turned up her nose at the smelly heap. "Ooh, Daddy, this is just a big pile of poop!" the little girl exclaimed, and she marched right out of that barn.

The second little girl, in the meantime, ran straight toward the pile and started digging frantically.

"What on earth are you doing, girl?" her father asked her.

"Oh, Daddy! With a pile this big," she said, "there must be a pony in here somewhere, and I'm gonna find him!"

It doesn't really matter whether or not the second little girl found her pony. What does matter is all the fun she had looking for it! She was a *cockeyed optimist*, and her belief in the innate goodness—and good news—in the world around her transformed every reality into something wonderful. In every problem she saw possibility; in every challenge she found a way to triumph. Even in the midst of adversity—even when she faced a huge pile of manure—she expected something good. This expectation was her first step to actually creating the reality that would fulfill it.

Whether you call it cockeyed optimism, positive thinking, or looking at the world through rose-colored glasses, this concept is certainly one of the keys to achieving health, wealth, and happiness. *Investor's*

Business Daily, a newspaper that has spent years studying leaders and successful people, lists a positive attitude as the number one trait of this high-powered group. It is the same trait that medical journals cite as a central factor in patients' recovery from serious diseases, such as cancer. Cockeyed optimism nurtures your emotions, tempers your logic, and magnifies your physical efforts—especially when you are in a position to spread your optimism to others in your organization.

Candy had been chief operating officer of DDB's Los Angeles office less than a year when she encountered the most severe financial problem of her career. She reviewed the account managers' annual revenue estimates in August and realized that the agency was roughly 20 percent short of its multimillion-dollar goal for the year. This was Candy's first year in the revenue "driver's seat," and she knew that her head would be the first one chopped off by the corporate guillotine if the group missed the target by 20 percent, which amounted to a huge, seven-figure number no matter how you looked at it! Generating 20 percent additional annual income from current and new clients in only four short months seemed a frightening, mind-freezing challenge. Candy spent the first day frantically searching her left brain for ideas—some rational pathway to success. Finally, she realized that her only hope was to be fearless, daring, and incredibly optimistic. Her first job was to convince her management team that they were up to the task—that they were capable of accomplishing a miracle!

First, Candy told her boss about the "little revenue problem." She and Dave Park had shared many crises over the years, but this was the first time he had turned white in reaction to bad news. She charged ahead and reviewed her ideas to add revenue, showing him that it was possible—and helping him regain his natural color and share in her optimistic outlook by the time the group met. Candy knew that if she and Dave both believed, they would be able to convince the rest of the team.

In the management meeting, Candy outlined the financial shortfall and detailed her list of opportunities. Several members of the team told her it was an impossible task (in a variety of colorful idioms reserved for such occasions).

"Look, I'm not saying this is a little problem," she told them (using a few idioms of her own). "But it is possible, and there are lots of ways to do it! We could do it with just one big new business win, or a bunch of smaller wins, or gains from existing accounts." They were still skeptical, so Candy challenged them to outdo her ideas with some big revenue possibilities of their own.

They did! The final list represented three times the revenue they needed. At this, the group became optimistic that they could succeed (after all, they only needed a 33 percent success rate to reach the target number). Then they committed to individual responsibilities, specific goals, and deadlines and set to work.

What happened? Miracles!

One temporary new account alone brought in half of the total revenue they needed and in just three months! The remainder of the money materialized—little by little—from a true potpourri of current and new client projects. By the end of the year the group had met the goal—and learned something even more valuable: they could achieve the impossible. All they needed was a little support, a little shove, from a couple of cockeyed optimists.

Cockeyed optimism can be the rocket fuel for business growth (as in this story) and for career growth. Just look at the very top of any organization. How many presidents and CEOs are pessimists, or even "objective," about their own abilities and the ability of their teams to beat the odds and triumph in the marketplace? The answer very likely will be none.

When Warren Bennis wrote *On Becoming a Leader*, he cited "optimism, faith, and hope" as the fifth of ten personal and organizational characteristics required for leaders to deal effectively with chaos and change in their businesses. Strong leaders demonstrate an optimistic view of life in all of their activities. After all, would you join the leader who announced, "This job will be really hard and we don't have much chance of succeeding, but follow me anyway!"? Or would you follow the leader who said, "Follow me! This job will be hard work, but it will be lots of fun and we have a great chance of achieving our goals!"?

It is the cockeyed optimists who rise to top management positions in dynamic, complex organizations, because they are the leaders who can triumph over every crisis. When they are faced with the most extreme challenges, they believe that success is not just possible but the inevitable outcome of their efforts.

Leadership and cockeyed optimism go hand in hand. If you want to be a great leader, you can begin by becoming a great optimist. The following four exercises will help you develop a new daily habit of cockeyed optimism. We encourage you not to select just the easy ones or the ones that seem the most obvious. If you truly desire to be a committed cockeyed optimist, then use all four exercises to ensure that this particular muscle called optimism is completely developed and a permanent part of the rest of your life.

1. Choose Your Words Wisely

In our very verbal world, there is no such thing as "objective reality," because once we use words to describe that reality we have interpreted it. We have made it subjective. And with those same words we have given the outside world the input necessary to interpret us. Words themselves have tremendous influence over our inner emotional states and the way the outside world perceives us. Yet we are very seldom truly conscious of that influence. All too often we choose words that build negative emotions or diminish our ability to act powerfully—and be perceived powerfully—in our world.

To illustrate this concept, we ask participants in our A Woman's Way of Leadership program to complete the following exercise. We invite you to play along, so you'll get a firsthand understanding of this idea:

1. Spend a few moments allowing yourself to feel the physiological sensations you experience when you're frightened. Did you feel your muscles tense, your stomach start churning, your breath quickening, your heart beating faster, your palms getting sweaty?
2. Now, stand up and shake yourself off to clear your thoughts and your feelings.
3. Next, take a couple of quiet minutes and allow yourself to feel the physiological sensations you experience when you're excited. Did you feel your muscles tense, your stomach start churning, your breath quickening, your heart beating faster, your palms getting sweaty?

"Aha!" Your physiological reactions are the same! But your ability to act dynamically in the outside world is certainly not. When your mind thinks "frightened," your cerebral cortex is bypassed and your body immediately goes into "fight or flight" mode. This explains why it is so difficult to think clearly when you are truly afraid. But when you change the label from "frightened" to "excited," you transform your subjective experience from unpleasant to pleasant. When you are excited, your cerebral cortex remains engaged, so your mind is as active as your body. You can still think!

Just imagine how much more successful—and fun—your life would be if you could simply interpret your experience of each new business challenge or crisis as excitement rather than fright. This is merely one example of how you can consciously change your experience of an event by using more positive language to describe it.

You can have a dramatic influence on your life by consciously using words that produce positive emotional states and empower you to reach ahead, not hold you back from taking the actions that will achieve your goals. Here are just a few examples to help you replace your negative interpretations with positive ones, leading you to more powerful actions:

- Instead of describing your emotional reaction as "angry" when a client asks for more facts to justify your recommendations, tell yourself that you are encouraged that the client is so interested.
- Instead of describing the amount of work and responsibility you are handling as "overwhelming," think of yourself as in demand.
- Instead of telling yourself that you are stupid in a new situation, remember that you are discovering and learning.

2. Choose a Mantra and Speak It at the Start of Every Day

A mantra is a kind of verbal formula, a special combination of words that are repeated several times in succession. For thousands of years the Hindus have used them to invoke their deities and have believed that mantras possess magical powers. In a similar way, we can use this magical power to set us on a positive, proactive mental and emotional course each day.

If this sounds too good to be true, just try a simple exercise. For the first three days, upon waking, set a positive expectation by speaking the following thought (or something like it) three times:

Today will be a fabulous day. I will be focused and productive at work. My decisions and my actions will be effortless. I will have fun.

At the end of each day, write down what you accomplished and how you were feeling during the course of the day.

For the next three days, upon waking, set a negative expectation by speaking the following thought (or something like it) three times:

Today will be a difficult day. I will experience lots of problems and frustrations at work. It will be hard to accomplish anything today. I will have a stressful day.

Go through the same writing exercise at the end of each day. After the six days, compare your notes to determine the impact that your mantra had on shaping your actions, your experiences, and your accomplishments.

This may seem like an artificial and ridiculous exercise. "After all," you may say to yourself, "people don't consciously start their day intending to make it hard for themselves." This is absolutely true. Nobody ever does it *consciously*. But every one of us has done it *unconsciously*. To break this negative-expectation habit, you must catch yourself in the act. The next time someone asks you how your day is going, be aware of your instinctive answer. Here's a hard-to-believe but true-life example from one of Candy's phone conversations with a new business associate:

"So, how are things going?" she asked, expecting to hear something positive.

"Terrible! Today's been a lousy day. Nothing's gone right."

"Well, today is almost over. Maybe tomorrow will be better."

"No, it won't. I know what I've got to do tomorrow, and it'll be just as bad as today."

"Well, after tomorrow it's the weekend." Candy was still struggling to help her friend find the silver lining at the edge of his very large, self-created cloud.

"Yeah, and the weekend will be terrible, too."

Of course, Candy's friend did have a terrible next day and a terrible weekend. And a lot of it was self-created. If he had merely changed his expectations, he would have set an entirely new chain of events in motion, and he would have transformed his experiences.

Choosing a mantra for yourself and reciting it a few times at the beginning of every day is simply a mechanism to convert your unconscious, negative attitudes into conscious, positive ones. It is a simple tool to help you develop a daily habit of cockeyed optimism.

3. Expect Abundance

Expectations and outcomes are not independent variables in your life. They are organically linked in your psyche, just as cause is linked to effect. Your expectations have a profound influence on the direction your life will take and on the outcomes that you will produce. Just how profound an influence it can have is demonstrated by a study of convicted criminals, cited in Brian Tracy's book *Maximum Achievement*: "90 percent of prisoners interviewed by psychologists reported that they had been told over and over again by their parents when they were growing up that 'Someday, you're going to end up in jail.'"[1] That's a pretty frightening correlation between expectations and outcomes, don't you think?

As an adult, you get to choose your own expectations. An inevitable part of this choice, particularly if you want to live in a world of abundance, is making the decision to leave behind any expectations of scarcity that may have been an integral part of your upbringing. Each American family has its elders who are Depression-era survivors. This experience of massive deprivation and scarcity left an indelible mark of financial fear on the entire generation. They saw fortunes disappear in a day, the successful become destitute, and the employed become job-less. Most of them carried these impressions deep within them for the remainder of their lives. They lived in a world governed by their own fears—of loss, of not having, of poverty.

One of Nancy's clients tells this story about her father, Harry, who was fourteen years old with seven brothers and sisters when the Great Depression began. Harry's father lost almost everything. Their family moved from a big white house on several acres of manicured lawn to a three-bedroom brownstone on a small, square lot. The kids picked fruits and vegetables on their neighbors' farms and took their pay in food so the family would have enough to eat. Clothes were passed down, hair was cut at home, shoes were worn only in winter. Harry lived in a world where there was always just barely enough for all and never a sur-plus. It was a world where must-have needs were met, but wished-for desires went unfulfilled.

For the rest of his life, Harry lived with the fear of not having enough money and of losing whatever he was able to acquire. He built a lucrative business and then lost it when he was drafted to fight in World War II. He never trusted the stock market, so while others were making huge returns in the eighties and nineties, the earning power of his money was actually shrinking as it sat in low-return, "safe" fixed-interest accounts. He worried so much about protecting what he had that he was never able to take the risk that is required to grow it into something bigger. Instead, he painstakingly worried it into something smaller. *He expected scarcity in his world . . . and that's exactly what he received.*

You don't have to be poor to suffer from a "scarcity mentality," liv-ing in fear that there will never be enough to fully satisfy the needs of all. Scarcity thinking is not just about money. It can dominate your thinking about almost everything in your life: power, friendship, love, acceptance, promotions, time, hobbies, respect. The list goes on and on. The fundamental principle in a world of scarcity is that someone gets more, and someone else gets less. This thinking puts you into a defensive mode of action in which your emphasis becomes *protecting* rather than *risking* and *growing*.

Women in business often fall prey to this thinking because they are typically competing on an uneven playing field with their male counterparts. But just like Harry, when you expect scarcity, you often receive it. This happens because your expectations cause you to behave in certain ways that actually create the outcome you fear.

Christina Rowland, a senior manager and team captain on a critical project for her company, began living in a world of power scarcity when her boss suddenly hired Breelynn Temple as a strategic consultant on Christina's project. He positioned Christina to the partnering company as the project's team leader and Breelynn as the strategy expert (a role previously owned by Christina).

Trouble arose straightaway. Breelynn began working directly with the partner company's most senior executive, often independently of Christina and her team. Christina was convinced that Breelynn was undermining her leadership on the project and her company's relationship with the partner company. The scarcity mentality for Christina was her belief that there could be only one strategic thinker on the project. Fearing loss of this role, she went into protection mode. Rather than keep her energies focused on the project, she redirected her focus to Breelynn. For weeks Christina fixated on what Breelynn was or was not doing. She became openly competitive with Breelynn, which created divisiveness within the entire team. Christina's boss interpreted the situation as a personality conflict and faulted Christina for creating the problem. He hired Nancy to coach Christina, in hopes that she would overcome her problem.

Nancy advised Christina that there was plenty of work for two senior strategists. She coached Christina to make full use of her own strengths, take on the role of an "abundance leader" rather than a scarcity-driven competitor to Breelynn, and direct Breelynn's talents instead of combatting them. Christina couldn't see how taking these steps would possibly benefit her, but she agreed to trust Nancy and take her coaching. She began giving specific tasks and responsibilities to Breelynn and treating her as a valuable part of the team.

Ironically, when Christina began including Breelynn as a team member in meetings, the partner company's key project manager began noticing some of the root issues that had originally disturbed Christina: the only ideas that Breelynn valued were her own; she often openly criticized other team members; she rarely shared credit. And when Christina reestablished her strategic ownership, her boss noticed that Breelynn's contributions were not valuable enough to overcome her other weaknesses. It wasn't long before he notified Breelynn that her services were no longer required.

Like Christina, you can reverse your scarcity thinking by consciously coaching yourself to expect that there will always be more than enough. When you live in a land of plenty, your actions are grounded in *receiving* rather than *struggling for*. You become empowered. You begin reaching for more because you expect to get it. When you expect success, your actions are much more likely to take you there. This happens because you are focusing your efforts in positive, proactive directions, not spending your physical and psychic energy in fear-based, defensive activities. Your thoughts, your energies, and your actions are devoted to the joyous areas of growth and expansion as opposed to the stress-filled areas of protection and control.

4. Ask Yourself Positive Questions

Your brain is responsible for coordinating and controlling your bodily functions, interpreting your sensory impulses, and exercising your emotions and thoughts. In short, it is designed to support all of your thought processes and your actions—to do everything possible to keep your life going.

One of your brain's primary responsibilities is to collect and store information in preparation for answering your questions and fulfilling your needs. Dr. Robert J. Maurer explains this function of the brain in his seminar series, "Creating a Successful Life." He contends (and research studies support) that how you view life is influenced by the questions you ask yourself. If you ask only negative questions, then negative information is what your brain gathers to answer you. But if you ask positive, empowering questions, your brain delivers positive, empowering responses. The list below shows how differently your brain will support you, depending on how you ask the question:

Negative Questions	*Negative Answers*
Why am I always getting passed over for promotion?	Because your analysis skills are poor, you are not participating with the team, you are not . . .
Why can't I ever get the plum assignments?	Because you're not charismatic, not smart enough, not outgoing enough . . .
Why can't I get a decent raise?	Because you're not working hard enough, not the most senior in the group, not well-liked by your boss, not . . .

Positive Questions	*Positive Answers*
What can I do to make sure I get the next promotion?	Take on that extra analytical assignment, make sure your boss sees what you are contributing to the team, come up with a great new product recommendation . . .
How can I get the next plum assignment?	Go to your boss and ask for it, tell him why you could do a great job on that assignment . . .
How can I get a 20 percent raise?	Deliver an outstanding assignment on project XYZ, and then ask for the raise, come up with a big idea to save money for the company, change companies . . .

These examples demonstrate that the very nature of your questions creates the beginnings of whatever success or failure will ultimately occur in your life. "Why?" questions are inherently negative and will keep you stuck in the problem. "What?" and "How?" questions are inherently positive, and in answering them you will find the opportunity or the solution that arises from the problem. You can effortlessly turn your world around by training yourself to ask positive questions so your brain can respond with positive, life-affirming answers.

This perpetually positive viewpoint is a sure sign of a cockeyed optimist.

Career-Enriching Concept #2: Establish Clear Boundaries for Your Identity and Your Time

Women who are especially career-driven often allow their personal identities to merge with their career identities. When this happens, a woman's sense of self-worth becomes completely defined by—and completely dependent on—her position and responsibilities within the company. This dependency marks her transition from the status of employee to the status of prisoner. But the bars and chains are of her own making.

Only when Candy began to consider leaving her advertising career did she realize the extent to which her identity had merged with her job. She had spent twenty years on a driven, persistent climb up the corporate ladder of her company. Finally, her business card said "Comanaging Director, Chief Operating Officer." Except it wasn't just her business card; it was her *identity card*. It told her and everyone around her that Candy Deemer was somebody important, somebody powerful, somebody smart, somebody successful . . . SOMEBODY. Who would she be without this job? Without this title? Until she could find substantive answers to these questions, Candy couldn't even think of leaving her job—and her identity—behind.

Nancy's coaching helped her find the solution. Nancy asked Candy to make a list of her talents and strengths. Through this exercise she realized that her self-worth, her power, and her career success were the result of her talents, not her title. To quote Nancy, "Talents, my dear, are permanent and portable." They will remain with you long after any job—or any career—has ended.

Mastering this separation between who you are and what you do is an incredibly freeing experience. It frees you from stress; it frees you from bondage to an organization that can devour you and your time.

Once you have reclaimed your independent identity, you will feel free to reclaim your time as well, to leave your company at night to be with your family and friends or leave the company for good if you find another, larger career opportunity. It is in this freedom that your power truly resides. Controlling the boundaries of your identity and your time are mandatory prerequisites if you want to live a balanced, harmonious life.

Professional, career-driven women are particularly prone to losing these boundaries. As we struggle up the ladder of male-dominated organizations, we buy into the belief that protecting these boundaries will have a negative impact on our careers. We believe that we have to be better, brighter, more aggressive, and harder working to outshine our automatically advantaged male peers. But this belief system leaves no room for boundaries.

The outside world often interprets this lack of boundaries as a sign of complete devotion to the company. In truth, this lack of boundaries is the warning system of a career that is about to hit troubled times. For what good is this kind of devotion if it isn't accompanied by results and effective leadership? How often is the overworked, workaholic manager actually performing below her capabilities because fatigue hampers her creativity, her emotional stability, and her decision-making powers? What message is the workaholic manager sending to her superiors about her ability to be an effective leader of the team? When her boss sees her working into the wee hours every night, long after many of her subordinates have gone home, who will he or she think is managing whom?

The next time you face a high-stress crisis in your company, just ask yourself: "Do I want the key decision maker to be the already stressed out and fatigued workaholic or the rested and ready-to-go executive?"

Here are three exercises to help you establish boundaries and then protect your new boundaries against would-be encroachers on your identity and your time.

1. Give Yourself an Identity Checkup

Make sure your self-identity is clearly separate from your work. Make a list of your talents and carry it around in your wallet. Look at it every week or so to remind yourself that the only person who owns these talents and the only person who can develop them further is *you*. They are merely on loan to your company while you are employed there.

2. Set Some Basic Boundaries on Your Time

Women are far too likely to keep their personal lives flexible to accommodate the time requirements of their work and of their needy coworkers. They make few personal time commitments to exercise, friends, entertainment, enrichment classes, or hobbies. Their flexible schedule translates into an empty personal life. Unwittingly, they have created the perfect growth environment for the virtually unlimited expansion of their work time.

Empty space doesn't like to stay empty. Neither does empty time. To keep your free time from becoming work time, schedule something else to fill it first. Then remind yourself that this free-time appointment on your calendar is just as important as any work-related meeting. Keep your commitment to it, just as you keep your commitments to your work. If something critical does require you to cancel it, *reschedule*, just as you would reschedule any other important work-related appointment.

If you are already in the workaholic cycle, here are two suggestions to begin establishing your time boundaries. First, make an ironclad promise to leave your work by a set (and reasonable) time the same three nights every week. Maybe you leave by 6 P.M. every Monday, Wednesday, and Friday so you can eat dinner with your family at 6:30. Track your actual performance on a weekly basis. If you're failing to meet this goal, look at your workload for tasks or responsibilities that can be delegated or eliminated. Don't be afraid to give a few of them to somebody else. After all, if it doesn't work, you can always take it back or delegate it anew.

Second, make a commitment to one regular, non-work-related activity every week. This could be dinner with friends, a class at the local college, an exercise class, volunteer time with a local charity, or any other social activity. The operative word here is *activity*. Just sitting passively at the movies will not do. When you are actively engaged with others, you are giving of yourself. This act of giving is what opens you up for receiving enrichment from others.

3. Start Saying No

We women are particularly reticent about saying no, even with our subordinates. As we keep saying yes, we get sucked into an expanded workload and an expanded workday. For example, when a subordinate asks for help with a project, the female boss will often say yes and end up doing part of the project herself. A male boss would have first encouraged the subordinate to work harder or longer to finish the project. Then, if necessary, he would have found another subordinate to help. But he would have left the responsibility for completion with the first subordinate, where it belonged. In this scenario, the male boss had a boundary already established, and he protected it. His "no" was also more empowering for his subordinate.

Once you are willing to say no when it's appropriate to protect your boundaries, your own value and power will increase within your organization. You will no longer be an "easy mark," because your ability to say no is precisely what makes your "yes" more meaningful. You and your time will become a precious resource, rather than something to be taken for granted.

As a first step in your "no" training, be conscious of every request for your time and attention at work and stop yourself from automatically saying yes. Take a deep breath, drink some water, do some quick doodles on your notepaper, or find something else that can function as your personal "pause button," an interrupter to stop your instinctive "yes" reaction. Then ask yourself a couple of simple questions to determine if "no" might be the wiser answer:

- What will I gain if I say yes, and what will I have to give up?
- Am I taking a big risk or a little risk if I say no?
- What does the employee gain if I say yes, and what does he or she gain if I say no?

The profound realization that the boundaries of your life are determined not by the outside world but by the inside world within you can be a critical transformation. Only you can change the time equations and the identity equations that add up to your life. Your career should be a highly ego-gratifying endeavor. But no matter how much you love what you do, remember that it is only *what you do*, not *who you are*. In this context, a life with boundaries holds more personal freedom—and offers more personal possibilities—than a life without them.

Career-Enriching Concept #3: Be Intentional Rather than Effortful

Intentionality is the difference between "I'll try" and "I'll do it." If you perform every action from the mind-set of intentionality, you will achieve the results you desire with far less effort. Intentionality magnifies the power of effort because it keeps your mental energies focused on the end result and your activities devoted to a process that will achieve the goals you desire. In his book *Flow: The Psychology of Optimal Experience*, author Mihaly Csikszentmihalyi says of intentions: "They act as magnetic fields, moving attention toward some objects and away from others, keeping our mind focused on some stimuli in preference to others."[2]

If you want proof of the magnetic properties of intentions, simply be aware over the next few days of the different results produced by coworkers who say "I'll try" when given a task versus those who say "I'll do it."

Nancy coaches her clients to clearly define the specific outcomes they desire from their actions, because she has learned from personal experience how powerful intentional actions are in achieving her own success. In Nancy's consulting business, she has made a commitment to complete a specific number of marketing telephone calls each week. Before making each call, she envisions a specific result. But occasionally she is so busy that these calls become a challenge just to complete, and she unconsciously slips into a "dialing for dollars" mode: she sits down and dials phone number after phone number, usually with few results. Why? Because she has shifted her focus to the completion of a task (accomplishing a certain number of marketing calls), rather than the achievement of a specific business result.

When this happens, Nancy reminds herself that even the simplest action is mightier when performed with intention. Before picking up the phone, she spends a minute thinking about the purpose of her call and the outcome she desires. Once she starts dialing, results "miraculously" occur. CEOs answer the phone, appointments are made, and relationships are initiated. Her intentionality has set the stage for her to be more powerful, effective, and successful in her business.

While Nancy is in her unconscious "try" mode, her thoughts are about the process: "I'll make twenty calls today." But when she is intentional, she is focused on results: "I'll schedule three appointments to talk about employee audits and individual coaching." With this intention, she has clearly identified what she is selling—audits and coaching—which helps her focus her conversation. And she has identified the result—an appointment—which means she will continue calling until three appointments have been scheduled. Only then, when she has achieved a specific result, is her task completed.

Women in particular tend to fill their language in the workplace with trying rather than intentions. This kind of language sounds less powerful, and it produces less powerful actions. Listen to yourself over the next few days to determine whether your language identifies you as a "trier" or a "doer." Be conscious of when, where, and how often you use that weak little word *try* and begin reprogramming yourself with alternative language. Replace *try* with *intend*, or better yet, with nothing at all. For example, if you would normally say, "I'll try to get that done today," switch to "I intend to get that done today," or the even more powerful "I'll get that done today."

Career-Enriching Concept #4: Listen to Yourself for Approval, Not Others

It is part of our human nature to desire the approval of others. It is also a necessary element of the Promotion Game that you learned in Chapter 7. External approval—from bosses, clients, peers, and others—is an important aspect of your professional advancement. But if you allow yourself to depend completely on this approval, it will become the primary gauge by which you determine your worth—and your worthiness. As a result, you abandon the most important career guide that you possess: you.

This is a particular danger for women, since we strive for acceptance into the higher ranks of the masculine business establishment that surrounds us. Constantly striving to earn the approval of others, and being on the watch for signs of that approval, puts us in danger of taking actions that are inconsistent with our own internal "knowing." Each time we take such an action, we deny the wisdom and value of Self. If we do it too often, Self simply stops speaking at all. Thus we begin a lifelong pattern of conforming and pleasing, instead of allowing ourselves to take ownership of our own thoughts, feelings, and actions.

"The need to conform to what others expect has been a major preoccupation for many working women," write Stanlee Phelps and Nancy Austin. "It is no surprise many women feel like impostors: They know that their insides don't match their outsides. They feel cheated and tired, but they are afraid to admit it."[3] Perhaps this is what women are talking about when they speak of achieving their career goals but losing themselves in the process.

If your need for external approval is strong, you are giving your power away and placing your own success and joy in the hands of others. According to Bill Cosby, "I don't know the key to success, but the key to failure is trying to please everybody."[4]

Shifting your mind-set away from dependence on the approval of others and toward dependence on the approval of Self can be frightening, because it requires you to take ultimate responsibility for your own thoughts and actions. You choose them. You own them. You enjoy the rewards they earn you, as well as the consequences.

Ann Hackman Rose can tell you a thing or two about relying on Self for approval. She had been the classic "supporter/nurturer," staying home to raise her children while her husband, Alvin, ran their family-owned Chicago-area franchise of Tastee-Freez International. "I stayed home, I was very pampered, and I loved it," she recalls.

But when Alvin died after a long and debilitating illness, Ann was thrust into the middle of some major decisions. Her first shock was financial: her new house was only half hers. The other half had been leveraged to pay a variety of business expenses. "I had no choice," she says of the experience. "I was wearing a ten-carat diamond ring and I pawned it to keep the business going."

Then Ann turned to her husband's friend, McDonald's founder Ray Kroc, for advice. He was blunt: "Ann, you have no qualifications to run this business. The smartest thing you can do is to sell it now, while you're still young. Then go find another man and get married again."

Ann—a Phi Beta Kappa graduate of Northwestern University—was crushed. "Ray was one of the most successful businessmen in America," she recalls. "And he wasn't the only man to tell me to sell. They all did. Even our accountant and the family attorney told me to sell the business and find another man to marry."

Ann knew that if she took over the business and failed, she would be jeopardizing her—and her children's—future. But Ann believed she could be successful. So she ignored all of the professional business advice and took her own. "I learned from the bottom up," she says. "Scrubbing floors, closing stores, working behind the counter. To get them [her employees and other franchisees] to respect me, that's what I had to do. They would never have challenged Alvin the way they challenged me."

As she learned the business, Ann added a new dimension: real estate. When Alvin passed away, most of their Tastee-Freez stores were on leased properties. Slowly and steadily, Ann began buying the properties in the better neighborhoods where her bigger, newer stores were located. Today, her real estate holdings are the most profitable part of her business. "If I didn't have the real estate company," she laughs, "I'd have been out of business a long time ago."

Ann Hackman Rose has been running her Chicago-area Tastee-Freez franchise for more than a quarter of a century. She still solicits others' opinions and considers their counsel before making a major decision. But she learned long ago that, ultimately, listening to her own "inner counsel" is her most potent decision-making tool.

Before you can be comfortable depending only on Self for approval, you must do as Socrates advised and, "Know Thyself." Ask incisive, reflective questions that will challenge you to probe more deeply into your strengths, your weaknesses, and the true nature of your character. Make an ongoing commitment to learn and to understand yourself at deeper and deeper levels. This is a commitment that characterizes leaders, according to Warren Bennis, who gives us these insights in his book, *On Becoming a Leader*:

> *Self-knowledge, self-invention are lifetime processes. Those people who struggled to know themselves as teenagers continue today to explore their own depths, reflect on their experiences, and test themselves. . . . All of the leaders I talked with agreed that no one can teach you how to become yourself, to take charge, to express yourself except you. But there are some things that others have done that are useful to think about in the process. I've organized them as the four lessons of self-knowledge. They are: One: You are your own best teacher. Two: Accept responsibility. Blame no one. Three: You can learn anything you want to learn. Four: True understanding comes from reflecting on your experience.[5]*

In completing the various exercises in the preceding chapters, you have already taken a quantum leap in self-knowledge. Consciously developing this deep awareness of your own strengths and vulnerabilities will help you establish the proper guideposts of your "listening" to others who are attempting to affect your actions and your decision making. It is important that you don't simply buckle under the pressure of their opinions, but that you listen to those opinions openly and let them sink in before judging them. If it rings true for you, own it and work with it. If not, throw it away. After all, it is your face in the mirror every day. If you're not proud of yourself, it really doesn't matter what anyone else thinks about you.

An international company hired Nancy to coach Joanna Broderick, a newly promoted executive who was having difficulty adjusting to the intensely political environment of the company's senior management. Joanna had been known for her decisiveness and clearheaded thinking . . . until she got promoted. Once in the competitive, backbiting culture of the company's senior ranks, she became so worried about making a decision that would be overturned by her bosses that she got stuck. She began using a plethora of delaying tactics to avoid making any decisions at all.

In discussing her problem with Nancy, Joanna finally admitted that she was in fundamental disagreement with several key priorities of top management. She felt that some of the decisions she was being told to make were even unethical. Nancy advised Joanna that she had some real soul-searching to do. She needed to decide if she would follow the advice of others or the advice of her Self in her decision making. Both pathways offered rewards and consequences. Joanna decided that her Self had to be her ultimate guide, even if it meant losing her job.

The day came when the company's executive VP directed Joanna to take an action that she believed was both unethical and illegal. Instead of doing it his way, she took a different—and legal—action to solve the problem. She lost her job because of her refusal to follow that top-management dictate.

Four months later, Joanna was happily employed in a higher-paying job at another company whose values better matched her own. She says she has no regrets, because through it all, she gained the strength and the wisdom to rely on her inner guides instead of on the whimsical forces swirling around her. She has walked through the corporate fire and lived to experience the euphoria of surviving with her Self intact.

This kind of competitive, political work environment is hard on everyone, but it is also a valuable teacher. When you are tempted to join the political game or go along with popular opinion, even though your internal guides are speaking differently, you betray yourself and your company in your failure to contribute your personal best to the larger community. Especially in a culture like this, your only source of powerful action is internal, in your own values and instincts.

Career-Enriching Concept #5: Focus Your Being in the Present

Our society offers a multitude of invitations to live anywhere but in the present. Particularly in today's business environment where employees have more work than time, the concept of multitasking has emerged as a trendy solution. At first glance this would seem to be an advantage for women, who have a special talent for juggling multiple priorities in their lives. But beware, and look deeper at this new phenomenon. Multitasking is about paying little bits of attention simultaneously to several different tasks. Isn't that the same thing as not paying enough attention to any single task to do it really well, or correctly?

In truth, multitasking takes our minds completely out of the here and now. It fragments our attention into a jumble of small pieces and diminishes the powers of our thinking by diffusing it across all of these pieces. Yet most top-level executives' success comes not from fragmentation but from focused concentration. They already know and practice what you are about to learn: *we can only create when our minds are clearly focused in the present moment.*

We are asking you to stop multitasking and keep your attention single-mindedly focused on the now. Instead of rushing through your day, live in each moment of that day. When you slow yourself down, your entire physical and mental being is centered in the present moment, and you can become grounded in the joy of *what is*, as opposed to the regrets about the past or frets about the future. If you stay centered on the here and now, your actions will be more dynamic, purposeful, and effective. Now that your mind is focused, rather than preoccupied, you will experience a more natural flow of new and innovative ideas. Other people will also sense in you a source of strength, for the person who is fully present to those around her is comforting and engenders trust.

One of Candy's bosses at DDB many years ago was a master at being in the present. Whenever she came to him with a problem or issue to discuss, he would set aside whatever materials he was working on, look directly at her, and stay in eye contact throughout the conversation. He never shifted his focus to the dozens of other crises on top of his desk or to the people who stood in the doorway waiting to enter. Only when the meeting was complete and all issues resolved did he move onto the next "moment."

During these conversations, Candy always felt an added sense of her own power and effectiveness. Without the need to compete with a myriad of other stimuli for his attention, she could concentrate on the issues at hand until they were resolved. In the absence of distractions, their meetings were more productive and shorter. Their being mutually in the present enriched their professional relationship, increased their productivity, and saved them time.

Candy once asked her boss how he was able to be so focused and calm in any crisis. He shared this secret: "My dad was a radiologist. When I was growing up, if he came home and told us he'd had a hard day, that meant that one or two of his patients had died. Even on my worst day in advertising, I know that nobody will die as a result of my decisions. So I figure that in my entire career, I'll never have a bad day."

That boss was Ken Kaess, who became president and CEO of DDB Worldwide in 2000, at the tender age of forty-six. His unprecedented rise through the ranks of this large, multinational advertising agency is proof of his many talents, one of which is the power of *being in the present*.

Even animals can tell if we are in the present or not. Nancy's dog, Bear, is her hairy, living, licky-face example of the power of being in the now. Nancy rescued Bear from an abusive home when he was a young adult. As a result, he has several unique behaviors. Unlike other dogs, he will not accept just any kind of petting attention. He is only willing to participate in such pleasures if the giver is totally, completely present with him. No reading while scratching his ears, no watching TV while petting his curly coat. And if Nancy wants to kiss his nose, she'd better be thinking about only one thing—kissing his nose. If her attention drifts for even a moment, he immediately breaks the connection and wanders away. Through Bear's ability to read and respond to Nancy's attention level, she realized that tangible energy is being given off when you are present. This energy simply doesn't exist when your mind or body are split in their attentions.

If you find yourself in the midst of a meeting and your thoughts stray to other things (past or future), then you are not in the now. If you feel impatient, hurried, or anxious for the meeting to end, then you are not being present to the people and issues in front of you at that moment.

Once you become aware of these thoughts and feelings, you can consciously choose to put them away, like storing them in a box inside your brain, so you can return to them at another time. Then you are free to devote your attention single-mindedly to the now.

Career-Enriching Concept #6: Accept Mistakes in Yourself and Others, and Learn from Them

The only sure thing about the business world is that it's not a sure thing. There is no way to guarantee 100 percent success from your plans and actions. Mistakes, glitches, and snafus are a fundamental part of a full, dynamic, and growing life. Successful people make far more mistakes than less successful people do, because they risk more. Consider Babe Ruth, the most outstanding batter in professional baseball. The year he set the record for major-league home runs, he also struck out more than anyone else. Is it possible that on the way to his 714 homers, it was his willingness to risk striking out that set the stage for his success? Of course!

In the game of business, great executives have some "Babe Ruth" qualities of their own: They see errors as a process of corrections rather than a process of failures. The executives that Warren Bennis studied for his book *Leaders* never even used the word *failure*. Instead they used a variety of more benign terms, such as *bungle, error, false start, glitch, mess, mistake,* and *setback. Failure*—the word—didn't exist in their vocabulary.[6]

These men accept falling down and getting back up again as a necessary part of the game of business. Women, however, are far more reluctant to take such risks. And we handle the mistakes we make differently from men. Author Adrienne Mendell posits in *How Men Think* that our childhood play patterns are what first create the differences between the sexes in these areas:

Research on gender differences shows that, in general, women do have a harder time than men when they err or fail. This difference evolves from the way the two sexes are traditionally raised. Compare the way boys and girls are socialized about mistakes:

Little boys play a lot of competitive team sports.
Little girls play dolls.

Little boys make a lot of mistakes playing team sports.
Little girls can't make a lot of mistakes playing dolls because there
are few or no rules.

When boys make mistakes, they are encouraged to go back and try
harder.
When girls make mistakes, they are comforted.

Boys learn that making a mistake may be embarrassing but not
fatal.
Girls learn mistakes are something to feel bad about.

Boys learn that you earn your team's respect by striving to
improve your skills after making a mistake.
Girls learn you will be consoled if you call attention to your
mistakes.[7]

Based on these distinctly different childhood lessons, it is no wonder women handle risk and mistakes so differently from men. We tend to personalize the event as confirmation that "I'm stupid" or "I'm no good." Rather than simply learning from a mistake and moving on, we hold on to the variety of emotions it triggered: shame, anxiety, self-doubt.

Candy and Nancy exemplify the career impact of these "sports versus dolls" play patterns. Candy was a classic tomboy during her entire childhood. Most of her friends were boys and most of her play involved team games like kickball, softball, and even "war." She carried the attitudes gained from this childhood into her adult career, so it was "natural" for her to become successful in the male-dominated business arena. In contrast, Nancy was a quiet, doll-playing little girl. Early in her career, she had difficulty with risk and competitiveness. Only when she began playing sports as an adult did she begin to deprogram those doll-playing attitudes from her childhood and become more comfortable in the competitive, risk-filled world of business.

Andrea Hardy, a senior tax manager in a major accounting firm, gives us another perfect example of the classic female reaction to mistakes. A week or two after one of her subordinates had completed the tax forms for a major corporate client and informed them of the amount of their final tax bill, Andrea discovered a $200,000 error in his calculations. When she brought it to her subordinate's attention, he dismissed the error and took no responsibility for correcting it. So even though it was not her mistake, Andrea personalized it as if she had been the culprit. She worked into the wee hours of the morning through the weekend searching unsuccessfully for a solution. On Monday, she told her boss— another male—and then waited for his tirade. He too nonchalantly dismissed it: "Not a big deal. The client made the mistake when they gave us the wrong information. You won't get any brownie points by making a big deal out of it. Just inform the client and then forget about it." Andrea had sacrificed her weekend and flogged her psyche mercilessly . . . for nothing!

Andrea's story is a real-life example of the four key results that Stephanie Riger and Pat Galligan found in their study of the distinctions between male and female responses to mistakes:

When men succeed, they point to self.
When men fail, they point outward.
When women succeed, they point outward.
When women fail, they point to self.[8]

Mistakes and failures hone you in ways that can never be imagined. When events go awry and you feel enmeshed in a mistake, how you respond influences your ongoing career success and your joy with yourself and your life. You can choose to internalize and personalize the event, which will merely keep you stuck in it, or you can choose to use it to spur you on to greater learning, better solutions, and renewed creativity and motivation.

Mistakes add immeasurably to our experience; when we choose to learn from them, they increase our wisdom as well. The lessons we take from life's mistakes can even help us survive truly life-threatening situations. Take this story from Joseph Jaworski's book *Synchronicity: The Inner Path of Leadership*:

> *During the early part of World War II, Kurt Hahn had been commissioned by the Royal Navy to help determine how to deal with an unusual phenomenon. When the Royal Navy's ships would go down in the frigid North Sea, a large proportion of the sailors would die before help could arrive. But a strange thing was happening—those who survived were almost all older people in their forties. The younger, seemingly more fit and hearty people in their twenties, were perishing. Hahn studied the situation and came to the conclusion that the older people were surviving because they had been through the trials and tribulations and exigencies of life itself. They had grown in body, mind, and spirit and had the will to live and to deal with extremely demanding new challenges. The younger people simply had not developed that kind of inner capacity.*[9]

People (and companies) who fear making mistakes and failures are limiting their future success because they are limiting their learning. As a manager, you must permit your subordinates to fail. In doing so, you will empower them to learn and grow. And you must give yourself the same latitude, for the same reason.

DDB Worldwide has codified this permission for almost twenty years, in a statement called The Four Freedoms, which is given to every new employee. One of the four was the Freedom to Fail, and here's what it says:

> *It is in the nature of creative talent to venture beyond the known, to poke into the unheard of, to pick its way through scary places, untrod by conventional minds. Because there are no assurances these idea-searching patrols will succeed, the seekers must be granted the latitude to fail in order to sustain their willingness to pursue again. It is the job of management to first point talented people in the right direction and then to judge their work. But if the approach to that work is responsible and intelligent, people must never be criticized for daring to fail.*[10]

A dynamic career is filled with creative ideas and innovative actions and decisions. In this context, mistakes are the one outcome that is guaranteed to happen along the way. When they do occur, focus not on blaming others, not on self-flagellation, but on *learning*. Diagnose what happened, acknowledge what you need to do differently next time, and move on. Remind yourself, periodically, that no one is perfect—not even you.

As you begin integrating these six Career-Enriching Concepts into your work life, you will be surprised at how changing your expectations can also change your reality. You may also be frustrated that you didn't do it sooner or that you can't do it all faster. Just remember that every new habit takes time and practice to develop—and we have just introduced you to not one but six magical, life-changing, new habits. These concepts are the energy boosters that enhance the power of your performance. They are the weights you add to the scale alongside your work to make the end result "pop up" more easily. They can transform your work from drudgery to delight, and they can extend your power—and your staying power—in your career journey.

CHAPTER 10

ENRICHING CONCEPTS FOR YOUR PERSONAL LIFE

Dance Lesson #10: A successful career is but one piece of a highly complex, multifaceted life. Once you understand where your career fits within the larger pattern, and which facets are most important, you will know what "having it all" means for you. This is your first step to living your life by design, rather than at random.

Women often get so caught up in the business of business that we forget to pay the proper attention to the rest of our lives. We pursue career success, yet we forget that succeeding in the rest of our lives requires some pursuit as well. To achieve joy and fulfillment in the larger domain called life, we must expand our focus beyond the single facet that is our career.

For example, when was the last time you contemplated any of these questions:

- Why do I work? What purpose does my work serve within the larger context of my life?
- Does the way I spend my time reflect who I am and who I hoped I'd be?
- Am I spending time on the things that are really important to me?
- What people and activities do I want in my personal life?
- What do I want my life to stand for?

With so many people and responsibilities vying for attention, it's easy to go off course in our lives. The special challenge that working women face is our tendency to say yes too much at work, and say no too much when it comes to our personal lives. This creates a debilitating imbalance that simply cannot continue, according to award-winning author and sociologist Barbara Ehrenreich: "Meaningful work and a balanced life are deep rooted and genuine human needs. Like any needs, they can be repressed or ignored for years at a time, but sooner or later they're going to assert themselves."[1]

Your career will always be demanding; so will your personal life. Whether you are single or married, with or without children, your personal life—like your work—is full of opportunities, possibilities, and options. The trick is to maintain the proper activities in each venue and the appropriate blend between them. There is no magic formula to balance this equation. In fact, there is no single right answer, since each of us is an individual, unique from all others. You are the only person who can define *balance* in your life, and you are the only one who can make the choices that will create it.

Why do women seem to struggle more than men with this idea of balance? Quite simply, it's because women carry tougher loads than men. For centuries, our primary role in life centered on family and home. Our entry into the ranks of full-time business workers is a relatively recent development. Our culture (and our male partners) simply have not yet adjusted to this massive change in the labor equation. So we carry a full load at the office in additon to carrying a full measure of the responsibilities at home. We are so accustomed to our female roles that we recognize the inequities only when they reach extremes, as Virginia Valian documented in her book, *Why So Slow?: The Advancement of Women*:

> *Married women who work for pay average about thirty-three hours of housework per week—about two-thirds of the total household work. . . . Overall, the partners had roughly equal professional commitments and responsibilities. The women, who were slightly better educated than their husbands and a few years younger, earned somewhat less money*

and were more intensely involved in their jobs. . . . Questioned independently, the wives and husbands agreed that the wives carried out more of all child care tasks but one—playing with the children. . . . Interestingly enough, women don't start feeling that they are taking on an uneven labor until they are doing about 75 percent of the household work. When they are doing 66 percent of the work they judge the division as fair to both parties."[2]

In this chapter, we offer you a new framework, the Life Diamond, to help you define what balance means in your life. In working with this framework, your first step will be to shift this paradigm from *balance*, which suggests the need to deal with only two opposing forces, to *harmony*, which accommodates the more complex realities of a working woman's personal life. You cannot balance a six-faceted life, but you can reach a point where you feel a sense of harmony—where the facets are working together as part of an integrated whole.

We will also offer you eight Life-Enriching Concepts to help you become more purposeful and selective about how you fill your personal time. As you begin to understand not just how to use your time, but why, you will also begin to shed those chronic attacks of guilt that so often plague the hearts of professional working women.

The Multifaceted Life Diamond

A satisfying and joyful life is multifaceted—a combination of involvement and activities in several different venues. Just as a diamond has many facets, so too does your life. Just as the number and reflective quality of the diamond's facets are key elements determining the quality of the stone, so it is with the quality of a life. The facets of your life do not exist in isolation from one another; they do not simply have individual reflections. They are linked in an interconnected pattern. While each facet has its own identity in the pattern, it also reflects on the others; they, in turn, reflect upon it. Your involvement and activities in one area affect your involvement and activities in another. The simplest example of this is work and family. Success and promotion at work reflect onto the facet of family by contributing an increased income and improved lifestyle. The slide into workaholism also reflects onto the family by reducing the time and attention that your spouse and children receive from you.

We have identified six facets and arranged them in a Life Diamond to give you a visual memory aid for the more complex pattern of multiple roles that characterize women's lives. Virtually all of your activities can be placed within one of these facets. Your spiritual or religious roles, for example, could be classified in community, self, and family. However, it is perfectly acceptable to categorize a group of similar activities as a unique facet, if you wish.

This diagram shows the six facets in relatively equal sizes, but this is rarely the reality of a life. Just as there is no one formula that defines a

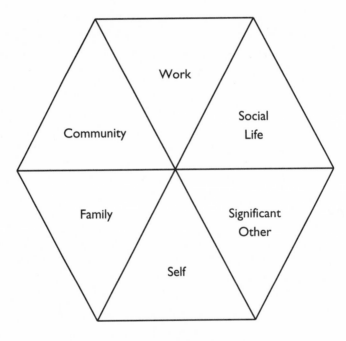

Life Diamond

harmonious life, there is no single, ideal size for each facet. At certain times in your life, certain facets will absorb more of your time and energy, while others will require less. Being active in all of them is not necessarily the ideal; it is often the guaranteed high-stress solution. Yet, restricting activities to only one or two facets is an indicator of a life that is highly limited in its possibilities. The cutting and arranging of your Life Diamond will not be easy, but the payoff will be huge to you, your family, your friends, and your life.

Following is a brief explanation of each of the six facets. As you read these descriptions, think about where you spend your time now and where you would *like* to spend your time. Chances are about 100 percent that you will recognize a gap between where you are and where you would like to be. Completing the Life Diamond exercises at the end of this section will help you understand this gap more clearly so you can start taking the steps to jump over it. These exercises will give you the insights to envision your ideal Life Diamond and the tools to actually achieve it.

Work

This facet is about your job, your career, what you do to earn money, how you make your living. Applying the six Career-Enriching Concepts from Chapter 9 is the first step to creating the free time you need for the other facets of your life.

Community

This facet covers the responsibilities and projects that you take on to support the various communities to which you belong: church (spiritual), professional associations, university alumnae groups, other affinity groups (such as PTA, ski clubs, singles clubs), and so on. This facet may require a purposeful effort if you are a single working woman. The various communities may not actively seek your involvement, so you have to be proactive about joining those that align with your goals and values.

For working mothers, the community facet becomes easily oversubscribed unless you are vigilant about accepting only those responsibilities and projects that align with your Heart's Purpose, your Defining Values, and your Destination Goals.

Social Life

The social life facet covers the lunches, dinners, cocktails, tennis matches, golf games, and so on that provide your entertainment as well as the development of business and personal relationships. It is a category that often reflects onto other facets (such as work and community), thus creating the "two-for-one deal" that we will discuss further in our eight Life-Enriching Concepts. For example, if you attend an awards dinner for your industry, it is both a social affair and a prime networking opportunity for your career.

The social life facet is one of the areas that can suffer from malnourishment if you are a working mother. With little free time, the simplest solution is often to cancel these activities or merge them with other facets—the "two-for-one deals." This is a perfectly viable—and often unavoidable—option, but there is a catch: When your social life becomes completely merged into other facets, you rob yourself of one piece of your own, independent identity and ego-separation from the more dominating areas of work and family. There is a little less of *you* in your Life Diamond.

Developing and maintaining a vital social life is a whole different kind of challenge for a single woman. Not only is work a consuming beast where you want to prove your prowess, but socializing in the outside world, beyond your working relationships, requires extra effort. Now, it's up to you alone to plan and organize your social activities before they can take place. If you want a well-rounded life, you must reach out and create it.

Family

The facet of family involves your emotional and social relationships with your immediate and extended family members. The warmth of a loving family relationship is a central support system for each of us, whether we are single or married. While we usually receive this support in our natural families, we can also create a support system by "adopting" family members.

If you are a working mother, this facet is probably rivaled most by the work facet for its dominance of your life.

Significant Other

We have created a separate facet for your significant other to ensure that this critical part of your personal life receives the specific attention required to nurture and grow this pivotal relationship. The working mother often unknowingly collapses spouse and children into one unit. The result is attention for the children and neglect of private time for the significant other. Yet the long-term health of a couple's relationship is determined by their ability to continue as a couple once their "nest" is emptied of children.

The single woman, too, can easily bury herself in her work and overlook the need for purposeful activity in this category. Looking for the perfect mate can be a wonderful adventure if you allow yourself to examine some new possibilities: golf courses, tennis courts, professional conferences, church and community groups, computer dating services, art galleries and museums, vacation tours, and college extension courses are just a few of the options. And the infamous blind date can occasionally work out famously. Candy and several of her friends (who married in their late twenties and early thirties) all met their husbands on blind dates.

Self

When a working woman becomes starved for time, self is usually the first facet that becomes starved for attention. While we willingly nurture others, we are reluctant nurturers of ourselves. This seems to us a selfish choice, and so it fills us with guilt. Yet spending time to care for self is precisely what enables us to then care for others. Only by learning to leave our guilt behind and embrace the value of nurturing ourselves will we ever be able to achieve the joy and harmony we seek in our own lives.

Assessing Your Facets and Learning to Refocus

Most career-driven people—both men and women—talk a lot about how important their family and personal lives are to them. But all too often they fail to walk the talk, so powerful and pervasive is the influence of *work*. While they are skilled at translating desire into action in their work environment, they fail to make the same translation in their personal lives. In his bestselling book *The Seven Habits of Highly Successful People*, author Stephen Covey gives a concise analysis of the problem and the solution: "The key is not to prioritize what's on your schedule, but to schedule your priorities."

The starting point, then, is to identify the priorities in your personal life and reduce or eliminate time-consuming activities that are not priorities. If you followed our coaching in Chapter 2, you've already established the criteria for determining your priorities. They are your Heart's Purpose, Activating Vision, and Defining Values. Just as they guide your career decision making, they should guide your decisions in the personal venues of your life. You can use them to determine which of your life facets are most important and to assess the appropriateness of your time and energy commitments.

Your next step is to look at the current state of your life, facet by facet. Make a list of your responsibilities and activities during the past month. When you have completed this list, estimate what percentage of your time was spent in each section of your Life Diamond. Your total should add up to 100 percent, not 120 percent or 140 percent!

Now, revisit your Heart's Purpose and Defining Values. Using these as your criteria, put a circle around only those responsibilities and activities that are in alignment with them. At the end of this exercise, any items not circled become candidates for reduction, delegation, or extinction. Ask yourself why you are doing them. What value are they contributing to you or to others? Are they helping or hampering your ability to achieve harmony in your life? These are like little specks of impurities in a diamond: they degrade the quality of the precious stone that is your life. Give yourself permission to eliminate them or assign them to someone else.

Your next step is to set some new targets for your time and then reapportion your 100 percent between each of your desired facets. By comparing your target with the actual time spent over the past month, you will know whether your challenge is to reduce or increase your involvement and activity level in each facet.

The point of all of this thinking, targeting, and tracking is to begin to build the kind of life that world-renowned mythology authority Joseph Campbell writes about in *An Open Life*: "People talk about the meaning of life; there is no meaning of life—there are lots of meanings of different lives, and you must decide what you want your own to be."[3] The challenge is not simply to decide what harmony means in your own life, but to persist until you achieve it.

In defining what harmony is for each of us, we are called to explore and determine the proper blending of giving and receiving, business and personal, work and play, doing and being, from our unique individual foundations of truth (Defining Values) and passion (Heart's Purpose). We are challenged to think not of maintaining a certain fixed equilibrium in our lives, but of achieving a certain pattern of ebb and flow— of chords and rhythms—much like constructing a symphony. Sometimes the chords will be complex and the rhythms slow; at other times single notes will dominate and the pacing will be staccato. The completeness comes not from the individual measures of music but from the mixtures of highs and lows, fasts and slows, in the total composition.

This symphonic concept of harmonics is more characteristic of women's lives than the simplistic idea of balance. It is balance, but on a higher, more complex, more integrated plain. It is about honoring what is most important to you and embracing the wholeness of who you are. It is a critical concept for women who juggle full-time employment against full-time personal life. On some days, work will consume the bulk of your attention, and that needs to be honored. At other times, it will be the rest of your life that receives your primary commitment of time and energy. And sometimes, taking care of self will be your number one priority (yes, really!).

Enriching Concepts to Simplify Your Life

If you have taken to heart the ideas in this chapter, you now have a Life Diamond with a list of your responsibilities and activities in each facet, and you have evaluated that list to determine where you want to enlarge it and where you want to shrink it. The first three of our eight Life-Enriching Concepts will help you make the reductions.

1. Think R.E.D.

To simplify your life, you have three choices: Reduce, Eliminate, or Delegate. Sometimes you will use all three choices to solve the same problem.

Martha used this "think R.E.D." approach when she found that she had overcommitted herself in the community area. She was a hard-charging senior manager in a PR firm and had finally convinced her employer to reduce her workweek from five days to four so she could spend more time with her two children. Her primary goal was to be more involved in their education. She began volunteering in their classrooms and was quickly identified as someone who could run things.

Suddenly, Martha found herself in charge of a library fund-raising campaign, a Girl Scout troop, and a Swim Club tournament. She had traded one ten-hour paid day at the office for twenty hours of unpaid volunteer time. Her balance equation had gone upside-down. To reverse it, she decided first to *eliminate* her lead role in the library campaign, since it was not in alignment with her goal of spending more time with her children. She found another volunteer and *delegated* the leadership role to her. Martha *reduced* her own weekly time commitment to the library project from the ten hours that she had been spending to lead the fund-raising effort to two hours as a telephone volunteer and advisor to the new chairperson.

2. Look for the Two-for-One Deals

As we mentioned earlier, each of the six life facets also reflects onto the others. A responsibility or activity is rarely confined to a single facet. For example, say you are an attorney and one of your largest clients shares your love of theater. So you get four tickets to the latest musical in town and attend with your boyfriend, your client, and your client's significant other. You have a lovely social engagement, but you are also building an important work-related relationship.

This is a two-for-one deal. The same activity, and the same time, works for you in two different life facets. And you thought there was no such thing as a 120-minute hour! Creating more of these kinds of hours will not only enrich your own life, it will enrich the lives of others. You will bring a new level of awareness, sharing, and relationship into many personal lives, including your own. So go ahead, take your daughter to work, invite your boss to share dinner with your family in your home, include your client in your foursome in a local golf tournament, hold that church planning meeting over a nice, social lunch.

3. The Word "No" Is a Wonderful Gift

The value of "no" was discussed in Chapter 9 as a Career-Enriching Concept. It is equally powerful in your personal life, where requests for your time and energies as a volunteer are never-ending. Churches, schools, amateur sports teams, scouting, college alumnae groups, women's groups, professional associations, and so forth all need a constant stream of volunteers to be successful. You simply cannot say yes to them all, no matter how deserving they are. To do so is to serve their needs and abandon your own. Yet it is natural to feel a measure of guilt whenever you deny your time to a worthy cause or organization. Here is where you will want to allow yourself to forego the guilt syndrome. First, remind yourself of your Heart's Purpose and Defining Values. Then evaluate requests for your time against these criteria. Ask yourself: "Do I *want* to say yes when I *should* say no?" Often it is our egos talking and not our true desires. When you make choices that are in alignment with your Heart's Purpose and Defining Values, you remain true to the direction you have chosen for your life. These are good decisions, and guilt has no place here.

Candy faced this issue of ego versus true desires when she was asked to take one of two volunteer positions on the board of the local PTA. Each position was a spot on a planned progression to becoming president, a title that has always been an "automatic ego target" for her. But not this time, thanks in large part to the two-and-a-half years of coaching she had done with Nancy! Candy consciously evaluated each position against one of her key priorities, which was to spend more time participating in her sons' classrooms. Both jobs would have required her to actually reduce the time she could spend in the classroom. She turned them down, and then called Nancy to share the joy of saying no for all of the right reasons.

Life-Enriching Concepts for Handling Adversity

Every life has its share of tough times. Whether we are dealing with routine frustrations, sudden difficulties, or situations of sadness and loss, the next two Life-Enriching Concepts can help us cope with these moments in our lives and come through them successfully.

4. Always Keep Your Sense of Humor, and Use It Often

The positive, pressure-relieving power of your sense of humor is as valid in your personal life as it is at work. Our sense of humor is that "sixth sense" that keeps us human at precisely those moments when we are tempted to behave inhumanely. It has held an important place in every culture and every era, from Aesop's fables to the cartoons of Dilbert; from the ancient myths of Greece and Rome to the relatively modern legends of Native Americans. In their book *Spiritual Literacy: Reading the Sacred in Everyday Life*, Frederic and Mary Ann Brussat write: "There is the Apache myth of the Creator giving human beings the ability to talk, to run, and to look. But He was not satisfied until He also gave them the ability to laugh. Only then did the Creator say, 'Now you are fit to live.' "[4]

You can never afford to take yourself or your life too seriously. In fact, studies have shown that laughter has a demonstrable positive impact on our health. When you laugh, all kinds of wonderful things happen to benefit your body and mind. Endorphins are released in your brain, which give you a natural high, and your respiratory system responds as if you were giving it an aerobic workout. Laughter also relieves pain. You can laugh only when you are physically relaxed. And the more relaxed you are, the less pain you feel. So funny books and movies are ideal pain relievers. Norman Cousins shared the healing power of laughter in his book, *Anatomy of an Illness*. He was suffering from a crippling disease and believed that his pervasive seriousness had caused it. He determined to reverse the condition with large doses of laughter. He watched slapstick comedies and tapes of old "Candid Camera" episodes. Eventually, his symptoms and his pain disappeared and he was able to resume a normal, healthy life.

So perhaps laughter really is the best medicine!

The Chinese are renowned for their ancient healing arts, such as acupuncture, tai chi chuan, and herbal medicines. So it is no surprise to see how they depict laughter in their written language. Authors Chungliang Al Huang and Jerry Lynch describe it this way: "In Chinese writing, laughter is depicted by the picture language of a human with arms and legs flung wide apart, head up to the sky, vibrating with mirth like bamboo leaves in the wind."[5]

Isn't that a wonderful image? Through laughter you contract muscles and alter your breathing patterns. Laughter certainly revitalizes the soul and heals the body. You can't experience the debilitating tension of stress when you are laughing—it is impossible. Try it!

5. Embrace the Imperfect in Yourself and Others

Every one of us is an imperfect being operating in a complex world. Yet how much stress and frustration do we create within ourselves and in those we love by striving constantly to ignore or correct or compensate or *perfect* that which is not—and never can be—perfect? Rather than waging this constant battle, we would be better served by embracing our imperfections and focusing our energies instead on learning the lessons that they can teach us. After all, our imperfections are what make us human. And our ability to love others despite their failings—to triumph despite our weaknesses—is the true nobility of human nature.

In the routine happenings of your life, embracing the imperfect can be as simple as making a conscious choice to overlook it. How often have you watched parents unwittingly sabotage their relationship with a child through criticisms and corrections over things that simply aren't important in the scheme of either life? Those parents so desperately want their child to excel that they fixate on the shortcomings. How different would the relationship be if the parent could simply shift focus and instead fixate on the child's strengths and achievements?

How much happier would each one of us be as adults if we could mute the voice of our "internal parent," ever-measuring us for our own weaknesses, mistakes, and "missings"?

An old adage states: What You Resist Persists. To choose to overlook imperfections is simply to stop resisting (and resenting) their presence. Once there is less mental and emotional energy swirling around the imperfections, you will be surprised at how unimportant they become. Some may even disappear. Is the change in perception or is it reality? Who cares! Either way you will be happier.

When Nancy was a teenager, she learned firsthand about the damage she could cause by focusing on others' imperfections. In this case, it was her brother, Jim. He was just two years younger than Nancy, so he was often her most zealous nemesis and an all-around pain in the butt; but just as often, he was her best friend, strongest ally, and confidante. Nancy began noticing that when she teased and picked at Jim's flaws, they were at war. But when she focused on his endearing qualities, they had a wonderfully alive, loving relationship. Nancy was to witness this phenomenon many times in her life before she finally realized that everyone shines when you spend your emotional energy on the good rather than the bad; when you focus on what's there, rather than on what's missing.

Occasionally, imperfections are of the more serious kind, and so are the consequences. This is precisely the time to open your arms and embrace. When the signals scream "Problem!" chances are pretty good that what is about to follow is "Solution!". Problems are the stage upon which new learning and insights occur.

As psychotherapist and former monk Thomas Moore wrote in *Care of the Soul*:

> *The soul presents itself in a variety of colors, including all the shades of gray, blue, and black. To care for the soul, we must observe the full range of all its colorings and resist the temptation to approve only of white, red, and orange—the brilliant colors. . . . Some feelings and thoughts seem to emerge only in a dark mood. Suppress the mood, and you will suppress those ideas and reflections.*[6]

Suppress the problem and you suppress the solution. So when your urge is to flee, stand your ground and walk through the storm. Give yourself the chance to reach the rainbow on the other side.

Life-Enriching Concepts to Increase Harmony

The pattern recorded by a seismograph is a good simulation of the look and feel of the pattern of our lives: long periods of little squiggles, interrupted at very rare intervals by a short period of peak activity. When the peak hits, we are centered and focused, directing our energies to solve whatever crisis it represents. We tend to feel most alive, most vibrant when we are caught up in the excitement and pain and gratification of handling these peaks. Yet we spend most of our lives down in the valleys. How centered, focused, and directed are we during those lulls? How much attention do we pay to the quality of our personal lives then? Do we look for ways to improve that portion of our lives? Or do we take a more passive approach and simply "leave well enough alone"?

Even our everyday lives are filled with tensions and pressures. They are simply more . . . routine. But consider how much happier, more satisfied, and more joyful your life would be if you could reduce and even release these tensions. You would experience an increase in the level of harmony in your relationships with your family and friends, and even within yourself.

6. Ask for What You Want and Tell the Truth

Intuition is truly second nature to women. In our efforts to support and nurture those around us, we are constantly using this skill to tune in to the wants and needs of our coworkers and subordinates, our friends and family, our significant other and our children. Because we do it, we assume that the men in our lives do it too. Wrong! We keep hoping that they will perceive our needs and respond, without any prompting from us. But they don't! Most men are not highly intuitive. The solution for this absence of intuition is more complete, direct, and honest communication. We need to *ask for what we want and tell the truth.*

Candy first encountered this concept in Warren Lyons' Joy of Singing! Corporate Confidence Workshop. It seems so simple, so commonsensical, and yet so few people do it. Candy certainly didn't. When she took the workshop, she had recently married and had been working overtime to be the perfect combination of career woman and wife. She was adjusting to her new state of cohabitation, after living alone for several years. A few of her husband's more mundane living habits were driving her nuts: leaving his dirty socks on the floor, never taking a turn to make the bed, leaving dirty dishes in the sink. They were irritating things . . . but, they were little things. So she said nothing. Instead, she hoped that her husband would somehow realize that these things were bugging her and change his ways on his own.

As time passed, Candy grew angrier. Her husband, Ken, remained oblivious. Then one night she came home from work, spotted two dirty socks on the bedroom floor, and blew up at Ken—complete with a few shouted expletives. Over socks! Ken was stunned, at both the problem and Candy's level of anger. How much easier it would have been if she had simply voiced her irritation when it first occurred—if she had simply asked for what she wanted, and told the truth—in a positive and nonjudgmental way: "You know, Ken, I'd really appreciate it if you could put your socks in the dirty-clothes basket in the closet." How simple! How easy! How painlessly effective!

Learning this one Life-Enriching Concept in The Joy of Singing! changed Candy's life (and probably had a lot to do with keeping her in a happy marriage). When you ask for what you want and tell the truth, you are behaving as an empowered individual. You are treating others in an empowering way, as well, because you are *asking*—not demanding or berating, not begging or nagging. You are offering the other person an opportunity to be a giver. And most people find this a very gratifying role. Sure, sometimes the answer will be a "no." But every "yes" makes life easier and more joyful—for you, and for those around you. So don't fall into the trap of not asking because you expect or hope that someone else will "figure out" your needs. Life is tough enough without adding yet another test to it! Stop expecting and start asking. It's one of the most positive actions you can take to increase the level of harmony in every venue of your personal life.

7. Create a Loving and Trusting Home, and Don't Worry About Tradition

This concept is primarily aimed at those of you who were raised in a "traditional" household in which the family ate dinner together several nights each week, Sundays saw crystal and silverware come out, Friday was family popcorn night, summers meant your own garden and fresh vegetables, holidays involved extensive decorating and even more extensive preparations of celebratory meals, and Mom stayed home, made your Halloween costume, and spent an entire afternoon baking holiday cookies with you.

Those homes and every one of those traditions were wonderful. But in today's world, there is simply not enough time in the day, month, or year for most working women to do an A+ job of "traditional" homemaking as well as an A+ job of professional career building. For those who insist on trying, the result is often a traumatizing injection of stress and anger into the household precisely at those times when you want yourself, your friends, and your family to experience an added infusion of peace, love, and joy.

So what is a good working woman to do? Keep yourself focused on delivering the peace, love, and joy part! Select those age-old traditions that are most important to you and easy to adopt, and then adapt to create new traditions that will enable you to have happy celebration, instead of stressful and exhausting ones.

Catherine Dunhill started inventing new traditions out of desperation one Thanksgiving. She had grown up in the quintessential American household where Mom stayed home with the kids, and Mom had a special passion for holidays. She baked, decorated, shopped, wrapped, cooked, and served. Every holiday was a warm (and calorie-filled) memory. Naturally, that became the standard for Catherine when she had her own family. The key difference was a demanding finance career that typically kept her at the office until 7:00 P.M. on Thanksgiving eve. She could routinely be found racing through the local grocery store at eight that night, poking the turkeys in hopes that one would be at least partially defrosted. She'd start cooking at 9:00 P.M., hit the sack around 2:00 A.M., and jump back out at six the next morning to finish cooking, cleaning, and setting the table in time for guest arrivals at two. By the time the turkey made it to the table at five, Catherine was mentally and physically exhausted.

After three years of this madness, Catherine's husband, Keith, suggested she stop worrying about tradition so much and find an easier way for herself.

The next year, she discovered the joys of ordering Thanksgiving dinner from a local gourmet take-out restaurant. The whole turkey came fresh-cooked and steaming hot in a foil-lined box. Ditto for the side dishes. Catherine's contribution was hors d'oeuvres and dessert. Voilá! She had founded a new tradition, and Thanksgiving became relaxing and fun for everyone.

This longing for the traditional also takes a toll on single working women, because for most of them, holiday traditions are indelibly bound to their memories of family. Their lack of spouse and/or children is often felt as a "missing," rather than as a conscious choice to be single. For these women, too, the emphasis on creating a loving, peaceful home can help them to fully enjoy what *is*, rather than long for what *is not*.

Nancy certainly felt this way every Thanksgiving, when she seemed to be the fifth wheel at her own family's celebration. Finally, she decided to do something to transform this depressing, unsatisfying holiday into a happy, fulfilling experience for herself. She posted a Thanksgiving open house invitation at a local homeless outreach organization. On Thanksgiving Day, Nancy got up at the crack of dawn and stormed into the facility's kitchen to cook a lavish homemade epicurean meal. The shelter was transformed into a loving family community, complete with overflowing table and an outpouring of love and caring. This occasion became a highlight of Nancy's year. She learned that by reaching out to others, she too was fulfilled. When she finally shed the *shoulds* and created her own tradition, Nancy experienced a joyous, fun, satisfying (and yes, tiring) holiday.

Isn't it ironic that holidays are the times of highest stress for us, when they should be the time of highest joy? Remembering the importance of love and peace and creating new traditions to fit your lifestyle are the keys to experiencing that joy again.

8. Take Time Each Week to Be Alone and Nurture Yourself

In your Life Diamond, self is the single facet that has the strongest reflective powers into every other facet. Self is the core facet in your life. The health of this facet can either add brilliance to or introduce darkness into every other area, both professional and personal. If you want to increase the joy and harmony in your life, your starting point must be to honor, nurture, and build the levels of harmony within yourself.

We certainly recognize the power of the self facet for our children, as evidenced by the emphasis both at school and at home on helping our children build a strong *sense of self* and learn to take proper care of themselves, physically, mentally, and emotionally. The primacy and power of this facet in our lives is no less when we are adults. Yet the first responsibility that we women tend to abandon when we become time-pressed is the responsibility of caring for ourselves. Working mothers in particular can become so single-mindedly focused on their responsibilities and activities in the work and family facets that they leave no time, energy, or even consideration, for what they might need for self.

To remain healthy and strong, every body and every mind needs a certain amount of exercise and rest, enrichment and pampering. It is easy for us to acknowledge this need in others (especially if they are our children); it is time we acknowledged it in ourselves.

For the majority of executive women who have coached with Nancy, this has been a predominant theme. It certainly was for Candy. Nancy knew this was a core "missing" that was negatively affecting other areas of Candy's life, so she made it her mission to shift Candy's thinking and behavior regarding self. While Candy was still working at DDB Worldwide, Nancy repeatedly coached her to take half an afternoon away from the office each week to do something nurturing with herself. It was not until Candy left the company that she began to take these breaks. She began by spending an hour alone at a local coffee shop in Manhattan Beach, sitting outside and sipping slowly on a hot, frothy double latte. Sometimes she would read a novel, other times write in her journal, and occasionally, simply sit and watch the world walking up and down the street. Candy found that taking these "coffee breaks" just once or twice a week would give her the mental and emotional reserves she needed to be more resilient and even-tempered at home. She found herself handling her children with more love and less loudness. Solving problems and resolving conflicts was nearly effortless and less laden with negative emotions. What a fantastic discovery!

Because we women are so quick to discard our self time, learning to give ourselves these breaks must be a conscious, regular effort if we want to reap the benefits. The key to ensuring that you get enough time for yourself is to make it a prescheduled part of your day or week, and then to give it the same level of importance as your business appointments. The only difference is that this is an appointment with *you*.

As unique individuals, each of us requires a different amount of time and different types of breaks to renew and rebuild our mental, physical, and emotional reservoirs. As you begin this journey of learning to take care of yourself, be sensitive to how much or how little you need and what kinds of breaks are most beneficial for you. How will you know? You will feel it, physically first, and then emotionally. As you reconnect with your feminine, nourishing self, you will feel your muscles relax. Often, these are muscles that you never even realized were tense. Your breathing will even out, and your heart rate will slow. Then, from deep within, a small bubble of contentment and joy will rise to your consciousness. You will feel a renewed connection with the external world.

Start with one or two hours of break time for the first three weeks. If you don't feel any difference in yourself, add an hour for the next three weeks. Keep adding until you feel that little reservoir of calm and serenity, contentment and joy, within you.

Your Journey to a Healthy Self

To help you begin your journey to a healthy self, we have provided a starter kit of alternative activities that you can try while you search for the kind of breaks that work best for you. We have created three categories, which are by no means exclusive or exhaustive: relaxation, feminine exercise, and pampering.

Whichever category or activity you choose, solitude is a critical component: this is your time to be with the most important person in your life: you! This does not mean that you have to sit in a field somewhere without a living soul in sight. But it does mean that you choose an environment where you are not interacting with anyone else. For example, Nancy loves to go to the movies and sit alone in the front row of stadium seats, where no one is next to her. The dark gives her space to just *be*. Two hundred people may be sitting in that same theater, and although Nancy is among them, she has created a situation of solitude. No one is pulling on her energy or requiring anything from her; she is free to experience a time of renewal of *Self*.

Relaxation

Candy's coffee breaks and Nancy's trips to the movies both fall into this category. Their minds and bodies are both in a relaxed state, which is different from a restful state. The latter implies a lack of awareness of outside stimuli, as in a mind and body asleep. Other relaxation activities include the following:

- *Soaking up the scene:* We receive pleasure from the pauses we take to observe the sights and sounds of the everyday scenes that surround us: a magnificent sunset over the breaking ocean waves, children giggling riotously over a playground game, a flock of birds flying in V-formation overhead, a beautiful flowering camellia with a hummingbird poised to sip its nectar. Observing nature is important to our wholeness; it renews the peace within and heals our fractured hearts. Author Douglas Preston writes:

  > *According to a new theory advanced by the Harvard biologist E. O. Wilson, called the biophilia hypothesis, the sacredness of the landscape is not some nebulous religious idea. It is rooted in our very genes. We do not love the beauty of the natural world by accident; we evolved to love it. This love is so profound that it is actually encoded in our genes, and it helped us survive in the landscape.*[7]

  This art of fully seeing and experiencing the everyday world has been an important part of many ancient cultures and religions, from the Celts of Ireland to the Zen Buddhists in ancient Japan. It can be even more beneficial as an antidote to the pressures and pace of twenty-first century life.

- *Journaling:* To write without structure, to put down one word after another on a piece of paper without linear direction, without end result in mind, is to access the feminine side of your brain—the right side. This is a powerful, creative, energizing tool. The unedited pouring forth that characterizes journaling is a stimulant for an internal process of replenishing both heart and mind. In her book *The Artist's Way* Julia Cameron recommends journaling every morning to support your ability to access the creative child within: "[to get us] to the other side of our fear, of our negativity, of our moods. Above all it gets us beyond our Censor. . . . morning pages [journaling] teach logic brain to stand aside and let artist brain [creativity] play."[8]

- ***Creating a place of sanctuary and silence:*** Embracing the creative power of solitude is an important journey to help women today stay connected with self. Being off the clock allows you the opportunity to get in touch with yourself at a deeper level, to discover who you are and dream of who you can be. This self-knowledge is an important foundation to guide the direction of your life. It enables you to respond thoughtfully and authentically to all that the universe has to offer.

  Your experience of silence will be heightened if you are in a "sanctuary"—a special place of solitude that is comfortable and aesthetically pleasing. This is your "do not disturb" zone. For Nancy, who is single, it is her entire home. For Candy, who is married with three active boys and a fifty-pound dog, it is her bathroom. If you're a runner, it may be the open road underfoot; if you're a reader, it may be the local bookstore.

  Lighted candles, soothing music, incense, special art or photos, and a beautiful view from the windows are just some of the aspects that transform a simple space into a special sanctuary where you can tap into the essence of that powerful, feminine side of yourself.

- ***Deep breathing:*** Oxygen is an essential for life, and deep breathing is a great way to instantly renew your brain, energize your body, release negative emotions, and relax overstressed muscles. The inward and outward patterns of your breathing are two opposing but harmonious forces. When you breathe in, you are inhaling all of the creative qualities of the universe. When you breathe out, you release all of your frustrations, fears, and limiting beliefs. Colin P. Sisson explains the relationship of breathing to emotions in his book, *Breath of Life*:

  If you watch a person experiencing a lot of emotion like fear or anger, you will find that their breathing is very restricted and controlled. That is because they are using the breath to try to suppress their feelings at that point. So, by suppressing the breath, particu-

larly by controlling the exhale, feelings and experiences are suppressed and held in the body. Every time we suppress something, the breathing becomes even more controlled, inhibited, and shallow.[9]

To experience the emotional release that accompanies deep breathing, simply breathe in deeply through your nose and hold for the count of four. Then exhale through your mouth to the count of four. Repeat this pattern several times. You will notice a significant reduction in stress. The beauty of this "break" is that you don't have to be alone to do it. But if you are by yourself, you can hum or make a sound on the exhale.

- *Meditation and contemplative prayer:* These two practices slow down both our own internal biorhythms and the rhythms of the world around us. They create a more receptive environment for a deeper listening to the seeds of truth and sacredness that God has planted within each one of us. Through meditation and contemplative prayer, we open ourselves to hear the heart of God and to receive his loving embrace. We experience comfort, wisdom, and inspiration.

Feminine Exercise

Certain forms of exercise strengthen your connection to your feminine energy, which is at the core of self. As a woman, your highest heart calling to yourself, your significant other, your children, your parents, and your friends takes place in a softer, rounded, more holistic domain, which is completely and utterly feminine. You are called to be the medicine woman who nurtures and supports, as opposed to the medical doctor who diagnoses and prescribes. In your personal domain, you are called to bring the aliveness of wisdom rather than the sterility of knowledge. The more rounded forms of exercise can help you rediscover, nourish, and reconnect with your feminine energy:

- *Dance:* Certain rhythms in music and dance have a vibrational power that literally resonates within our bones. When we allow ourselves to feel that vibration and move in sync with it, we create a deeper physical connection with the rhythms of our souls. As author Anthony Lawlor wrote, "Dancing imitates the rhythms of the cosmos and the divine play of creation. . . . Through dance the body can swing to the music of the soul."[10]

Two videos that can help you free your body and your being are *The Wave* by Gabrielle Roth,[11] and *The African Healing Dance* by Wyoma.[12] Both videos use dance to help you get in touch with your inner being for healing and personal growth.

- *Yoga or tai chi chuan:* These two examples of Asian and Indian exercise forms combine breathing and an element of meditation with a more fluid (and nonaerobic) form of physical movement. While one benefit of these types of exercise is certainly improved physical conditioning, they are also designed to help you achieve a greater level of inner peace and spiritual connection.

- *Walking:* This exercise can cover a broad range of physical exertion. An aerobic but nonstressful walk provides the level of mental and physical relaxation that boosts your connection to the feminine within you, helps you rebuild your internal emotional reservoirs, and increases your mental creativity. Nancy walks with her dog almost every morning. She finds it a magical time of awareness building. On these walks, Nancy is not pressing for time, or miles, or achievement of any kind. She is simply experiencing the joy and wonder of life around her, reconnecting to earth's energy. It revitalizes her and renews her feelings of closeness to God.

Pampering

Your body is the physical evidence of your presence and individuality in the world. From the moment of our birth, tactile stimulation is a primary need and a core method of connecting with others and reconnecting with Self. Your body is a source of natural wisdom and strength, but it can only support you if you honor and nurture it. The more you care for your physical being, the stronger it becomes at helping you transcend the challenges of a stressful life. Understanding this important function of your physical being will help you to view pampering your body as a responsibility rather than a selfish indulgence.

- *Luxurious bath:* Our bodies are 75 percent water, so it is natural that we enjoy an external connection with this most important element of our being. Life cannot exist without water. Throughout history, humankind has experienced the healing and purifying effects of water. Soaking and nurturing yourself in the bath is one of the most relaxing, renewing sensations you can give yourself. The very act of taking a bath brings you back to the most protected and contented stage of your life, when you were in your mother's womb, free of responsibility—even free of gravity!

  Luxuriating in the solitude and quiet of a twenty- or thirty-minute bath allows you to revive and reconnect with the essence of your female energy. It is a time not just of cleansing the body but also renewing and rebalancing the mind and the soul. Special oils and soaps, fluffy towels, a warm room, gentle music, pleasant scents, soft colors, and the glow of candles add ambiance to the room and enhance the pleasure of the experience. They transform an everyday routine into a luxurious ritual.
- *Massage:* The external benefits of massage are the soothing of tired, tense, sore muscles and the stimulation of pores and blood vessels to enhance the flow of energy through the body. But massage also brings a valuable internal benefit. It soothes a tired psyche and revitalizes the energy of mind and spirit.
- *Creaming, oiling, and caressing your body:* This is yet another way to satisfy and nurture your body with loving, tactile care. Like the bath, you can surround yourself with a safe, warm environment. This kind of tactile stimulation and care taking is not only healthy for your skin; it is healthy for your psyche. Time stops and the world ceases to exist for this time.

The ability to love and nurture another is perhaps our most divine gift as human beings. It is certainly a special gift of women. But you cannot give what you do not possess. Only by taking the time each week to love and nurture yourself can you create the emotional reservoir that will enable you to love and nurture others. This is the single, most important enriching concept in this book.

And so we have arrived at the end of our journey together. We began with professional self, looking far into the future to create an Activating Vision for our careers. And we finished with personal self, looking at the present to identify which Life-Enriching Concepts will help us integrate the different facets of our lives into a single, harmonious whole. We have, step by step, accepted responsibility for our choices and learned the powers of our feminine talents.

All that remains now is to make the choice to use these talents as the foundation for leadership. Once you do, you will experience a level of success far more meaningful than simply a higher position on the corporate ladder. You will experience the freedom, the power, and the inner peace that come from being true to yourself—your *feminine* self.

NOTES

Chapter One

1. Jacquelyn Wonder and Priscilla Donovan, *Whole-Brain Thinking: Working from Both Sides of the Brain to Achieve Peak Job Performance* (New York: William Morrow and Company, 1984): 25, 29.
2. Patricia Sellers, "Patient but Not Passive," *Fortune*, vol. 144, no. 7 (October 15, 2001): 193.
3. Patricia Sellers, "These Women Rule," *Fortune*, vol. 140, no. 8 (October 25, 1999): 94–126.
4. Patricia Sellers, "The 50 Most Powerful Women in American Business," *Fortune*, vol. 138, no. 7 (October 12, 1998): 76–96.
5. Patricia Sellers, "These Women Rule," *Fortune*, vol. 140, no. 8 (October 25, 1999): 94–126.
6. Pat Heim and Susan K. Golant, *Hardball for Women: Winning at the Game of Business* (Los Angeles: Lowell House, 1992): 8.

Chapter Two

1. Pat Heim and Susan K. Golant, *Hardball for Women: Winning at the Game of Business* (Los Angeles: Lowell House, 1992): 16.
2. Mary Catherine Bateson, *Composing a Life* (New York: Penguin Group, 1990): 34.

3. "Oprah!" July 12, 1999, broadcast.

4. Carol Kinsey Goman, *This Isn't the Company I Joined: Seven Steps to Energizing a Restructured Work Force* (New York: Van Nostrand Reinhold, 1997): 195.

5. Robert Fritz, *The Path of Least Resistance* (New York: Ballantine Books, 1984): 138.

6. Jacqueline McMakin, with Sonya Dyer, *Working from the Heart: A Guide to Cultivating the Soul at Work* (New York: HarperCollins Publisher, 1993): 12.

Chapter Three

1. Brian Tracy audiotape series, "Psychology of Achievement" (New York: The Nightingale-Conant Company).

2. Rachel Naomi Remen, M.D., *Kitchen Table Wisdom: Stories That Heal* (New York: Riverhead Books, 1996): 66.

3. David Whyte, *The Heart Aroused: Poetry and the Preservation of the Soul in Corporate America* (New York: Bantam Doubleday Dell Publishers, 1994): 218–219.

4. E. Holly Buttner and Dorothy P. Moore, "Women's Organizational Exodus to Entrepreneurship: Self-Reported Motivations and Correlates with Success," *Journal of Small Business Management* (January 1, 1997): 35.

5. Ibid., 34.

Chapter Four

1. Margaret Wheatley and Myron Kellner-Rogers, *A Simpler Way* (San Francisco: Berrett-Koehler Publishers, 1996): 49.

2. Anthony Robbins, *Awaken the Giant Within* (New York: Summit Books, 1991): 77.

3. David Whyte, *The Heart Aroused: Poetry and the Preservation of the Soul in Corporate America* (New York: Bantam Doubleday Dell Publishers, 1994): 280.

Chapter Five

1. Judy B. Rosener, Ph.D., *America's Competitive Secret: Utilizing Women as a Management Strategy* (New York: Oxford University Press, 1995): 46.
2. Matt Siegel, "The Perils of Culture Conflict," *Fortune*, vol. 138, no. 9 (November 9, 1998): 258.
3. Richard C. Whiteley, *The Customer Driven Company: Moving from Talk to Action* (Reading, MA: Addison-Wesley, 1991): 13.

Chapter Six

1. Morgan W. McCall and Michael M. Lombardo, *Off the Track: Why and How Successful Executives Get Derailed*, Technical Report No. 21 (Greensboro, NC: Center for Creative Leadership, 1983), in Robert H. Rosen, Ph.D., with Lisa Berger, *The Healthy Company: Eight Strategies to Develop People, Productivity, and Profits* (Los Angeles: Jeremy P. Tarcher, Inc., 1991): 50.
2. Charles Handy, *The Age of Unreason* (Boston: Harvard Business School Press, 1990): 211.
3. Steven F. Hayward, *Churchill on Leadership: Executive Success in the Face of Adversity* (Rocklin, CA: Prima Publishing, 1997).
4. Warren Bennis, *On Becoming a Leader* (Reading, MA: Addison-Wesley, 1989): 91.
5. Marianne Williamson, *A Woman's Worth* (New York: Random House, 1993): 125.
6. Stanlee Phelps and Nancy Austin, *The Assertive Woman* (San Luis Obispo: Impact Publishers, 1997): 91.

Chapter Seven

1. Ira Chaleff, *The Courageous Follower: Standing Up to and for Our Leaders* (San Francisco: Berrett-Koehler Publishers, 1995): 26.

2. Donna Fisher and Sandy Vilas, *Power Networking: 55 Secrets for Personal and Professional Success* (Austin, TX: MountainHarbour Publications, 1992): 7.

Chapter Eight

1. Bonita C. Long and Sharon E. Kahn, *Women, Work, and Coping: A Multidisciplinary Approach to Workplace Stress* (Montreal: McGill-Queen's University Press, 1993): 91–92.
2. Patricia Sellers, "These Women Rule," *Fortune*, vol. 140, no. 8 (October 25, 1999): 94–130.
3. Ibid., 119.
4. Patricia Sellers, "The 50 Most Powerful Women in American Business," *Fortune*, vol. 138, no. 7 (October 12, 1998): 80.
5. Ann M. Morrison, et al., "Breaking the Glass Ceiling: Can Women Reach the Top of America's Largest Corporations?" *Los Angeles Times* (July 26, 1987): 10.
6. Deborah Tannen, Ph.D., *You Just Don't Understand: Women and Men in Conversation* (New York: William Morrow and Company, 1990): 38–39.
7. Ibid., 75.
8. Norma Carr-Ruffino, Ph.D., *The Promotable Woman: 10 Essential Skills for the New Millennium*, Third Edition (New Jersey: Career Press, 1997), 79.
9. Pat Heim and Susan K. Golant, *Hardball for Women: Winning at the Game of Business* (Los Angeles: Lowell House, 1992), 270.
10. Carol Kinsey Goman, *This Isn't the Company I Joined: Seven Steps to Energizing a Restructured Work Force* (New York: Van Nostrand Reinhold, 1997): 99.
11. Ibid., 100.
12. Julia Cameron, *The Artist's Way: A Spiritual Path to Higher Creativity* (New York: Jeremy P. Tarcher/Penguin Putnam, 1992): 38.
13. Michael Michalko, *Cracking Creativity: The Secrets of Creative Genius* (Berkeley: Ten Speed Press, 1998): 283.

14. Nancy Chodorow. *Feminism and Psychoanalytical Theory* (New Haven, CT: Yale University Press, 1989).
15. Lucy McCauley, "The State of the New Economy Voices," *Fast Company* (September 1999): 122.

Chapter Nine

1. Brian Tracy, *Maximum Achievement* (New York: Simon & Schuster, 1993): 51.
2. Mihaly Csikszentmihalyi, *Flow: The Psychology of Optimal Experience* (New York: Harper & Row, 1990): 27.
3. Stanlee Phelps and Nancy Austin, *The Assertive Woman* (San Luis Obispo: Impact Publishers, 1997): 46.
4. Vicki Spina, *Success 2000: Moving into the Millennium with Purpose, Power, and Prosperity* (New York: John Wiley & Sons, 2000): 191.
5. Warren Bennis, *On Becoming a Leader* (Reading, MA: Addison-Wesley, 1989): 55–56.
6. Warren Bennis, *Leaders: The Strategies for Taking Charge* (New York: Harper & Row Publishers, 1985): 69.
7. Adrienne Mendell, M.A., *How Men Think: The Seven Essential Rules for Making It in a Man's World* (New York: Fawcett Columbine, 1996): 127.
8. Pat Heim and Susan K. Golant, *Hardball for Women: Winning at the Game of Business* (Los Angeles: Lowell House, 1992): 219.
9. Joseph Jaworski, *Synchronicity: The Inner Path of Leadership* (San Francisco: Berrett-Koehler Publishers, 1996): 100.
10. Reprinted with permission of DDB Worldwide, 2002.

Chapter Ten

1. Elizabeth Perle McKenna, *When Work Doesn't Work Anymore: Women, Work, and Identity* (New York: Delacorte Press, 1997): 55.

2. Virginia Valian, *Why So Slow?: The Advancement of Women* (Cambridge: The MIT Press, 1998): 39–40.

3. Joseph Campbell, *An Open Life: Joseph Campbell in Conversation with Michael Toms*, edited by John M. Maher and Dennie Briggs (New York: Harper & Row, 1989): 110.

4. Frederic and Mary Ann Brussat, *Spiritual Literacy: Reading the Sacred in Everyday Life* (New York: Scribner, 1996): 350–351.

5. Chung-liang Al Huang and Jerry Lynch, *Thinking Body, Dancing Mind: TaoSports for Extraordinary Performance in Athletics, Business, and Life* (New York: Bantam Books, 1992): 128.

6. Thomas Moore, *Care of the Soul* (New York: Harper Perennial, 1992): 136.

7. Douglas Preston, *Talking to the Ground: One Family's Journey on Horseback Across the Sacred Land of the Navajo* (Albuquerque: University of New Mexico Press, 1996): 137.

8. Julia Cameron, *The Artist's Way: A Spiritual Path to Higher Creativity* (New York: Jeremy P. Tarcher/Penguin Putnam, 1992): 12–13.

9. Colin P. Sisson, *Breath of Life* (Auckland, New Zealand: Total Press Ltd., 1989): 45.

10. Anthony Lawlor, *A Home for the Soul: A Guide for Dwelling with Spirit and Imagination* (New York: Clarkson Potter Publishers, 1997): 92–93.

11. Gabrielle Roth, *The Wave* (Bluehorse Films, Raven Recording, 1993). Call 201-76-RAVEN or 800-76-RAVEN.

12. Wyoma, *The African Healing Dance* (Sounds True, 1997). Call 800-333-9185.

CREDITS

Page 66: Excerpt reprinted with permission of the publisher. From *A Simpler Way*, copyright © 1996 by Margaret Wheatley and Myron Kellner-Rogers, Berrett-Koehler Publishers, Inc., San Francisco, CA. All rights reserved. 1-800-929-2929.

Page 71: Excerpt reprinted with the permission of Simon & Schuster Adult Publishing Group from *Awaken the Giant Within* by Anthony Robbins. Copyright © 1991 by Anthony Robbins.

Page 115: Permission granted by the Center for Creative Leadership, Greensboro, NC. www.ccl.org. Copyright 1983, *Off the Track: Why and How Successful Executives Get Derailed*. All rights reserved.

Page 116: Excerpt reprinted by permission of Harvard Business School Press. From *The Age of Unreason* by Charles Handy. Boston, MA, 1990, p. 211. Copyright © 1990 by Harvard Business School Publishing Corporation, all rights reserved.

Pages 139 and 226: Excerpts from *The Assertive Woman*, Fourth Edition, copyright © 2002 by Stanlee Phelps and Nancy Austin. Reproduced for Interven Partners by permission of Impact Publishers, Inc., P.O. Box 6016, Atascadero, CA 93423. Further reproduction prohibited.

INDEX

ABOUT THE AUTHORS

Nancy Fredericks and Candy Deemer offer executive coaching, customized consulting, and several proprietary courses through their company, Interven Partners. Their client companies include Warner Brothers Pictures, DDB Worldwide, Allergan, Danone Waters of North America, KPMG, Walt Disney Studios, AEGON, Motorola, Hughes Electronics, and the Los Angeles County Employees Retirement Association.

Interven's flagship proprietary program is A Woman's Way of Leadership, a course that helps professional women identify and overcome barriers to their performance to achieve success within their organizations. This course makes extensive use of the concepts and tools from *Dancing on the Glass Ceiling*.

Candy and Nancy are also experienced public speakers. They are insightful and entertaining, and they encourage plenty of audience participation.

To learn more about Interven's services, A Woman's Way of Leadership, or the authors' speaking availability, contact them at 562-690-3975, or at their corporate website, www.interven.com.